'To protect people against mass atrocity crimes remains a crucial issue of these turbulent times. This book provides a timely analysis on the norm of responsibility to protect and identifies the challenges to norm diffusion. Rietveld problematizes the EU normative claims and highlights the agency of regional organizations in internalising a global norm. A mandatory reading to better understand regional security.'

—**Stefania Panebianco,** *Jean Monnet Chair and Associate Professor, University of Catania, Visiting Professor, MES-MUNDUS Master Programme at LUISS-Guido Carli, Rome*

'Rietveld's piercing analysis reveals how regional organizations like the EU and ECOWAS have struggled to prevent atrocities and protect vulnerable populations. This book makes a timely contribution to our understanding of how global norms like the Responsibility to Protect are locally constructed, modified, and operationalised.'

—**Simon Adams,** *President of the Center for Victims of Torture. Former Executive Director of the Global Centre for the Responsibility to Protect*

Regional Approaches to the Responsibility to Protect

This book studies regional approaches to the Responsibility to Protect (R2P) in Europe and West Africa.

The work assesses how and to what extent the European Union (EU) and the Economic Community of West African States (ECOWAS) have internalised the norm, both generally, in institutions, policies, and programs and specifically, in crisis situations of R2P concern, such as the 2011 Libyan crisis and 2012 Malian crisis. It provides a historical analysis of how the two regional organisations have dealt with questions of sovereignty, security, and human rights since their founding, as well as an analysis of some of the European and West African roots of the R2P norm. This reflects the notion that global norms are often informed by local and regional practices and that this needs to be recognised in order to fully understand regional responses to alleged global norms. The book uses process tracing to trace the regional internalisation of R2P and has benefited from qualitative research interviews with EU- and ECOWAS-stakeholders. One of the key findings is that ECOWAS and West Africa have delivered a key contribution to the norm construction of R2P, a finding insufficiently recognised in the current literature.

This book will be of much interest to students of the Responsibility to Protect, EU human rights and foreign policy, African politics, security studies, and International Relations in general.

Jochem Rietveld is Research Associate at the Centre for the Study of Existential Risk, University of Cambridge, UK, and holds a PhD in International Relations and Comparative Regionalism from LUISS Guido Carli, Italy/University of Warwick, UK.

Global Politics and the Responsibility to Protect

Series Editors

Alex J. Bellamy

University of Queensland

Sara E. Davies

Griffith University

Monica Serrano

The City University of New York.

The aim of this book series is to gather the best new thinking about the Responsibility to Protect into a core set of volumes that provides a definitive account of the principle, its implementation, and its role in crises, that reflects a plurality of views and regional perspectives.

Implementing the Responsibility to Protect
A Future Agenda
Edited by Cecilia Jacob and Martin Mennecke

The Responsibility to Protect in Darfur
From Forgotten Conflict to Global Cause and Back
David Lanz

Constructing the Responsibility to Protect
Contestation and Consolidation
Edited by Charles T. Hunt and Phil Orchard

Protecting the Global Civilian from Violence
UN Discourses and Practices in Fragile States
Timo Kivimäki

Covid-19 and Atrocity Prevention in East Asia
Edited by Mely Caballero-Anthony and Noel M. Morada

Advocacy Networks and the Responsibility to Protect
The Politics of Norm Circulation
Sarka Kolmasova

Regional Approaches to the Responsibility to Protect
Lessons from Europe and West Africa
Jochem Rietveld

For more information about this series, please visit: www.routledge.com/Global-Politics-and-the-Responsibility-to-Protect/book-series/GPRP

Regional Approaches to the Responsibility to Protect

Lessons from Europe and West Africa

Jochem Rietveld

Routledge
Taylor & Francis Group
LONDON AND NEW YORK

First published 2023
by Routledge
4 Park Square, Milton Park, Abingdon, Oxon OX14 4RN

and by Routledge
605 Third Avenue, New York, NY 10158

Routledge is an imprint of the Taylor & Francis Group, an informa business

British Library Cataloguing-in-Publication Data
A catalogue record for this book is available from the British Library

ISBN: 978-1-032-13763-6 (hbk)
ISBN: 978-1-032-13771-1 (pbk)
ISBN: 978-1-003-23073-1 (ebk)

DOI: 10.4324/9781003230731

Typeset in Bembo
by Apex CoVantage, LLC

Contents

Acknowledgements

This book is based on doctoral research undertaken at LUISS Guido Carli and the University of Warwick, as part of the Marie Curie Horizon 2020 European Joint Doctorate programme GEM-STONES. Special thanks are due to my PhD supervisors, Prof. George Christou of the University of Warwick and Dr. Daniela Huber of the Istituto Affari Internazionali (Rome), where I completed a non-academic placement during my PhD. I could not have wished for better supervisors, given all the time and effort they invested in supporting my doctoral research. Their critical but constructive feedback on multiple iterations of my PhD chapters have really improved the quality of my research.

I also thank Prof. Sonia Lucarelli and Prof. Stefania Panebianco as external readers of the first submission of my doctoral research at LUISS Guido Carli. Their insightful comments helped sharpen my research for its final submission.

Special thanks are also due to all of those interviewed for this research. The interviews provided me with rich information and they often challenged me to rethink and re-evaluate important aspects of my research, which has been invaluable.

I would also like to thank the editors of this book series, Alex Bellamy, Sara Davies, and Monica Serrano. Two anonymous reviewers provided very helpful comments on my book proposal, for which I am grateful. Their comments helped me in transforming my doctoral research into a manuscript. Special thanks also to Andrew Humphrys, Devon Harvey, and Bethany Lund-Yates for their wonderful support throughout the publication process.

Last, but certainly not least, I thank my family, friends, and colleagues for their support throughout my doctoral research and the manuscript writing process. Special thanks go to my fiancée Nikita, for being there for me every step on the way.

This research would not have been realised without funding from the European Union, the specifics of which are indicated below.

This research has received funding from the European Union's Horizon 2020 research and innovation programme under the Marie Sklodowska-Curie Grant Agreement No 722826.

Abbreviations

AFISMA	African-led International Support Mission to Mali
AIPECT	African Institute for Peacebuilding and Conflict Transformation
ALDE	Alliance of Liberals and Democrats for Europe
ASEAN	Association of Southeast Asian Nations
AU	African Union
CAP	Common Agricultural Policy
CEE	Central and Eastern Europe
CFSP	Common Foreign and Security Policy
CSDP	Common Security and Defence Policy
CSO	Civil Society Organisation
DEVCO	Directorate-General for International Cooperation and Development
EC	European Community
ECHR	European Convention on Human Rights
ECOMOG	ECOWAS Cease-fire Monitoring Group
ECOWARN	ECOWAS Warning and Response Network
ECOWAS	Economic Community of West African States
ECPF	ECOWAS Conflict Prevention Framework
ECSC	European Coal and Steel Community
EDC	European Defence Community
EEAS	European External Action Service
EEC	European Economic Community
EP	European Parliament
EPC	European Political Community; European Political Cooperation
EU	European Union
EUFOR	European Union Force Bosnia and Herzegovina
EULEX	European Union Rule of Law Mission in Kosovo
FRY	Former Republic of Yugoslavia
GCR2P	Global Centre for the Responsibility to Protect
GUE/NGL	Confederal Group of the European United Left – Nordic Green Left
HI	Humanitarian Intervention

HLP	High-Level Panel on Threats, Challenges, and Changes
ICC	International Criminal Court
ICG-G	International Contact Group on Guinea
ICISS	International Commission on Intervention and State Sovereignty
ICJ	International Court of Justice
ICTY	International Criminal Tribunal for the former Yugoslavia
IEC	Independent Electoral Commission
IR	International Relations
ISIS	Islamic State of Iraq and the Levant
ISP	(Directorate) Integrated Approach for Security & Peace
LRA	Lord's Resistance Army
MEP	Member of European Parliament
MINUSMA	United Nations Multidimensional Integrated Stabilization Mission in Mali
MNLA	Movement for National Liberation of Azawad
MSC	Mediation and Security Council
MSF	Médecins Sans Frontières
NATO	North Atlantic Treaty Organization
NGO	Non-Governmental Organisation
OAU	Organisation of African Unity
OIC	Organisation of Islamic Cooperation
OSCE	Organization for Security and Cooperation in Europe
PMAD	Protocol on Mutual Assistance in Defence
PNA	Protocol on Non-Aggression
PRISM	Prevention of Conflicts, Rule of Law/ Security Sector Reform, Integrated Approach, Stabilization, and Mediation
RSC	Regional Security Complex
RSG	Regional Security Governance
RUF	Revolutionary United Front
SEA	Single European Act
SG	Secretary General
TAN	Transnational Advocacy Networks
UK	United Kingdom
UN	United Nations
UNDP	United Nations Development Program
UNGA	United Nations General Assembly
UNOCI	United Nations Operation in Côte d'Ivoire
UNPROFOR	United Nations Protection Force
UNSC	United Nations Security Council
US	United States
VP/HR	(EU) Vice-President/High Representative
WANEP	West African Peacebuilding Network
WEU	Western European Union

1 Introduction

International norms and regional organisations

Ever since the adoption of the Responsibility to Protect (R2P) at the World Summit in 2005, much discussion has focused on what role regional organisations can play in the implementation of the new norm. The role of regional organisations was a central topic of the 2011 UN Secretary General yearly report on R2P and the subsequent debate in the UN General Assembly (UNGA) (UN 2011). This research aims to shed light on this topic and, more specifically, it aims to uncover how and to what extent regional organisations have internalised the norm of R2P, which forms the research question of this book. The European Union (EU) and the Economic Community of West African States (ECOWAS) will serve as regional case studies to investigate this question. In order to unpack the research question, this project will assess the International Relations (IR) literature on norms, the evolution of the norm of R2P, and the role of regional organisations in peace and security.

Norms have been closely studied in the IR literature since the constructivist turn in the 1990s. Finnemore and Sikkink (1998) delivered a key contribution with their norms life cycle model, which investigated how global norm entrepreneurs diffused new global norms, which after reaching a certain threshold, cascaded through the international community and subsequently became internalised by other states. This first wave of norm scholarship tended to have a cosmopolitan, Western bias, though, as it investigated how transnational norm entrepreneurs, often Western, spread supposedly 'good global norms' globally, to places in developing countries with 'bad local norms' (Acharya 2004). It was Acharya (2004) who addressed this bias and gave agency to actors from the Global South, through new concepts such as 'norm localisation', 'norm subsidiarity', and 'norm circulation' (Acharya 2004, 2011, 2013). Other scholars criticised the implicit assumptions of 'norm linearity' and norm stability inherent in the early norms literature (Welsh 2013; Wiener 2004). Finally, a new generation of norm scholars, of which Bloomfield (2016) is one of the main representatives, noted that earlier norms scholarship had the tendency to privilege norm entrepreneurs and successful normative change, while undertheorising opponents of normative change and their strategies, so-called 'norm

DOI: 10.4324/9781003230731-1

antipreneurs'. Adding these norm antipreneurs and other, 'in-between roles' to the analysis adds analytical depth to the norms literature and takes away the bias towards successful normative change (Bloomfield 2016).

The discussion of norms and the development of the literature around it, which will be comprehensively done in the theory chapter of this book, is key as the object of study in this book is the regional internalisation of the R2P norm. A final key aspect of this book is the regional element, as the object of study is the *regional* internalisation of the norm of R2P. To contextualise how regional organisations have approached the R2P norm, the analytical framework of this book will first discuss the increasing security role of regional organisations in general. One strand of the literature, while importantly recognising the increasing importance of regional organisations in security governance, has mostly discussed regional organisations vis-à-vis their usefulness for the UN in global governance (Suominen 2005; MacFarlane 2014; Kefale 2015), which risks downplaying their agency. The regional security governance literature and the regional security communities literature take the agency of regional organisations more seriously. Recognising this agency is necessary if one wants to get an understanding of the regional rationales behind engaging with the R2P norm, which go beyond UN calls upon regional organisations to implement the norm (UN 2011). Other topics which will be discussed in this light are the role of power in regions, regional hegemony, and regional leadership. These discussions will culminate in the formulation of a number of regional factors deemed relevant to the likelihood of regional internalisation of the R2P norm.

The Responsibility to Protect (R2P)

Although many regional roots were already in place and fed into it, as this book will demonstrate, the norm of R2P in its 'global form' emerged in the early 2000s through the work of the International Commission on Intervention and State Sovereignty (ICISS) in 2001, which was set up by the government of Canada. Canada took this step in response to a key, and often heated, debate of the 1990s, which revolved around the tension between state sovereignty and intervention in the case of mass atrocity crimes. This question was poignantly asked by UN Secretary General Annan in his 2000 Millennium Report, in which he wondered "if humanitarian intervention is, indeed, an unacceptable assault on sovereignty, how should we respond to a Rwanda, to a Srebrenica, to gross and systematic violation of human rights that offend every precept of our common humanity?" (United Nations 2000). After the ICISS' work, more stages of norm building followed, most notably through the work of the High-Level Panel on Threats, Challenges and Changes (HLP) (2004) and the Secretary General's Report 'In Larger Freedom' (2005). Finally, important revisions to the norm were made during the 2005 World Summit Negotiations, in which R2P was one of the agenda items. One major revision was that the criteria for intervention, which the ICISS had formulated and which the

HLP had endorsed, were dropped, as several states had reservations about this (Bellamy 2009). At the World Summit, the international community eventually came to endorse the new notion of R2P, in paragraphs 138 to 140 in the World Summit Outcome Document (UNGA 2005). In these paragraphs, they recognised "that each individual state has the responsibility to protect its populations from genocide, war crimes, ethnic cleansing and crimes against humanity" (UNGA 2005). The international community should, as appropriate, encourage and help states to exercise this responsibility and it should be prepared to take collective action when national authorities manifestly fail to protect their populations from atrocity crimes (UNGA 2005).

The 2005 World Summit Outcome Document marked the culmination of a long period of norm building of R2P. This would not stop new innovations, though. For instance, in 2009, in preparation for the first formal debate in the UN General Assembly (GA) since the adoption of the norm, the adviser to the Secretary General came up with a pillar approach to operationalise R2P (UNGA 2009). Pillar one constitutes "the protection responsibilities of the State", Pillar two refers to "international assistance and capacity-building", while Pillar three deals with "timely and decisive response" (UNGA 2009, 2). Other innovations have been made by states such as Brazil and China in the aftermath of the 2011 Libyan intervention. Brazil came up with the concept of 'responsibility while protecting', which emphasises enduring accountability of those states implementing a Security Council mandate (Tourinho et al. 2015), while China coined the term 'responsible protection' (Fung 2016). This shows that R2P, like all international norms, is not 'set in stone' but is continuously discussed, contested, and (re-)assessed at all levels of governance.

The theoretical and methodological approach

This research is at the crossroads of the study of international norms and regional security governance in the field of International Relations. The research follows an empirical approach, rather than a normative approach, which means it will analyse empirically how and to what extent regional organisations have internalised the norm of R2P, rather than engaging with some of the normative or ethical questions around R2P.

The theoretical approach in this book is constructivist, acknowledging the intersubjective nature of norms and the reflexive nature of social actors. This research builds on insights from a substantial body of constructivist literature on norm emergence, diffusion, and internalisation. One of the foundational works on international norms, Finnemore and Sikkink's (1998) norm life cycle model, forms the starting point of this book, while it is also indebted to Acharya's work (2004, 2011, 2013), which demonstrated the important normative role of local actors, particularly in the Global South, and corrected the Western-centrism of the early norms scholarship.

This book focuses on *regional* approaches to the R2P norm for a variety of reasons. First, the UN has explicitly called upon regional organisations to help with the implementation of the norm (UNGA 2005; UN 2011). Given the historical development of R2P, UN statements should convey significant authority on the norm. R2P in its 'global form' was initially negotiated and adopted at the UN level during the 2005 World Summit, and key debates (first the informal annual UN General Assembly dialogues, and since 2018 the formal debates on the topic) and innovations, such as the 2009 Pillar Structure, directly emanated from the UN (UNGA 2005, 2009, 2018). Given the UN's authority on R2P, its statements are expected to frame expectations in the international community regarding who should be at the forefront of engaging with R2P. Whether regional organisations subsequently take up this role and whether they have the relevant capacity and authority to do should, however, be subject to empirical analysis. This analysis will be an integral part of the wider assessment of how and to what extent regional organisations have internalised the norm of R2P.

More empirically, it can also be observed that regional organisations have increased their role in security governance over the years, as widely reported in the regional security governance literature (Buzan and Waever 2003; Kirchner and Sperling 2007; Kirchner 2011). So, in that sense, there is also an empirical argument to be made for a regional focus in research on the internalisation of the R2P norm, which has a clear security dimension behind it.

In short, the choice for a focus on regional organisations has been predominantly informed by explicit authoritative UN references to their role, and, more empirically, their reported rising importance in security governance.

Two regional case studies are used to analyse the regional internalisation of R2P: the EU and ECOWAS. The EU and ECOWAS differ in many aspects that are deemed relevant for the regional diffusion and internalisation of R2P: whereas the EU is a Western regional organisation, is deemed to have a low risk of mass atrocity crimes, is generally seen as a security community, and has two permanent Security Council members, ECOWAS is an African (sub-) regional organisation, is deemed to have a medium to high risk of mass atrocity crimes, is generally seen as a hegemonic power system, and has no permanent Security Council members. The case selection thus follows Mill's logic of a most different systems design (George and Bennett 2005; Mahoney 1999; Mill 1843). The fact that the organisations differ in many aspects is important in terms of case selection: to better understand the drivers of regional norm diffusion and internalisation of R2P, one has to look at regional systems that are very different from one another to understand which factors matter and which do not or only to a lesser extent.

Within the two regional cases, a selection of case studies relevant to R2P has been made. In the EU chapter, the cases include the Libyan crisis, the Syrian crisis, the refugee crisis, and the Rohingya crisis. These cases are chosen as they all have an atrocity-component, either through potential threats or actual commission, and they show variance in what R2P measures have been taken. In the Libyan crisis, the responsibility to react was activated with a military intervention, whereas in the Syrian crisis and the Rohingya crisis measures stayed limited to formal support, the responsibility to prevent, and the application of sanctions. The refugee crisis is relevant as it is the only case where R2P 'hit home', whereas the other cases concern external crises. For ECOWAS, the cases include the Guinean crisis, the Ivory Coast election crisis, and the Mali crisis. In the Guinean and Ivory Coast crises, only preventive measures and sanctions were employed, whereas in Mali, ECOWAS eventually deployed troops after the French Serval operation started. For ECOWAS, all cases concern internal crises, as ECOWAS generally does not operate outside its own region.

The methodology used to empirically apply the analytical framework is qualitative in nature. I draw on George and Bennet's (2005) and Lupovici's (2009) method of process tracing to analyse how the norm of R2P has evolved over time, and more specifically, what some of the regional roots of R2P are and how the norm has been internalised at the regional level (back from the global level) over time. This method is particularly used in the case studies in the two empirical chapters, in which I trace the development of a case while simultaneously assessing what signs of R2P internalisation are visible in the case. Process tracing should reveal how and to what extent the regional organisations have internalised and diffused the norm of R2P, while also uncovering how processes of local norm construction have fed into the R2P norm prior to the 2001 ICISS report, arguably R2P's 'founding document'.

Interviews with EU officials and experts were conducted during two research visits in Brussels, in June 2018 and February 2019. Next to that, interviews were conducted remotely through Skype. Interviewees included academics, EU officials, a UN official, and NGO staff. While planning a research visit to Abuja, Nigeria, security concerns were flagged in the research visit evaluation process (Nigerian national elections were coming up at the time), which unfortunately forced me to reconsider traveling to the region. Through a 'snowball method', I still managed to speak to ECOWAS officials and NGO staff in the region remotely in the period from April 2019 to February 2020. All interviews were structured and I generally provided my interviewees with a list of questions a few days prior to the interview. I allowed interviewees to deviate from my questions as this often resulted in interesting information and I asked follow-up questions not covered by my list of questions.

Structure of the book

After this introductory chapter, Chapter 2 develops the analytical framework of this book. It first discusses the norms literature at large, which culminates in a discussion of different normative contexts and the implications they have for norm entrepreneurs and antipreneurs who respectively aim to change and defend the normative status quo. The different aspects of norm internalisation of R2P, encompassing formal support for R2P, and the three components of R2P – the responsibility to prevent, the responsibility to react, and the responsibility to rebuild – are captured in a final set of factors that aim to answer how and to what extent regional organisations have internalised R2P. The concepts of absorption, accommodation, and transformation, which stem from the Europeanisation literature, are used to capture the depths of change in response to R2P, and they answer to what extent the regional organisations have internalised R2P. Second, the chapter comprehensively discusses the regional security governance literature which will result in the identification of several regional factors that are expected to have an impact on the likelihood of internalisation of R2P.

A contextual overview of how the EU and ECOWAS have dealt with questions of security, sovereignty, and human rights historically is presented in Chapter 3, the contextual chapter of this book. These three broad themes have been selected as they are all highly relevant to the norm of R2P. The contextual overview starts in the years the regional organisations were founded and analyses how the organisations approached the three themes against a changing historical context, from the era of decolonisation and the Cold War to the post-Cold War period. A key finding in this chapter is that some of the terminology that is now associated with R2P is actually already visible in the protocols that ECOWAS adopted in the 1990s and early 2000s, suggesting that some of the origins of the norm actually lay in the West African region. The chapter also provides some comparative reflections on how the EU and ECOWAS have historically dealt with security, sovereignty, and human rights.

Chapter 4 is the first empirical chapter, focusing on the EU's internalisation of R2P. It assesses the regional normative status quo at the time when R2P emerged, which is characterised by conditional notions of sovereignty. It subsequently analyses the positions EU actors have taken on R2P, both at the institutional level and at the level of member states, since the norm was adopted at the 2005 World Summit. The European Parliament (EP) has emerged as the EU's chief R2P norm entrepreneur, expressing strong support for the norm since the very start and ensuring it stays on the political agenda in Brussels. The remainder of the chapter is allocated for case studies – the Libyan crisis, the Syrian crisis, the refugee crisis, and the Rohingya crisis – which are guided by the different aspects of internalisation of R2P. The Libyan crisis is important as it is the only analysed crisis in which the military component of the responsibility to react was activated. The Syrian crisis offers sobering conclusions as the international community has failed to offer meaningful protection to the Syrian people more than a decade into the country's civil war. The EU has, however, used many of the R2P tools at its disposal during the crisis. The refugee crisis is telling as it is the only 'EU-internal crisis' analysed in this book, and it demonstrates that the EU particularly struggles when 'R2P hits home'. Finally, the Rohingya crisis demonstrates prevention failures, while at the same time showing that the EU is improving its activities related to responsibility to rebuild after atrocity crises. Some comparative reflections pertaining to the different components of R2P – the responsibility to prevent, react, and rebuild – are offered towards the end of the chapter. This then culminates in a discussion that sets out to answer the research question of this book with regard to the case of the EU. The concepts proposed by the Europeanisation literature come in use here. Before the conclusion, the chapter will revisit the regional factors as identified in the analytical framework of this book and assess them against the evidence presented in the chapter.

Chapter 5 has the same aim as Chapter 4 but analyses ECOWAS' internalisation of R2P. It again starts by assessing the regional normative status quo at the time when R2P emerged, which was also characterised by qualified notions of sovereignty due to the emerging regional intervention practice and architecture in West Africa since the late 1980s. The chapter then proceeds by analysing the positions ECOWAS-actors have taken on R2P, both at the institutional level and at the level of member states, since the norm's global adoption in 2005. It shows that Ghana and Nigeria have been two important R2P norm entrepreneurs in West Africa. The case studies in this chapter are the crises in Guinea, Ivory Coast, and Mali, where internalisation of R2P will be assessed with the help of the different aspects of internalisation of R2P. The case of Guinea had ECOWAS respond to atrocities taking place in a post-coup context. The Ivory Coast is a telling case as the norm conflict between R2P and the norm to uphold constitutional maintenance and assumption of power led to a diluted message to the followers of Ouattara, who, next to defeated President Gbagbo's followers, engaged in atrocity crimes as well. The crisis in Mali is an important one as it was the only one among the analysed cases in which ECOWAS' engagement with the military component of the responsibility to react and the responsibility to rebuild could be assessed (Mali was the only case in which ECOWAS responded with sending troops which later had a rebuilding mandate as well under MINUSMA) (UN 2022). After the case studies, some comparative reflections with regard to the different components of R2P are offered, which will pave the way for a discussion that aims to answer the research question of this book for the case of ECOWAS. The Europeanisation literature concepts will again be used as a yardstick for assessing the depths of normative change in response to the R2P norm. Before the concluding section, the chapter will revisit the regional factors and assess them based on the chapter's empirical findings.

The conclusion provides a summary of the main findings of this book in Chapter 6. It concludes that both the EU and ECOWAS have contributed to the norm building of the R2P norm, through extant practices and institutions, such as the ECOWAS protocols and mechanisms, and through the work of influential norm entrepreneurs such as Kofi Annan and Bernard Kouchner. With regard to norm internalisation, the EU seems to have engaged in norm accommodation, changing existing policies and institutions to integrate R2P without a complete overhaul of existing practices and institutions. The regional discourse has significantly changed though as R2P has become the default discourse when atrocity cases are concerned. ECOWAS, on the other hand, has mounted a transformative response to the region's security challenges since the 1980s and through these efforts helped inspire the development of the R2P norm. Its response to the R2P norm in its 'UN-form' post-2005 has been one of norm absorption as a result: as there were already extensive institutions and policies in place to prevent and respond to atrocities, there was no need for a very transformative response to R2P in the post-World Summit era. The chapter also offers comparative reflections between the EU and ECOWAS based on the contextual and empirical chapters. The regional factors are further explored and compared in this part of the chapter and a call is made for further regional case studies to test them, as in the context of this research they mostly served as explorative factors rather than robust hypotheses. Finally, the chapter provides a discussion of contributions to the literature, some of the limitations of this research, and avenues for future research on regional organisations and R2P.

Bibliography

Acharya, Amitav. 2004. "How Ideas Spread: Whose Norms Matter? Norm Localisation and Institutional Change in Asian Regionalism." *International Organisation* 58 (Spring): 239–275. DOI:10.1017/S0020818304582024.

Acharya, Amitav. 2011. "Norm Subsidiarity and Regional Orders: Sovereignty, Regionalism, and Rule-Making in the Third World." *International Studies Quarterly* 55 (1): 95–123. DOI:10.1111/j.1468-2478.2010.00637.x.

Acharya, Amitav. 2013. "The R2P and Norm Diffusion: Towards a Framework of Norm Circulation." *Global Responsibility to Protect* 5 (4): 466–479. DOI:10.1163/1875984X-00504006.

Bellamy, Alex. 2009. *The Responsibility to Protect. The Global Effort to End Mass Atrocities.* Cambridge: Polity Press.

Bloomfield, Alan. 2016. "Norm Antipreneurs and Theorising Resistance to Normative Change." *Review of International Studies* 42 (2): 310–333. DOI:10.1017/S026021051500025X.

Buzan, Barry and Ole Waever. 2003. "Security Complexes: A Theory of Regional Security." In *Regions and Powers: The Structure of International Security* (Cambridge Studies in International Relations). Cambridge: Cambridge University Press, 40–82. DOI:10.1017/CBO9780511491252.007.

Finnemore, Martha and Kathryn Sikkink. 1998. "International Norm Dynamics and Political Change." *International Organisation* 52 (4): 887–917. DOI:10.1162/002081898550789.

Fung, Courtney. 2016. "China and the Responsibility to Protect: From Opposition to Advocacy." *United States Institute for Peace.* www.usip.org/publications/2016/06/china-and-responsibility-protect-opposition-advocacy.

George, Alexander L. and Andrew Bennett. 2005. *Case Studies and Theory Development in the Social Sciences.* Cambridge, MA: MIT Press.

Kefale, Asnake. 2015. "Regional Organisations and Security Governance: A Comparative Assessment of IGAD and ASEAN." LSE Global South Unit Working Paper Series, no. 1/2015. London: LSE.

Kirchner, Emil. 2011. "The EU as a Regional and Global Security Provider." In *The Security Governance of Regional Organizations*, eds. Emil J. Kirchner and Roberto Dominguez. New York: Routledge, 25–45.

Kirchner, Emil and James Sperling. 2007. *EU Security Governance.* Manchester and New York: Manchester University Press.

Lupovici, Amir. 2009. "Constructivist Methods: A Plea and Manifesto for Pluralism." *Review of International Studies* 35 (1): 195–218.

MacFarlane, S. Neil. 2014. "Regional Organisations and Global Security Governance." In *International Organisation and Global Governance*, eds. T.G. Weiss and R. Wilkinson. London; New York: Routledge, 471–483.

Mahoney, J. 1999. "Nominal, Ordinal, and Narrative Appraisal in Macro-Causal Analysis." *American Journal of Sociology* 3: 1154–1196.

Mill, John Stuart. 1843. "Chapter VIII: Of the Four Methods of Experimental Inquiry." In *A System of Logic*. New York: Project Gutenberg Ebooks.

Suominen, Kati. 2005. "Globalizing Regionalism: Harnessing Regional Organizations to Meet Global Threats." *UNU-CRIS Occasional Paper* 11: 1–24.

Tourinho, Marcos, Oliver Stuenkel and Sarah Brockmeier. 2015. ""Responsibility while Protecting": Reforming R2P Implementation." *Global Society* 30 (1): 134–150. DOI:10.1080/13600826.2015.1094452.

United Nations. 2000. *We the Peoples: The Role of the United Nations in the Twenty-First Century: The Millennium Report*. New York: United Nations.

United Nations. 2011. "The Role of Regional and Subregional Arrangements in Implementing the Responsibility to Protect." A/65/877 – S/2011/393. https://undocs.org/A/65/877 (February 18, 2020).

United Nations. 2022. "Mandate." *United Nations Peacekeeping*. https://minusma.unmissions.org/en/mandate-0 (July 15, 2022).

United Nations General Assembly. 2005. *2005 World Summit Outcome. Resolution 60/1.* (October 24). GA/RES/60/1. New York: United Nations General Assembly.

United Nations General Assembly. 2009. *Implementing the Responsibility to Protect. A/63/677.* https://undocs.org/A/63/677 (April 13, 2020).

United Nations General Assembly. 2018. "Responsibility to Protect." www.un.org/pga/72/2018/06/25/formal-debate-of-the-general-assembly-under-agenda-item-the-responsibility-to-protect-and-the-prevention-of-genocide-war-crimes-ethnic-cleansing-and-crimes-against-humanity/ (July 14, 2022).

Welsh, Jennifer M. 2013. "Norm Contestation and the Responsibility to Protect." *Global Responsibility to Protect* 5 (4): 365–396.

Wiener, Antje. 2004. "Contested Compliance: Interventions on the Normative Structure of World Politics." *European Journal of International Relations* 10 (2): 189–234.

2 Analytical framework for assessing norms, regional organisations, and the Responsibility to Protect

Introduction

While the UN has attributed an important responsibility to regional organisations to implement the norm of the Responsibility to Protect (R2P), it is a matter of debate how and to what extent these organisations have responded to this call (UN 2011). The analytical framework that will be developed in this chapter aims to provide the analytical tools to answer the research question of this book: how and to what extent have regional organisations internalised the norm of the Responsibility to Protect (R2P)?

The analytical framework aims to make several key contributions to the existing literature on norms and regional security by:

- Adding to existing understandings of norm internalisation;
- Introducing the concept of local norm construction;
- Theorising the impact of regional factors on the ability and willingness of regional organisations to internalise the norm of R2P.

Regarding the latter, the link between regional security governance systems and normative change is something that has not been explicitly theorised in the existing literature, neither in the norms nor in the regional security governance literature, so this will be one of the main contributions of this book.

Importantly, this book leaves the origins of the R2P norm open, in the sense that it does not assume from the outset that R2P is a global norm originating from the United Nations (UN). Key to this research is the notion that global norms, such as R2P, often have local roots ('local' is broadly conceived here and can refer to the 'regional' as well) (Acharya 2004, 2011, 2013). If one truly wants to understand processes of (regional) norm internalisation of alleged 'global norms', it is important to acknowledge that such processes are dynamic. That is, norms do not simply flow from the global to the local level but can 'travel' between different levels of governance (Acharya 2004, 2011, 2013). This notion has not always received the attention it should in the existing literature, with studies frequently taking the R2P norm as a 'global UN-norm' which is then internalised, institutionalised, or implemented by other

DOI: 10.4324/9781003230731-2

actors. While these studies are important in their own right, they run the risk of missing out on the local and regional 'priors' of alleged 'global norms', which contain vital information on the genealogy of alleged 'global norms' and their likelihood of subsequent take-up and internalisation by different regions and regional organisations (Acharya 2004).

Apart from theoretical reasons, this book also focuses on the regional dimension of R2P internalisation for empirical reasons. First, the UN's call on regional organisations to be at the forefront of implementing R2P has raised expectations in the international community. Given the historical developments of R2P at the global level, UN statements should convey significant authority on the norm. R2P was initially negotiated and adopted at the UN level during the 2005 World Summit, and key debates (first the informal annual UN General Assembly dialogues, and since 2018 the formal debates on the topic) and innovations, such as the 2009 Pillar Structure, directly emanated from the UN (UNGA 2009; Acharya 2012; Welsh 2013). Given the UN's authority on R2P, its statements are expected to frame expectations in the international community regarding who should be at the forefront of engaging with R2P. Its call upon regional organisations to be partners in the implementation of R2P also fits into a long historical tradition of UN-regional cooperation in the area of security governance that dates back at least to the 1945 San Francisco conference (Acharya 2012). Whether regional organisations subsequently take up this role and whether they have the relevant capacity and authority to do so should be subject to empirical analysis, which is conducted in the empirical chapters of this book. The second empirical reason for focusing on the regional dimension is that the role and importance of regional organisations in security governance has reportedly increased over time, as documented by the regional security governance literature (Buzan and Waever 2003; Kirchner and Sperling 2007; Kirchner 2011; MacFarlane 2014; Kacowicz and Press-Barnathan 2016). This provides another rationale to study regional approaches to the R2P norm, rather than, for instance, national approaches.

The analytical framework I propose aims to identify the regional roots of the R2P norm pre-2005, and it assesses how and to what extent the norm has been internalised by the two regional organisations under analysis, the EU and ECOWAS, post-2005. The framework is rooted into two bodies of literature: the norms literature and the regional security governance literature. This chapter will provide a short review of both literatures and distil their relevance for the project at hand. This research is at the intersection of these two literatures, as it is both interested in questions of norm emergence, diffusion, and internalisation, and how these processes with regard to the R2P norm play out at the regional level, which relates to regional security governance. The main contributions the analytical framework aims to make are thus to theorise the intersection between normative processes and regional security governance, to introduce the concept of local norm construction, and to further theorise the concept of norm internalisation. This chapter will now begin with a discussion of norms and how this book understands and will use this concept.

Defining norms in relation to the Responsibility to Protect (R2P)

This research adopts a constructivist approach to norms, acknowledging the intersubjective nature of norms and the reflexive nature of social actors. Actors operate in a 'social environment' inhabited by a wide variety of other actors, so actors' behaviour takes place in socially dense context. Actors are reflexive as they are able to learn from their own behaviour and the feedback that their social environment provides to them (Checkel 1998). With regard to norms, this research defines norms as 'shared expectations of appropriate behaviour for actors with a given identity' (Katzenstein 1996). It needs to be acknowledged that when norms become deeply ingrained, they may also affect actors' identities, as poststructuralists have been acute in arguing (Hansen 2006). However, this research focuses on how 'R2P' as a norm – being adopted at the 2005 World Summit while in and by itself being informed by various local and regional practices – has raised behavioural and institutional expectations internationally and has subsequently affected discursive, behavioural, and institutional change at the regional level. This is not to say that R2P may not have likewise affected the identity of regional actors. Such an analysis, however, falls outside the scope of this book. Having positioned this research in the constructivist approach, having defined norms, and having positioned R2P within this, it is now time to look at how norms emerge and develop over time.

R2P and the norm life cycle: a critical evaluation

This section will discuss the normative concepts, processes, and actors that are relevant to the question of how and to what extent the norm of R2P has been internalised regionally. It will therefore focus on the norms literature, which deals with concepts such as norm emergence, diffusion, internalisation, localisation, and contestation. These concepts are crucial to this research, as it aims to explain how and to what extent the norm of R2P has been internalised at the regional level. Finnemore and Sikkink's (1998) norms life cycle model provides a good starting point to engage with these concepts. The following section will therefore start with a discussion of their model. Subsequently, it will discuss the main critiques of the model and propose ways forward. Key insights are derived from Acharya's body of work, especially from those pertaining to the local and regional roots of global norms (Acharya 2004, 2011, 2013). This discussion will introduce the concept of local norm construction. Bloomfield's (2016) article also provides a compelling way forward in the way it conceptualises different roles related to processes of normative change.

Finnemore and Sikkink (1998) published a formative piece on global norms that continues to be referenced in the wider norms literature that has emanated from it. The authors create a model to explain normative change, in which norm entrepreneurs construct new norms and convince states to adopt them, which after a process of 'norm cascades' (in which the norms gain increasing support in the international community) leads states to internalise new norms. The authors identify three stages: stage 1 refers to norm emergence, stage 2 to 'norm cascade', and stage 3 to internalisation. Stages 1 and 2 are separated by a tipping point, at which a critical mass of states (norm leaders) has embraced the new norm (Finnemore and Sikkink 1998, 895). During the first stage, norm entrepreneurs use persuasion to convince a critical mass of states to embrace a new norm. The second stage, in which norms 'cascade' through the international community, "is characterised more by a dynamic of imitation as the norm leaders attempt to socialise other states to become norm followers" (Finnemore and Sikkink 1998, 895). In both stages, norm diffusion manifests itself, as a new norm spreads through the international community, with an increasing number of actors (states in this case) encountering a new norm and starting to adopt it. The third stage, at the far end of the norm cascade, refers to a process of norm internalisation, in which "norms acquire a taken-for-granted quality and are no longer a matter of broad public debate" (Finnemore and Sikkink 1998, 895).

For an emergent norm to reach a threshold and move towards the norm cascade stage (stage 2), it must become institutionalised in specific sets of international rules and organisations (Finnemore and Sikkink 1998, 900). The authors argue that "institutionalisation contributes strongly to the possibility for a norm cascade both by clarifying what, exactly, the norm is and what constitutes violation (often a matter of some disagreement among actors) and by spelling out specific procedures by which norm leaders coordinate disapproval and sanctions for norm breaking" (Finnemore and Sikkink 1998, 900). At the same time, they acknowledge that "institutionalisation is not a necessary condition for a norm cascade," and that it "may follow, rather than precede, the initiation of a norm cascade" (Finnemore and Sikkink 1998, 900). A tipping point would be reached after norm entrepreneurs have persuaded a critical mass of states to become norm leaders and adopt new norms. Concerning this "critical mass", the authors hypothesise that about one-third of the total states in the system has to adopt the norm (based on preceding empirical research) and that the support of "critical states, without which the achievement of the substantive norm goal is compromised" is needed (Finnemore and Sikkink 1998, 901). These can be pivotal states in the substantive issue area, such as land-mine producing states for the land-mine treaty, or states with a certain moral stature, such as South Africa under Mandela (Finnemore and Sikkink 1998, 901).

At the far end of a norm cascade, "norms may become so widely accepted that they are internalised by actors and achieve a "taken-for-granted" quality that makes conformance with the norm almost automatic" (Finnemore and Sikkink 1998, 904). This process refers to the third stage of the life cycle model, norm internalisation. Finnemore and Sikkink (1998, 904) note the paradoxical nature of internalised norms: on the one hand they can be extremely powerful (because behaviour according to the norm is not questioned), while on the other hand, they can be very hard to discern (because actors do not seriously consider or discuss whether to conform).

While providing a first comprehensive account of norm diffusion and internalisation and continuing to serve as an important frame of reference in the norms literature, Finnemore and Sikkink's (1998) norm life cycle model has been criticised on multiple accounts. Scholars have taken issue with its linear take on normative evolution (Wiener 2009; Welsh 2013; Acharya 2013); its assumption of norm stability (Van Kersbergen and Verbeek 2007; Wiener 2009; Krook and True 2012; Welsh 2013); its cosmopolitan and Western bias (Acharya 2004); and the absence of a discussion of actors resisting normative change, so-called 'norm antipreneurs' (Bloomfield 2016). In this section, I will address these critiques one by one and I will also discuss ways forward.

Norm linearity and stability

First, Finnemore and Sikkink's account was criticised by post-positivists for its linearity and its assumptions about norm stability. On the former, a range of authors criticised Finnemore and Sikkink that they implicitly assumed that global norms developed linearly, from norm emergence to internalisation, which leaves little room for contestation and which would miss out on important circular normative dynamics (Wiener 2009; Welsh 2013; Acharya 2013). Regarding norm stability, multiple scholars contended that the early scholarship on norms assumed 'norm stability', i.e. that the content of norms becomes 'fixed' post-norm adoption or institutionalisation. Post-positivist scholars have criticised this notion, as to them, norms continue to be contested post-adoption as the meanings and understandings of norms continue to evolve given new circumstances and crises and varying cultural expectations (Wiener 2008; Welsh 2013). This can then potentially lead to backsliding, differential interpretations of a norm's meaning (Wiener 2009), or the need to reformulate norms (Van Kersbergen and Verbeek 2007). Having briefly addressed the criticisms of norm linearity and stability of the early norms literature, I will now discuss the two remaining critiques in further depth, given their strong relevance to this research. These critiques address the moral cosmopolitanism and the bias towards successful normative change of the early norms literature.

The cosmopolitan and Western bias

Acharya (2004) takes issue with what he identifies as the cosmopolitan and Western character of the first wave of norms scholarship. Norms scholarship of the 1990s (e.g. Finnemore and Sikkink 1998; Risse-Kappen 1994; Ropp and Sikkink 1999 amongst others) would have privileged the role played by transnational (almost invariably Western) actors, as they operated as key actors in these works. Effectively, this bias led to a conception of norm diffusion as teaching by Western actors to local actors, almost invariably actors in developing countries (Acharya 2004, 242). This downplayed the agency role of these local actors, while implicitly reserving the category of norm entrepreneurs exclusively for Western actors. The first wave of norms scholarship thus suffered from a too narrow scope of normative agency with a strong bias towards transnational, Western actors.

Acharya (2004, 242) problematises this notion of passive local recipients of global norms and the somewhat patronising account of Western transnational agents teaching 'good global norms' to actors in the developing world, in the hope of replacing 'bad local norms'. He offers a clear alternative with the concept of 'norm localisation', which "describes a complex process and outcome by which norm-takers build congruence between transnational norms (including norms previously institutionalised in a region) and local beliefs and practice" (Acharya 2004, 241). This concept shifts the analytical attention from transnational norm entrepreneurs to local actors, which would actively reconstruct foreign ideas with the aim of increasing the congruence of these ideas with local beliefs and practices (Acharya 2004, 245). Linking foreign ideas with existing beliefs may bring renewed legitimacy to the latter and could also enhance the profile and prestige of local elites (Acharya 2004, 246).

A blind spot of Acharya's (2004) localisation model is that it does not fully address the issue of norm entrepreneurship. It endows local actors with agency and a certain degree of entrepreneurship, as they "prune" and "graft" global norms to make them resonate with local priors. At the same time, this gives them at best a 'reactive entrepreneurial role' (as they alter global norms already 'out there') as opposed to a 'proactive entrepreneurial role' (which would have them promote their own norms on the global stage). Acharya (2011, 97) later addresses this issue with the concept of 'norm subsidiarity', which he describes as "a process whereby local actors create rules with a view to preserve their autonomy from dominance, neglect, violation, or abuse by more powerful central actors." Norm subsidiarity differs from localisation as it involves norm-making as opposed to norm-taking or norm-adjustment and it is more critical (instead of redefining global norms for local usage, it involves rejecting them and forwarding alternatives) (Acharya 2011, 97–98). The aim of 'subsidiarity norms' would be to strengthen regional autonomy and minimise outside influence, especially guarding against great power hypocrisy (Acharya 2011, 100). Finally, the concept of 'norm circulation' brings the processes of norm localisation and subsidiarity under one roof, providing a circular account of norm diffusion and internalisation (Acharya 2013). In this article, Acharya (2013) also recognises and elaborates on the contributions local actors make to international norms. This notion of local norm construction will have a central place in the analytical framework of this book and will now be discussed in further depth.

Local norm construction: the local roots of global norms

One of the key arguments in this book is that global norms often have local and regional roots and this aspect needs to be acknowledged if one wants to truly understand how these norms are diffused and internalised at the regional level.

Acharya's work has been critical in recognising this fact, and this is why his concepts and frameworks will help to contextualise the concept of local norm construction that will be proposed in this book.

Building on the critique of Acharya of the first wave of norm scholarship, it is important to further look into processes of local norm emergence and construction. I propose the following definition for local norm construction: "the process through which local actors build new norms". The concept of local norm construction adds to the existing literature, particularly to Acharya's work, but it gives local actors even more of an agency role. To illustrate the added value of this new concept, it will be helpful to distinguish it from some of Acharya's key concepts that have been previously discussed, i.e. norm localisation, subsidiarity, and circulation. The concept of norm localisation has local actors fit global norms with existing local priors, while norm subsidiarity sees local actors resist global norms that interfere with their local autonomy, while supporting those that support it (Acharya 2004; 2011). Arguably, Acharya's norm circulation comes closest to capturing local norm construction. He argues that "some supposedly global norms can have a regional context in terms of their origins. One should not assume – as most norm scholars do – that regions merely adopt or adapt global norms; it can be the other way around" (Acharya 2013, 469–70). He also asserts that norm creation is not solely the business of powerful states. On the contrary, weak states can create regional and global norms as well (Acharya 2013, 470).

Some sections of Acharya's article, however, still reveal an implicit assumption that there is a global norm to which locally constructed norms and local feedback contribute, which is, for instance, evident in the following quote:

> "At the same time, locally-constructed norms in similar issue areas (including those in the West or non-West) might be exported to the transnational space and acquire a global resonance, thereby modifying the definition or promotion *of the more globally prominent norm/s* in similar issue areas This multiple-agency, two-way, multi-step process of norm diffusion, based on resistance, feedback and repatriation, is the essence of my idea of norm circulation. Such circulation does not imply the weakening of *the norm*. Instead, it can lead to the strengthening of *the norm* and enhance the prospects for application and compliance."
>
> (Acharya 2013, 471, emphasis added)

There is thus a need to further conceptualise and understand processes of local norm construction. The expectation is that actors primarily engage in local norm construction to deal with a particular, concrete problem or set of problems in their local environment. These local norms can in a later stage find global resonance if they address problems that are experienced beyond their own region or even globally, and therefore contribute to norm building at the global level. The difference with some of Acharya's concepts is that this is not a case where local norms contribute to existing global norms (as is the case with subsidiarity and circulation), but where they help build new global norms. The concept of 'universalisation', in which a local norm is one-to-one universalised to become a global norm, comes close to capturing this dynamic (Acharya 2013). However, more often than not, it is expected that the local-global dynamic will be slightly more complex than that, as global norms will be constructed through different and multiple 'local inputs'.

This raises the question under which conditions local norm construction can be expected to contribute to global norm building. A few tentative scope conditions can be identified at this stage. First, as already noted, there should be a degree of similarity in experienced policy challenges in and beyond the local context. This means that the local norm being constructed is likely to speak to other localities and contexts as well. Second, the newly construed local norms should enjoy a degree of success or at least show potential in the local context, which could make it an attractive candidate for mimicking and adoption beyond the local context. Third, local norm construction is facilitated if some local actors emerge as global norm entrepreneurs and elevate the newly construed local norm as a building block of global normative solutions. With regard to this research, I will analyse to what extent R2P was built 'locally' in Europe and West Africa, i.e. to what extent local roots of the R2P norm can be identified in these two regions, which has repercussions for how the 'global UN-norm' was shaped and subsequently internalised by the regional organisations post-2005. This analysis will be conducted in the contextual and empirical chapters of this book.

It is now time to address another key point recognised in the more recent norms literature: the fact that normative change does not always come about and that norm entrepreneurs may actually fail or run into significant opposition in their normative endeavours.

The bias towards norm entrepreneurs and successful normative change

Finnemore and Sikkink (1998) acknowledge that norm entrepreneurs will not ordinarily receive a red-carpet treatment when they construct and advocate for new norms. The frames these entrepreneurs build to help carry their message "enter a contested normative space, in which they encounter embedded alternative norms and frames with their own understanding of appropriateness and interest" (Finnemore and Sikkink 1998, 897). All the same, the authors leave these avenues for resistance and contestation somewhat undertheorised. They do not really address from which sides contestation is to be expected, what sort of strategies of resistance is to be expected and how the process of contestation between new and embedded norms, as well as between competing understandings of a new norm is likely to play out. Bloomfield (2016, 321) aims to fill this gap with the concept of 'norm antipreneurs', which refers to "actors who defend the entrenched normative status quo against challengers." He argues that "recognising a clear distinction between entrepreneurs and antipreneurs" can actually facilitate "the construction of a spectrum of various roles", which actors might assume throughout the processes of norm contestation (Bloomfield 2016, 321). This well help in correcting the emphasis on norm entrepreneurs and successful normative change in the literature.

Bloomfield (2016) creates a norm dynamics role spectrum for these different types of roles, ranging from norm entrepreneurs to norm antipreneurs. The norm entrepreneurs at one side of the spectrum are all from the same normative community, they agree on the need for change and they are also largely on the same page when it comes "to the content of the norm that should be promoted to achieve it" (Bloomfield 2016, 330). These 'pure entrepreneurs' were introduced in the first wave of norms scholarship, to which Finnemore and Sikkink (1998) belong. The actors slightly more towards the centre are called 'competitor entrepreneurs'. Bloomfield (2016) links this to Wiener's (2004) concept of 'contested compliance', the notion that norms are subject to contestation from both norm setters and norm followers. Wiener (2004) seems to focus mostly on constructive contestation: norms are contested with the aim of making them more responsive to actors' needs, not to completely resist or reject them. Hence, competitor entrepreneurs agree on the need for change, they share basic normative understandings with the 'pure entrepreneurs' and contestation is thus limited to rivalry over which normative answer best fulfils the need for change (Bloomfield 2016, 316). The roles at the left side of the spectrum[1] – those just discussed – are already quite well-developed in the norm dynamics literature according to Bloomfield. His key theoretical contribution is on the other side of the spectrum.

On the right side of the spectrum, Bloomfield (2016) hypothesises one will find 'pure antipreneurs'. They belong to a radically different normative community than the norm entrepreneurs and they reject the need for change, which makes them "resist implacably" (Bloomfield 2016, 331). Related to this, I expect norm antipreneurs will organise 'counter-campaigns' to new norms. Pertaining to the norm of R2P, one should see norm antipreneurs campaign on sovereignty, territorial integrity, regime security, and the right to govern internal affairs without external interference. These principles will serve as 'counter norms' to R2P, to undermine the R2P campaign and to point at the deficits of the R2P norm. Antipreneurs could argue that norms as sovereignty and non-intervention are deeply enshrined in international law and are morally desirable, as they promote political and cultural diversity and protect 'the weak' against 'the strong' (Ayoob 2004). Making sovereignty and non-intervention look natural, 'the way things have always been done' and 'ought to be done' ('naturalising the 'sovereignty-discourse'), implies discrediting the rival discourse of R2P. Antipreneurs can warn for the disruption and harm that R2P could bring to the international order (thus exploiting the second blocking opportunity), such as being used as a tool by the strong to legitimise interventions in weaker states whenever this suits their preferences (Ayoob 2004). As a strategy, antipreneurs might even securitise the existing normative framework, arguing that the guiding principles of international relations, such as state sovereignty, and non-intervention (referent objects), are at an existential risk because of the R2P campaign (existential threat) (Buzan and Waever 2003).

This idea of 'counter-campaigns' resembles Acharya's norm subsidiarity model, which Bloomfield (2016) links to the actions of norm antipreneurs. Acharya (2011, 97) defines norm subsidiarity as "a process whereby local actors create rules with a view to preserve their autonomy from dominance, neglect, violation, or abuse by more powerful central actors." The two main effects of norm subsidiarity Acharya (2011) identifies are a 'challenging/resisting effect' and a 'supportive/strengthening effect'. The former refers to the way local actors use subsidiary norms to offer normative resistance to central actors, while at the same time claiming "the right to formulate rules and deal with their own issues without intervention by any higher authority" (Acharya 2011, 101). The latter involves local support for existing common global norms which are vital to preserving local autonomy (Acharya 2011, 101). Acharya (2011) mentions norms as sovereignty, territorial integrity, and non-intervention as examples – among others – of global norms that 'weaker states' invoke and support. With the 'counter-campaigns', I expect norm antipreneurs to resist the normative change that R2P would bring about by expressing support for existing global norms which preserve local (or regional) autonomy, such as sovereignty and non-intervention. The idea of counter-campaigns thus speaks to both the challenging/resisting and the supportive/strengthening effects of Acharya's (2011) norm subsidiarity.

The more moderate position on the right side of the spectrum belongs to the 'creative resisters', a role conception introduced by Campbell-Verduyn (2016). 'Creative resisters' are not from the same normative community as the entrepreneurs, "but perhaps because they are forced by circumstance or maybe because they have been partially persuaded by the entrepreneurs they concede that some (minimal) change is acceptable or necessary" (Bloomfield 2016, 331). They therefore "yield some ground while still essentially defending the status quo" (Bloomfield 2016, 331). Depending on the extent 'creative resisters' are willing to compromise, they may be engaging in norm localisation or norm subsidiarity. If they tend towards the middle of the spectrum, signalling a willingness to compromise, localisation is the likely option. If, however, they tend more to the right of the spectrum, signalling a preference to resist, norm subsidiarity is a more likely strategy.

Having discussed the various normative 'role types' as identified by Bloomfield (2016), it is now time to assess how the normative status quo in the two regional organisations under analysis, the EU and ECOWAS, can be fruitfully analysed. Scholars should start by investigating the normative status quo in the regions under analysis and ask themselves which norms are entrenched in the region, which are unstable, and which norms are contested or are 'good candidates' for contestation (Bloomfield 2016). The latter is expected to apply to unstable norms. With regard to this research, it is important to get an understanding of regional understandings of the norm of sovereignty: which 'sovereignty understandings' are dominant in the region? Are these in line with traditional understandings of sovereignty (i.e. emphasising absolute sovereignty, territorial integrity, regime security, etc.) or with more qualified notions of sovereignty (i.e. emphasising qualified sovereignty, balancing sovereignty with human rights considerations, prioritising human security over state security, regional experiences with sovereignty pooling, etc.)? The status of sovereignty in the region at the time R2P as a norm emerges will be called the 'normative status quo', i.e. the normative situation as it is in the early 2000s. One needs to bear in mind that the 'normative status quo' does not have to imply a stable normative context with regard to a specific norm. For example, a regional normative status quo may be characterised by qualified notions of sovereignty, i.e. traditional notions of sovereignty are already contested and may not enjoy majority support in the region under analysis. When R2P as a norm emerges against that normative context, norm entrepreneurs are expected to be advantaged over norm antipreneurs, as there is no need to problematise traditional understandings of sovereignty in the region. The structural factors underpinning the 'normative status quo' consist of embedded and contested norms, but also institutional factors. In the case of R2P, one relevant institutional factor would be decision-making procedures on regional interventions. If decision-making procedures make it difficult to reach regional agreement on interventions, for instance because of a 'unanimity-rule', this may prove an impediment to internalising the more robust aspects of R2P. This is just one example of how structural factors can inhibit or facilitate normative change at the regional level.

Generally speaking, in the context of an entrenched normative status quo, antipreneurs are expected to be advantaged over entrepreneurs. Given the stability of the normative status quo, antipreneurs will be well-positioned to seize the two blocking opportunities. Entrepreneurs, on the other hand, will face an uphill battle in problematising the status quo and promoting a new norm to solve the issue (Bloomfield 2016). Concerning the two blocking opportunities, it will be relatively easy for norm antipreneurs to maintain there are no problems with the current status quo, which means they will generally not have to focus on the new norm entrepreneurs propose ('if there is not a problem, one does not need a 'solution'). Even in the unlikely case entrepreneurs have some success in problematising the entrenched normative status quo, antipreneurs can still refer to the costs generally associated with change ('sunk costs'), the unproven track record of the new norm and/or other specific problems they have with this new norm (Bloomfield 2016). As norm entrepreneurs will face an uphill battle problematising the status quo and promoting a new norm to solve the issue, they might have to compromise. Instead of aiming to replace or fundamentally change the normative order, they may have to try to adjust it (Bloomfield 2016).

In the context of an unstable normative status quo, the roles are reversed. Now, entrepreneurs are expected to be advantaged over antipreneurs. Entrepreneurs will be well-positioned to seize the opportunity presented by the crisis or structural shift to problematise the status quo and advocate for a new norm to address the problem. Given that the status quo is unstable, antipreneurs will find it difficult to seize the two blocking opportunities: first, it will be difficult to maintain there are no problems with the current status quo, which makes it hard for antipreneurs to seize this blocking opportunity. This means they will have to focus on the new norm entrepreneurs propose ('there might be a problem, but this is not the way to solve it'). Clearly, this situation puts antipreneurs on the defence (Bloomfield 2016). Given the unstable status quo and the difficulty antipreneurs will likely have in seizing the two blocking opportunities, their preferred strategy of 'implacable resistance' may not pay off. Instead, they may be forced to adopt an intermediary position, such as 'creative resistance' to defend the status quo to a more limited extent (Bloomfield 2016, 332). It needs to be acknowledged, though, that there is no determinacy in actors' behaviour and strategies given set contexts, as norm antipreneurs may, for instance, still engage in principled opposition against a new norm, even in the face of an unstable normative status quo that works against them.

The regional security governance literature

It is now time to turn to the regional security governance literature to synthesise this with the norms literature for the purpose of this book. The regional security governance literature can provide insights into the role that regional organisations can play vis-à-vis regional security in general and R2P in specific. This discussion will lay the groundwork for the identification of several regional factors that theorise the gap between the norms and regional security governance literature, with a focus on the R2P norm.

In the literature, regional organisations are often seen as ideal actors to implement R2P, as they enjoy certain advantages in comparison with other international actors. They would have a better understanding of the root causes of conflicts and local conflict dynamics and they would enjoy more legitimacy on the ground than global actors like the UN (Suominen 2005; MacFarlane 2014; Kefale 2015). This particular branch of the literature has the tendency to focus on the utility the regional actors have for the UN and other global actors in the field of peace and security, thereby downplaying their agency. The regional security governance and region building literature seems to more seriously address the agency role of regional organisations. This part of the analytical framework will analyse the theories and concepts proposed by these strands of the literature to assess the role regional actors can play in implementing security norms like R2P.

Kacowicz and Press-Barnathan (2016, 299) define regional security governance (RSG) as "the development and dynamics of security arrangements in a given region, institutionalised through regional and sub-regional organisations that share understandings, rules, and practices in the security realm." According to the authors, RSG is more and more performed by multi-purpose regional organisations, like the EU, as opposed to those specifically founded for security purposes, like NATO (Kacowicz and Press-Barnathan 2016, 300). They also observe that regionalism in the developing world is often of a defensive nature in the sense that it developed out of concern about extra-regional great power intervention. Regionalism here thus serves the goal of boosting sovereignty to mitigate state concerns over regime survival (Kacowicz and Press-Barnathan 2016, 302). This makes this type of regionalism fundamentally different from that in the EU, which is characterised by the pooling of sovereignty. With regard to R2P, the defensive nature of regional projects in the developing world might explain resistance from some developing countries to R2P, as they might believe the norm carries the potential to infringe on regional integration projects and national sovereignty.

In their discussion of regional security governance, Adler and Greve (2009) argue that different orders and systems of governance can actually overlap, and it is important to understand the reasons for these kinds of overlap. For instance, there seems to have been a return to a balance of power rationale in Europe with the question of NATO membership of Ukraine and Georgia. This is seemingly at odds with Europe's security community, which is defined by "dependable expectations of peaceful change," but the authors argue that the coexistence of different systems of governance is actually quite widespread (Adler and Greve 2009, 66). In the context of this research, the notion of overlapping systems of security governance is interesting, as it may provide insights into the normative contestation of R2P at the regional level. Some systems of security governance, such as security communities, seem – at least in theory – to be more receptive to norms like R2P, than others, such as balance-of-power systems. The balance of power logic demands foreign policies to be focused on state security, either through national defence investments ('internal balancing') or alliances ('external balancing') (Adler and Greve 2009). Norms such as R2P are in such a system of peripheral concern, as spending foreign policy resources on these issues might compromise the objective of guaranteeing the security of the state. A security community, on the other hand, subscribes to shared norms and values and facilitates peace among its members (Adler and Greve 2009). This could allow member states to focus on matters beyond state security, such as the defence of human rights through for instance R2P. The norm-based nature of security communities further increases the attention for human rights issues.

Adler and Greve (2009) borrow the notion of security communities from Deutsch (1957), who pioneered the concept. Deutsch (1957, 2) uses the term to describe "a group of people which has become integrated", meaning "they have attained, within a territory, a sense of community, and of institutions and practices strong enough and widespread enough to assure, for a 'long' time, dependable expectations of 'peaceful change'." Deutsch distinguishes between two types of security communities: the amalgamated and pluralistic ones. Amalgamated security communities are created when two or more previously independent states form a common government. This type of security communities is rather rare in history. The formation of the United States out of the previously independent states is an important example of such an amalgamated security community (Deutsch 1957). Pluralistic security communities are a less ambitious alternative, which can arise out of a process of integration between states that retain their sovereignty (Deutsch 1957). Deutsch (1957) argues that these pluralistic security communities are easier to establish and maintain than their amalgamated counterparts. The EU is a key example of a pluralistic security community, as it grew out of a process of integration between states that retained their formal sovereignty.

Multiple authors have investigated the role that regional powers play in regions. Lake (1997; 2009) and Adler and Barnett (1998) have argued that unipolar systems dominated by a regional power would generally produce a more peaceful regional order. Adler and Barnett (1998, 40) hold somewhat optimistic assumptions about regional powers, though, as they argue that power can work as a catalyst for regional integration processes: weaker states would be attracted to it in their search for security and protection, while the regional powers themselves would use their power to develop a common regional identity. This presupposes that regions with a strong regional power would be likely candidates for developing peaceful regional orders. It also assumes that all regional powers share an interest of commitment to peace-fostering regionalisation (Lopez 2014). The behaviour of the regional hegemon has important repercussions for how actors in the region will perceive the norm of R2P: if states in the region feel threatened by the regional hegemon, they might treat a norm involving intervention with considerable scepticism. If, however, states in the region have a positive perception of their regional power and see their regional project as fostering peace, they might have fewer concerns about the norm.

This critical evaluation of the dual importance of material and more subjective factors, such as self-perception and leadership aspirations, in determining regional leadership is relevant to this research: it is important to see how the regional powers in the regional case studies perceive themselves and their interests concerning the region, as this may shine light on their willingness to take up leadership roles in the normative sphere. It has been argued, for instance, that Germany's past has made it reluctant to play a leadership role in Europe when it comes to R2P, especially because of unease with the 'robust side' of the norm (Brockmeier et al. 2014, 444). Another significant line of enquiry is to see whether Nigeria, given its position as strongest state in the West-African region, sees a leadership role for itself in the region, possibly providing some sort of hegemonic stability. If this could be established, this would likely have repercussions for the norm internalisation of R2P in ECOWAS. Given Nigeria's dominance in the region, it may be better able to shape the discourse on R2P around its preferences than in a region with multiple powers, such as Europe. Also, if Nigeria takes an interest in R2P, it might make it part of the rules of the regional system and enforce it when needed as a regional hegemon (Gilpin 1981).

To wrap up, the literature discussed in this section will be useful in assessing the role of regional organisations in implementing security norms like R2P.

The discussion will provide insights into what sort of regionalism developed in the different regions under analysis and how this influenced regional normative positioning towards the R2P norm. What follows now is a brief discussion of regional actor types, related to expected predispositions towards R2P. This will set the stage for the identification of a number of relevant regional factors and their expected impact on the likelihood of internalisation of R2P. It needs to be stated at the outset that regional actor types and regional factors are not assumed to affect internalisation in a linear way and much will depend on contextual and case-specific factors. It is an important first attempt, though, to theorise the regional-normative-R2P link, which is currently insufficiently addressed in the literature.

Regional actor types

Based on the review of the regional security governance literature, I expect different types of regional actors to deal with the norm of R2P in different ways. Leaving for the moment aside if they can be objectively categorised as certain regional actor types or if this is more a matter of self-perception, I distinguish between the following three regional actor types: regional security communities, balance-of-power systems, and hegemonic systems (Adler and Greve 2009; Destradi 2008). It is expected that these types deal with R2P in different ways, also conditioned by how their regional actor type manifests itself, which I will explicit below. For every regional actor type, I will briefly describe its characteristics, followed by its likely perception and implementation strategies of the norm of R2P.

Regional security communities are characterised by dependable expectations of peaceful change and highly institutionalised interactions and context (Deutsch 1957). Besides, they subscribe to shared norms and values (Adler and Greve 2009). This section will refer to pluralistic security communities, which arise out of a process of integration between states that retain their sovereignty, as opposed to amalgamated security communities, which are created when two or more previously independent states form a common government (Deutsch 1957). The norm of R2P could fit an environment that is characterised by peaceful change, as state sovereignty and regime security are largely taken for granted and not of direct concern. This provides opportunities for widening the concept of security to include considerations like human rights and mass atrocity prevention. This begs the question how regional security communities will internalise and implement different aspects of R2P. Given the highly institutionalised nature of regional security communities, they are likely to embed new norms in their existing institutional structures (Adler and Greve 2009). How regional security communities will internalise R2P, besides, depends on many factors, such as capacities and the region's self-image. For instance, if the region has states with strong military-strategic cultures, it may be inclined to focus on internalisation of the 'robust side' of R2P. If its expertise is, however, more in the diplomatic and humanitarian sphere, it may be more likely to focus on the internalisation of the prevention side of R2P. Various capacities and expertise can of course overlap in regions as well. Apart from capacities, 'self-perception' of the region and actors within the region matters. Regional security communities may, for instance, be inclined to export their 'home model' of dependable expectations of peaceful change outside the region, therefore contributing to peaceful interactions in other regions, which would mean more a focus on prevention than on reaction in terms of R2P (Adler and Greve 2009).

Balance-of-power systems are generally characterised by a pervasive security dilemma, insecurity and a peace that cannot be taken for granted. These dynamics force states to rely on self-help and balance against external threats (Adler and Greve 2009). The institutional context tends to be loose and interactions between states often have a zero-sum character. State actors in a balance-of-power system are likely to perceive the norm of R2P with a degree of indifference or even contempt. Given their enduring quest for security, their priority is with sovereignty and the security of the state. That sits uneasily with the aim of R2P to open the box of security and to prioritise human security over state security. States will most likely see norms like this as an unnecessary distraction at best or in opposition to their goal of survival in an insecure environment at worst, especially when R2P is seen as a tool that could legitimate outside intervention. In terms of internalisation, actors could see R2P as irreconcilable with their objectives. In that case, they could refuse to internalise the norm. Otherwise, an ad hoc implementation is likely. Given the fact that balance-of-power systems are usually loosely institutionalised, it is unlikely that actors will institutionalise norms, especially when these new norms are far off their balance-of-power logic (Adler and Greve 2009). New norms might provide a new consideration that can be used on a case-to-case basis, alongside other considerations. Whether the norm is invoked and will inform policy action will thus depend on case-specific peculiarities instead of being informed by a standardised, institutionalised approach.

Hegemonic systems generally consist of three types: one in which hegemons provide so-called 'hegemonic stability' and play a largely positive role in their region and one in which they dominate to further their own interests and therefore play a largely negative role in their region. A third possibility is a system in which the regional hegemon is relatively absent in regional affairs, a 'hegemonic isolationist system'. Regional systems characterised by hegemonic stability generally foster peaceful regional orders. They often have relatively well-developed regional institutions and positive-sum interactions between states (Gilpin 1981; Lake 1997, 2009; Adler and Barnett 1998). On the contrary, 'hegemonic dominance systems' (Destradi (2008) refers to these systems as 'empires') are characterised by assertive behaviour from the hegemon, which creates a security dilemma and security threats for the weaker states in the region. These regional systems will generally be loosely institutionalised with predominantly zero-sum interactions between states, at least between the hegemon and the other states in the region. For the weaker states, this will mean they have to decide whether they will bandwagon with or balance against the hegemon (Destradi 2008). The likely perception of R2P depends on the type of hegemonic system. Under hegemonic stability, regional hegemons generally take a leadership role within their regions and their regional role tends to be positively perceived by other regional states, which might reduce fears of hegemonic abuse of R2P. Under hegemonic dominance, on the contrary, weaker states may fear that the hegemon may abuse the norm for interventions in the region. In the latter case, the weaker states may be willing to accept and internalise the primary responsibility to protect but resist the international community side, as this could be seen as intruding upon national sovereignty. As a strategy, they can try to build a coalition of weak states in the region to resist against the third pillar in international fora. In hegemonic isolationist systems, it is difficult to hypothesise the likelihood of internalisation of R2P. In any case, in these types of systems, states in the region cannot depend on the regional hegemon to lead the regional internalisation process.

An example of a hegemonic isolationist system would be medieval China. China was for a long time throughout its history a rather isolationist regional power in Asia despite having significant resources: even before Europeans started their global discoveries, China had an impressive fleet that went as far as Africa, but then decided to abolish it to focus on home affairs (Edwards 2017). These examples demonstrate there is nothing natural or 'automatic' about hegemons pursuing a policy of providing hegemonic stability, just because they have the means to do so. So, rather than assuming that hegemons or leaders share the same kind of identity, interests, and objectives, it makes sense to investigate whether regional powers are likely to take up a leadership role given the way they see themselves and how their perceived interests frame their policy towards their regions (Lopez 2014, 66).

Regional security governance factors and R2P

Based on the literature and the discussion above, one can expect several regional factors to influence the likelihood of internalisation of R2P at the regional level. It is important to reiterate that these factors do not have to affect internalisation in a linear fashion, and much will depend on contextual and case-specific factors. The factors are useful in the sense that they give an indication of which factors are expected to play a role when it comes to regional internalisation of R2P. They therefore contribute to theorising the intersections between the norms and the regional security governance literature, one of the key theoretical contributions of this book.

The first factor is the fear of the use of hard power, which is operationalised as expressed concern by states about past, current, or potential future use of hard power in the region. The expectation here is that in a region where there is fear of the use of hard power, one would expect more concerns in the region about R2P. After all, states might fear that R2P could serve as legitimisation of intervention (Bellamy 2005). These concerns of states might, in turn, negatively affect the likelihood of internalisation of R2P at the regional level. If

R2P could potentially be used as a 'Trojan horse', why incorporate the norm into regional policies and discourse? Hard power is here defined as "the ability to coerce, growing out of a country's military and economic might" as opposed to soft power, which Nye (2004, 256) defines as "the ability to get what you want through attraction rather than coercion and payments." The expectation here is that if hard power – whether used by regional or external powers – plays a prevalent role in a regional system, one would expect more concerns in the region about R2P. After all, smaller states in a region might fear R2P will be abused by more powerful states in- or outside the region to legitimise an interventionist agenda. This dynamic could negatively affect the likelihood of internalisation of R2P at the regional level.

A second factor concerns regional actor type and the self-image of the regional organisation and actors within the region. Here, it is important to see if the regional organisations in question perceive themselves as (close to) one of the ideal types. The many references to 'Europe as a peace project', both by officials and academics, and the extensive literature on 'civilian power Europe', cosmopolitan Europe, and the EU as a 'normative power' indicate that the EU can be classified as a security community and also perceives itself that way (Von der Leyen 2019; Tusk 2019; Duchene 1972; Habermas 2003; Manners 2002). Dependable expectations of peaceful change are the norm in the EU, and it is currently unconceivable that this will change (Adler and Greve 2009). ECOWAS sees itself as an economic integration project and as one of the pillars of the African Economic Community (ECOWAS 2022). In terms of regional system types, ECOWAS can be best characterised as a regional hegemonic system. The literature on ECOWAS is rich with references to the role played by the regional hegemon, Nigeria. Nigeria also tends to see itself as regional leader or hegemon, as evidenced by statements from its officials, and so do the smaller states in the region (Adebajo 2000; Lopez 2014).

The expectation is that if a regional actor perceives itself as a regional security community, this could positively affect the likelihood of internalisation of R2P. Dependable expectations of peaceful change make for a stable security environment (Deutsch 1957; Adler and Barnett 1998), which would, in turn, allow states to explore wider concepts of security, beyond national security. This may make these types of regional systems receptive to the norm of R2P, which resonates stronger with 'human security' than with traditional notions of security. Self-perception as a regional hegemonic system comes with less clear expectations with regard to the likelihood of R2P internalisation, first and foremost given the diversity of possible subtypes of hegemonic systems, which will be further discussed below. The self-image of actors within the region also matters in framing responses to the R2P norm. For instance, the self-image of Germany makes it reluctant to engage with the 'robust side' of R2P, whereas the self-images of the UK and France facilitate their engagement with this aspect of R2P, given cognitive priors related to intervention in their national strategic cultures (Brockmeier et al. 2014). Finally, the self-image of middle powers often leads them to take leadership in niche issues. It will be instructive to see if one can witness this type of 'middle power leadership' related to R2P within the EU and ECOWAS (Behringer 2013).

The expectations with regard to R2P internalisation in hegemonic regional systems are more diffuse than in regional security communities and depend largely on the (self-)perceptions of and the role(s) played by the hegemon in the region. As previously discussed, three distinct regional hegemonic systems are identified: hegemonic stability systems, hegemonic dominance systems, and hegemonic isolationist systems. In hegemonic stability systems, the hegemon plays a constructive role, promoting hegemonic stability. If there is an interest in R2P in the region, the hegemon may ensure a stable institutionalisation of the norm within the region in line with its own preferences, which corresponds with the 'hegemonic stability thesis' (Gilpin 1981). In this type of hegemonic system, weaker regional states are expected to generally have a positive view of the hegemon, which should reduce fears of abuse of R2P and therefore decrease the likelihood of regional resistance against R2P by weaker states. In hegemonic dominance systems, on the contrary, the hegemon plays a dominant role, narrowly pursuing its own interests. This will likely negatively affect the likelihood of regional R2P internalisation. Weaker states in the region are likely to particularly resist the third pillar of R2P, as they fear interventions from the regional hegemon (Destradi 2008). In hegemonic isolationist systems, the hegemon plays an absent role, resulting in only very limited engagement with the region. In this case, it is an open question how the region will respond to the norm of R2P. In any case, states in the region cannot depend on the hegemon to provide resources and guidance for internalising the R2P norm at the regional level in this context.

A third factor entails the available and preferred policy resources in a region and its expected impact on R2P internalisation. The expectation is that the availability of and expertise in particular policy resources, whether these are diplomatic, economic, institutional, or military, will influence which aspects of R2P regional actors are *able* to internalise and which they are not able to internalise, or to a more limited extent. A preference for particular policy resources may, in the same vein, influence which aspect(s) of R2P regional actors are *willing* to internalise and which aspects to a lesser extent.

The fourth and final factor is the degree of regional institutionalisation and the expected impact on R2P internalisation. The general expectation is the higher the degree of regional institutionalisation one witnesses, the higher the chance of an institutional response to new global norms such as R2P. The logic here is that regional organisations that operate in a dense institutional environment will be – by their very nature – inclined to formulate institutional responses to R2P, with the opposite being the case for regional actors operating in more loose institutional environments. An example of the latter would be balance-of-power systems, where the ever-pervasive quest for security often precludes regional institutionalisation and where new 'global norms' will often be met with ad hoc, and case-by-case responses at best (Gallagher 2012). In short, the expected divergent regional responses to the

R2P norm reflect the different natures of the regional organisations under analysis, which will impact on their approaches to norm diffusion pressures emanating from the global level: while heavily institutionalised regional organisations are expected to respond through creating new institutions and policies, more loosely institutionalised regional organisations are expected to respond in a more ad hoc manner to diffusion pressures or be altogether unresponsive, if the 'global norm' in question has a poor regional fit (Acharya 2011).

Specific aspects of norm internalisation of R2P

Having discussed the regional factors, one can now explore the ways through which specific R2P provisions can be internalised: fundamentally, what should one see to be able to speak of internalisation of the R2P norm? This book provides the following definition to norm internalisation: "the process through which actors effect change in response to a norm in terms of discourse, institutions, and policies, with the aim of adhering to and living up to the key tenets and obligations of that norm." This definition is in line with Checkel's (1997, 477) 'elite learning mechanism', a diffusion mechanism which entails a process of learning leading agents to adopt prescriptions embodied in international norms. Checkel (1997, 477) asserts that "norms are internalised and constitute a set of shared intersubjective understandings that make behavioural claims; their adoption is anything but instrumental" (Finnemore and Sikkink (1998, 904) similarly argue that "norms may become so widely accepted that they are internalised by actors and achieve a "taken-for-granted" quality that makes conformance with the norm almost automatic" (Finnemore and Sikkink 1998, 904). The proposed definition in this book, however, further specifies where one should see this "taken-for-grantedness" when it comes to norm internalisation, namely in discourse, institutions, and policies.

Directly related to R2P, the changes in discourse, institutions, and policies should be tailored to effectively meet the expectations of R2P and its component parts raised in the various areas, i.e. the responsibility to prevent, react, and rebuild. To take the responsibility to prevent as example, for an actor to have internalised this component of R2P, one would expect it to express rhetorical support for it, provide institutional means to engage with it (i.e. officials, organisations, and divisions), and devise specific policies to implement it, such as creating atrocity prevention policies or integrating atrocity prevention in existing policies and programmes. This conceptualisation of norm internalisation presupposes 'respect for the letter and the spirit' of the norm. This would rule out merely instrumental or strategic applications of the norm, when actors apply it out of self-interest or for other instrumental reasons, as indicative of norm internalisation of R2P (Checkel 1997).

Before proceeding with a discussion of how norm internalisation can be specifically measured, it is helpful to highlight how this concept differs from related concepts in the literature, such as 'norm consolidation' and 'norm implementation'. Norm consolidation, a concept widely used by Crossley, is primarily used to assess a norm's status in contemporary international society through its place in the norms life cycle and its effect on international practice (Crossley 2016, 27). Norm internalisation differs from norm consolidation in the sense that the former is actor-specific, whereas the latter assesses the status the norm enjoys in the wider population of actors. Norm implementation, on the other hand, is very practically oriented and refers to the specific measures that need to be taken to operationalise a norm (UNGA 2009; Welsh 2013). Arguably, implementation is part of norm internalisation, but internalisation goes deeper than that (De Franco et al. 2016).

What needs to be specified then is how norm internalisation can be measured. This can be done through assessing the degree of discursive, institutional, and policy change one observes in response to the norm. Has R2P made inroads in the discourse of regional institutions and officials? Have new institutions been created or have existing institutions been adapted to implement the norm? And, finally, have policies and programmes been created or adjusted to implement R2P? Measuring norm internalisation both has a quantitative and a qualitative component. Pertaining to the quantitative component, the frequency of references to the norm in regional discourse can, for instance, indicate urgency and importance assigned to the norm. More qualitatively, one will have to assess how and to what extent changes in regional discourse, institutions, and policies are in line with the expectations raised by the various aspects of R2P. The concepts of the Europeanisation literature will serve as an important yardstick here. They are able to capture conceptually the depths of change and provide an ordinal measurement to this. In case one witnesses quite shallow changes in terms of discourse and policies, this might reflect a process of norm absorption, whereas the creation of significant new policies and institutions and the overhaul of existing policies may be indicative of a process of norm transformation. This conceptualisation will be further discussed in the next section.

It is evident that more often than not, actors' internalisation of R2P will fall short of perfect internalisation, consistent with all the different aspects of the norm, or total 'non-internalisation'. Therefore, each R2P provision will benefit from a number of 'qualifiers': qualifying what internalisation should look like and at the same time providing an idea of to what extent actors will internalise the norm. It is to this categorisation we turn now.

Table 2.1 shows the different aspects of internalisation of R2P. The first aspect of internalisation is formal support for the R2P norm, and it holds that if one sees mentioning of R2P in formal documents or speeches, this could be an indication of norm internalisation of R2P in terms of formal support. This general statement will benefit from several qualifiers. Mentioning of R2P in formal documents or speeches could be an indication of norm internalisation, depending on (1) the author of the document or the person giving the speech (the higher ranked the official, the more authority references to R2P in the document or speech convey), (2) the type of document (which agency or ministry produces the document? The more important the document, the

Table 2.1 Different aspects of internalisation of the R2P norm

1	Formal support	*If we see mentioning of R2P in formal documents or speeches, this could be an indication of norm internalisation of R2P, depending on:* *Authoritative support: the author of the document/person giving the speech, the type of document, the setting of the speech, the way of addressing the topic, the frequency of addressing the topic*
2	Responsibility to prevent	*If actors engage in preventive efforts in (imminent) R2P cases, this could be an indication of norm internalisation of the norm of R2P, depending on:* *Authoritative support: references made to R2P/the responsibility to prevent as a reason to become involved;* *Practice: consistency between prescribed and taken preventive action;* *the level of engagement*
3	Responsibility to react a) sanctions	*If we see the application of sanctions in an R2P case (imminent or ongoing mass atrocity crimes), this could be an indication of norm internalisation of the norm of R2P, depending on:* *Authoritative support: references made to R2P/the responsibility to react as a reason to become involved;* *Practice: the degree to which the sanctions are tailored towards R2P ends; the seriousness of the sanctions*
	b) military action	*If we see military action in an R2P case (imminent or ongoing mass atrocity crimes) authorised by the UN Security Council, this could be an indication of norm internalisation of the norm of R2P, depending on:* *Authoritative support: references made to R2P/the responsibility to react as a reason to become involved;* *Practice: the degree to which military action is tailored towards R2P ends; the level of military engagement*
4	Responsibility to rebuild	*If actors are engaged in rebuilding activities after a conflict that represents an R2P situation, this could be an indication of internalisation of the (rebuilding component of the) norm of R2P, depending on:* *Authoritative support: references made to R2P/the responsibility to rebuild as a reason to become involved;* *Practice: the degree to which the rebuilding efforts are tailored towards R2P ends; the seriousness of rebuilding efforts*

more authority references to R2P in it convey), (3) the setting of the speech (the more important the venue, the more authority references to R2P in the speech convey), (4) the way of addressing the topic (are references to R2P generally positive, neutral, or negative? This is of key importance to assess formal support. In addition, do references to R2P provide any clues about how to internalise and implement R2P?), and (5) the frequency of addressing the topic (the more references to R2P are made, the more urgency and importance the references to R2P in the document or speech convey).

For the three different components of R2P, the responsibility to prevent, react, and rebuild, it is useful to refer to Crossley's (2016) work. Crossley (2016, 82) defines the responsibility to prevent as the responsibility "to address both the root causes and the direct causes of internal conflict and other man-made crises putting populations at risk." In terms of operationalisation of this R2P component, one should assess if "international actors seek to become engaged early on in a conflict, prior to an escalation of political violence that may lead to the perpetration of R2P crimes," and if " 'prevention' is given as a justification for early involvement in political crises" (Crossley 2016, 150). The responsibility to prevent is captured by the second aspect of R2P internalisation, and it holds that if actors engage in preventive efforts in (imminent) R2P cases, this could be an indication of norm internalisation of the norm of R2P. This would depend, however, on (1) references made to R2P as a reason to become involved (authoritative support), (2) consistency between preventive actions taken and preventive actions prescribed by the R2P norm (practice), and (3) the level of engagement (practice).

When a crisis has passed the preventive stage, reactive measures are warranted. Crossley (2016, 82) defines the responsibility to react as the responsibility "to respond to situations of compelling human need with appropriate measures, which may include coercive measures like sanctions and international prosecution, and in extreme cases military intervention." In order to assess if states live up to their pillar two and three obligations, "it is necessary to establish whether states consistently respond to R2P crimes, and whether the responses taken conform to the principles underpinning R2P as a norm" (Crossley 2016, 119). As the third aspect of internalisation shows, the responsibility to react has a sanctions component, which includes coercive measures and international prosecution, (aspect 3a) and a military component (aspect 3b). Concerning sanctions, their application in an R2P case can be an indication of norm internalisation of R2P, depending on (1) references made to R2P as a reason to become involved (authoritative support), (2) the degree to which the issued sanctions are tailored towards R2P ends, i.e. preventing and responding to mass atrocities (practice), and (3) the seriousness of the sanctions (practice). Similarly, military action in an R2P case can be an indication of norm internalisation of R2P, depending on (1) references made to R2P as a reason to become involved (authoritative support), (2) the degree to which the military actions are tailored towards R2P ends, i.e. preventing and responding to mass atrocities (practice), and (3) the level of military engagement (practice).

Once a crisis or conflict with an atrocity component has dissipated, the need for reactive measures diminishes, while there is usually a vast amount of rebuilding to do, both in physical and societal terms. Physical infrastructure has been destroyed, intergroup trust has plummeted, and political and societal institutions have decayed. Crossley (2016, 82) defines the responsibility to rebuild as the responsibility "to provide, particularly after a military intervention, full assistance with recovery, reconstruction, and reconciliation, addressing the causes of the harm the intervention was designed to halt or avert". As the fourth and final aspect of R2P internalisation outlines, if actors are engaged in rebuilding activities after a conflict that represents an R2P situation, this could be an indication of internalisation of the rebuilding component of the norm of R2P, depending on (1) references made to R2P as a reason to become involved (authoritative support), (2) the degree to which the rebuilding efforts are tailored towards R2P ends, i.e. preventing and responding to mass atrocities (practice), and (3) the seriousness of rebuilding efforts (practice).

Types of internalisation

The discussion so far has dealt with the different aspects of internalisation of R2P, in terms of the content or 'building blocks' of R2P, ranging from the expression of formal support for the norm to the implementation of rebuilding measures in the post-atrocities phase. Arguably, this addresses the 'how-aspect' of the research question, i.e. showing how actors internalise the R2P norm: some actors may focus on prevention and rebuilding, whereas other actors focus on reaction. Finally, actors may only pay lip service to the norm through formal support but leave the substantive aspects of R2P that need policy action, such as prevention, reaction, and rebuilding, untouched. While important, this discussion still leaves the 'to what extent' aspect of the research question largely unaddressed. Relevant here is how far and deep internalisation of R2P reaches, i.e. how much institutional, political, and discursive change actually takes place in response to the norm.

The depths of change reflect different types of internalisation. The Europeanisation literature is particularly instructive in this regard. This body of literature focuses on the question of how much domestic change occurs in response to EU legislation, norms, and practices (Börzel and Risse 2003). Three types of normative change are particularly distinguished: absorption, accommodation, and transformation. Absorption occurs when actors incorporate norms into their programs and domestic structures, but without substantially modifying existing processes, policies, and institutions. The degree of change is low (Börzel and Risse 2003, 69–70). Accommodation happens when actors accommodate normative pressures by adapting existing processes, policies, and institutions without changing their essential features and the underlying collective understandings attached to them. One way of doing this is by 'patching up' new policies and institutions onto existing ones without changing the latter (Héritier 2001). The degree of domestic change is modest. Transformation occurs when member states replace existing policies, processes, and institutions by new, substantially different ones, or alter existing ones to the extent that their essential features and/or the underlying collective understandings are fundamentally changed. The degree of change is high (Börzel and Risse 2003, 70).

While this model has been developed in the context of the Europeanisation literature, its relevance to the argument and overarching question in this book is evident. The question is in this case not how much change occurs in response to EU legislation, norms, and practices, but how much change at the regional level occurs in response to the norm of R2P. This is why the empirical chapters will address not only which aspects of R2P the regional organisations under analysis have internalised (addressing 'the how' part of the research question, focusing on the content of R2P) but also how much change has actually occurred institutionally, politically, and discursively at the regional level compared to when R2P was not yet around (addressing the 'to what extent' part of the research question, focusing on the depths of change in response to R2P).

A framework for assessing the internationalisation of R2P at the regional level

Having discussed the various building blocks of this research, it is now time to discuss how these come together in an analytical model. Figure 2.1 is a visual representation of this analytical model. It makes sense to follow the chronology of the norm life cycle model when discussing the model. First, I will discuss the regional roots of the R2P norm in both regions and regional organisations: to what extent has R2P been 'built' locally and to what extent can one trace some

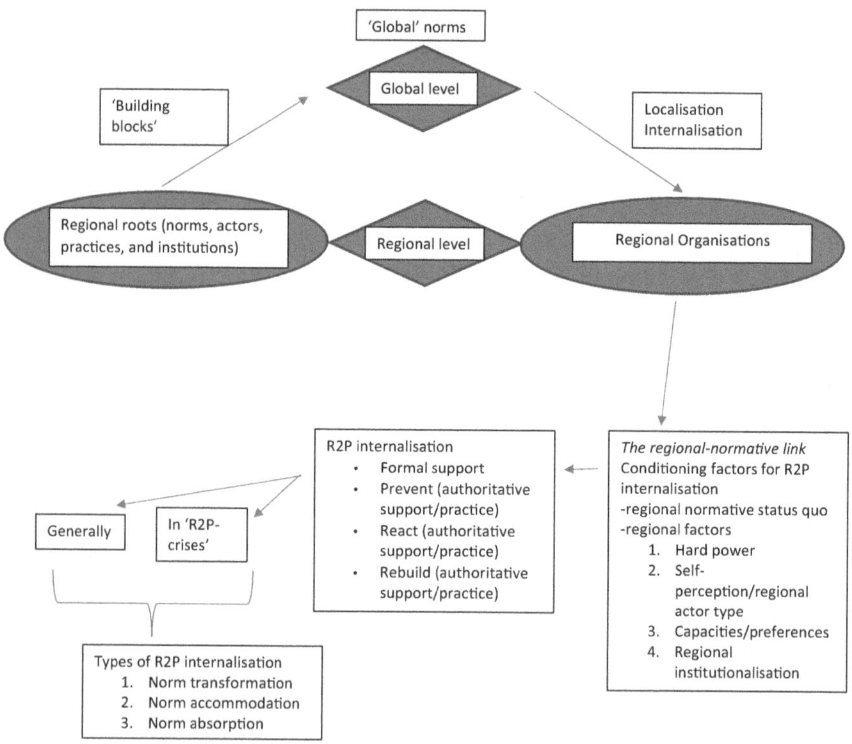

Figure 2.1 Analytical model of norms, R2P, and regional organisations

Source: Author's creation

of its roots back to the regions under analysis? This analysis will be conducted in both the contextual chapter – in which I analyse the development of some of the key norms and concepts related to R2P from the moment of the ROs founding until the 2005 World Summit – and the empirical chapters. Second, I will analyse the normative status quo in both regions when the norm of R2P emerges at the global level in the early 2000s. Central questions here are what kind of understandings of sovereignty were dominant in the regions at the time, how these are related to R2P's qualified understanding of sovereignty, what role R2P norm entrepreneurs and antipreneurs played in this period, and what kind of structural factors influenced the normative status quo and whether these factors tended to be facilitating or inhibiting of R2P at the regional level. The regional factors identified in this chapter will both get a place in the general discussion of how the norm of R2P has been internalised at the regional level and how the norm has been internalised concretely during actual crisis situations. Towards the end of the empirical chapters, the regional factors will be systematically discussed based on the empirical evidence presented in these chapters. The chapter will assess the internalisation of the various components of R2P – prevent, react, and rebuild – as well as formal support for the norm in a reflection on the case studies and explore where internalisation is incomplete. Finally, based on all the above, I will provide a qualitative assessment of the extent to which R2P has been internalised at the regional level, i.e. how and to what extent the norm has reshaped regional discourse, institutions, and policies in line with the R2P norm. The concepts of the Europeanisation literature will serve here as a yardstick of normative change.

Conclusion

This chapter has outlined the analytical framework that will be used to guide the empirical analysis of this research. Finnemore and Sikkink's (1998) norms life cycle model has proven useful in giving a general account of norm diffusion and internalisation. The main critiques of the model, which have been addressed in this chapter helped in providing nuance to the analysis of how the norms literature has developed since, and aided in building the analytical model of this research. Jointly, the concepts introduced in the analytical model will help answer the research question of this book: how and to what extent has the norm of R2P been diffused and internalised at the regional level?

While taking on board the different critiques and refinements of the norm life cycle model in general, a key theoretical contribution of this research will be to explore processes of local norm construction of R2P, based on the notion that many global norms have local and regional roots (Acharya 2004, 2011, 2013). This demonstrates that scholars who study global norms need to critically and seriously engage with the local roots of these norms. Another core contribution is the theorisation of the link between norms and regional security governance, which is currently largely missing in the literature. This research also speaks directly to Bloomfield's (2016) work, when assessing the normative status quo's in the regions and the role played by different regional actors in the normative struggles around R2P.

The factors formulated in the chapter provide concrete ways to analyse the empirical information in this research. First, the discussion around the normative status quo shows that the normative context is an important factor in determining the strategies of actors and their likelihood of achieving success in particular normative struggles. Second, the regional factors theorise which regional factors are expected to have an impact on the likelihood of internalisation of R2P at the regional level and therefore contribute to theorising the regional-normative dimension of this research. Third, the specific norm internalisation factors allow for thinking about the ways specific R2P provisions (such as prevention, reaction, and rebuilding) can be internalised and what one should observe in this regard. The qualifying statements under each provision will help to detect the nuance in between internalisation and non-internalisation and show how the regional organisations under analysis have internalised R2P. Finally, the concepts of absorption, accommodation, and transformation, derived from the Europeanisation literature, will allow to assess the depths of change in response to the norm of R2P. These latter three concepts will therefore address the 'to what extent' part of the research question.

Note

1 Left and right here have no political-ideological connotation in the ordinary sense but refer to different positions on the entrepreneur/antipreneur spectrum, with the entrepreneurs, on the left, proposing normative change and antipreneurs, on the right, opposing this.

Bibliography

Acharya, Amitav. 2004. "How Ideas Spread: Whose Norms Matter? Norm Localization and Institutional Change in Asian Regionalism." *International Organization* 58 (Spring): 239–275. DOI:10.1017/S0020818304582024.

Acharya, Amitav. 2011. "Norm Subsidiarity and Regional Orders: Sovereignty, Regionalism, and Rule-Making in the Third World." *International Studies Quarterly* 55 (1): 95–123. DOI:10.1111/j.1468-2478.2010.00637.x.

Acharya, Amitav. 2012. "Comparative Regionalism: A Field Whose Time Has Come?" *The International Spectator* 47 (1): 3–15. DOI:10.1080/03932729.2012.655004.

Acharya, Amitav. 2013. "The R2P and Norm Diffusion: Towards a Framework of Norm Circulation." *Global Responsibility to Protect* 5 (4): 466–479. DOI:10.1163/18759 84X-00504006.

Adebajo, Adeyeke. 2000. "Nigeria: Africa's New Gendarme?" *Security Dialogue* 31 (2): 185–199. DOI:10.1177%2F0967010600031002005.

Adler, Emanuel and Michael Barnett. 1998. *Security Communities*. Cambridge: Cambridge University Press. DOI:10.1017/CBO9780511598661.

Adler, Emanuel and Patricia Greve. 2009. "When Security Community Meets Balance of Power: Overlapping Regional Mechanisms of Security Governance." *Review of International Studies* 35 (1): 59–84. DOI:10.1017/S0260210509008432.

Ayoob, Mohammed. 2004. "Third World Perspectives on Humanitarian Intervention and International Administration." *Global Governance* 10 (1): 99–118. DOI:10.1163/19426720-01001009.

Behringer, Ronald M. 2013. "The Dynamics of Middlepowermanship." *Seton Hall Journal of Diplomacy and International Relations* 14 (2): 9–22.

Bellamy, Alex. 2005. "A Responsibility to Protect or a Trojan Horse? The Crisis in Darfur and Humanitarian Intervention after Iraq." *Ethics and International Affairs* 19 (2): 31–54. DOI:10.1111/j.1747-7093.2005.tb00499.x.

Bloomfield, Alan. 2016. "Norm Antipreneurs and Theorising Resistance to Normative Change." *Review of International Studies* 42 (2): 310–333. DOI:10.1017/S026021051500025X.

Börzel, Tanja and Thomas Risse. 2003. "Conceptualising the Domestic Impact of Europe." In *The Politics of Europeanisation*, eds. Kevin Featherstone and Claudio Radaelli. Oxford: Oxford University Press, 55–78. DOI:10.1093/0199252092.003.0003.

Brockmeier, Sarah, Gerrit Kurtz and Julian Junk. 2014. "Emerging Norm and Rhetorical Tool: Europe and a Responsibility to Protect." *Conflict, Security & Development* 14 (4): 429–460. DOI:10.1080/14678802.2014.930587.

Buzan, Barry and Ole Waever. 2003. "Security Complexes: A Theory of Regional Security." In *Regions and Powers: The Structure of International Security* (Cambridge Studies in International Relations). Cambridge: Cambridge University Press, 40–82. DOI:10.1017/CBO9780511491252.007.

Campbell-Verduyn, Malcolm. 2016. "Additional Categories of Agency: 'Creative Resistors' to Normative Change in Post-Crisis Global Financial Governance." In *Norm Antipreneurs and the Politics of Resistance to Global Normative Change*, eds. Alan Bloomfield and Shirley Scott. New York: Routledge, 140–158.

Checkel, Jeffrey. 1997. "International Norms and Domestic Politics: Bridging the Rationalist-Constructivist Divide." *European Journal of International Relations* 3 (4): 473–495. DOI:10.1177%2F1354066197003004003.

Checkel, Jeffrey. 1998. "Review: The Constructivist Turn in International Relations Theory." *World Politics* 50 (2): 324–348. DOI:10.1017/S0043887100008133.

Crossley, Noële. 2016. *Evaluating the Responsibility to Protect: Mass Atrocity Prevention as a Consolidating Norm in International Society*. New York: Routledge.

De Franco, Chairo, Christoph Meyer and Karen Smith. 2016. "Europe and the European Union." In *The Oxford Handbook of the Responsibility to Protect*, eds. Alex Bellamy and Tim Dunne. Oxford: Oxford University Press, 391–408. DOI:10.1093/oxfordhb/9780198753841.013.21.

Destradi, Sandra. 2008. "Empire, Hegemony, and Leadership: Developing a Research Framework for the Study of Regional Powers"' *GIGA Working Papers* 79, http://repec.giga-hamburg.de/pdf/giga_08_wp79_destradi.pdf.

Deutsch, Karl. 1957. *Political Community and the North Atlantic Area: International Organization in the Light of Historical Experience*. Princeton: Princeton University Press.

Duchene, Francois. 1972. "Europe's Role in World Peace." In *Europe Tomorrow: Sixteen Europeans Look Ahead*, ed. Richard Mayne. London: Fontana/Collins, 32–47.

ECOWAS. 2022. "Basic Information." www.ecowas.int/about-ecowas/basic-information/ (May 3, 2022).

Edwards, Jim. 2017. "500 Years Ago, China Destroyed its World-dominating Navy because its Political Elite was Afraid of Free Trade." *The Independent*, 5 March. www.independent.co.uk/news/world/americas/500-years-ago-china-destroyed-its-world-dominating-navy-because-its-political-elite-was-afraid-of-a7612276.html (April 20, 2018).

Finnemore, Martha and Kathryn Sikkink. 1998. "International Norm Dynamics and Political Change." *International Organization* 52 (4): 887–917. DOI:10.1162/002081898550789.

Gallagher, Adrian. 2012. "A Clash of Responsibilities: Engaging with Realist Critiques of the R2P." *Global Responsibility to Protect* 4 (3): 334–357. DOI:10.1163/1875984X-00403004.

Gilpin, Robert. 1981. *War and Change in World Politics*. Cambridge: Cambridge University Press. DOI:10.1017/CBO9780511664267.

Habermas, Jurgen. 2003 "Making Sense of the EU: Towards a Cosmopolitan Europe." *Journal of Democracy* 14 (4): 86–100. http://doi.org/10.1353/jod.2003.0077.

Hansen, Lene. 2006. *Security as Practice: Discourse Analysis and the Bosnian War*. London: Routledge.

Héritier, Adrienne. 2001. "Differential Europe: National Administrative Responses to Community Policy." In *Transforming Europe. Europeanization and Domestic Change*, eds. Maria Green Cowles, James A. Caporaso and Thomas Risse. Ithaca, NY: Cornell University Press, 44–59. DOI:10.7591/9781501723575-004.

Kacowicz, Arie and Galia Press-Barnathan. 2016. "Regional Security Governance." In *The Oxford Handbook of Comparative Regionalism*, eds. Tanja A. Börzel and Thomas Risse. Oxford: Oxford University Press, 296–329. DOI:10.1093/oxfordhb/9780199682300.013.15.

Katzenstein, Peter. 1996. "Introduction: Alternative Perspectives on National Security." In *The Culture of National Security: Norms and Identity in World Politics*, ed. Peter Katzenstein. New York: Columbia University Press, 1–32.

Kefale, Asnake. 2015. "Regional Organisations and Security Governance: A Comparative Assessment of IGAD and ASEAN." LSE Global South Unit Working Paper Series, no. 1/2015. London: LSE.

Kirchner, Emil. 2011. "The EU as a Regional and Global Security Provider." In *The Security Governance of Regional Organizations*, eds. Emil J. Kirchner and Roberto Dominguez. New York: Routledge, 25–45.

Kirchner, Emil and James Sperling. 2007. *EU Security Governance*. Manchester and New York: Manchester University Press.

Krook, M.L. and J. True. 2012. "Rethinking the Life Cycles of International Norms: The United Nations and the Global Promotion of Gender Equality." *European Journal of International Relations* 18 (1): 103–127. DOI:10.1177%2F1354066110380963.

Lake, David. 1997. "Regional Security Complexes: A Systems Approach." In *Regional Orders: Building Security in a New World*, eds. David Lake and Patrick Morgan. University Park, PA: The Pennsylvania State University Press, 45–67.

Lake, David. 2009. "Regional Hierarchy: Authority and Local International Order." *Review of International Studies* 35 (1): 35–58. DOI:10.1017/S0260210509008420.

Lopez, Elisa. 2014. "Discourses and Practices of the Regionalisation of Foreign and Security Policies: The Cases of West Africa and South America." Ph.D. diss. University of Warwick and LUISS Guido Carli.

MacFarlane, S. Neil. 2014. "Regional Organizations and Global Security Governance." In *International Organization and Global Governance*, eds. T.G. Weiss and R. Wilkinson. London; New York: Routledge. DOI:10.4324/9781315301914.

Manners, Ian. 2002. "Normative Power Europe: A Contradiction in Terms?" *Journal of Common Market Studies* 40 (2): 235–258. DOI:10.1111/1468-5965.00353.

Nye, Joseph. 2004. "Soft Power and American Foreign Policy." *Political Science Quarterly* 119 (2): 255–270. DOI:10.2307/20202345.

Risse-Kappen, Thomas. 1994. "Ideas Do Not Float Freely: Transnational Coalitions, Domestic Structures, and the End of the Cold War." *International Organization* 48 (2): 185–214. DOI:10.1017/S0020818300028162.

Ropp, C. Stephen and Kathryn Sikkink. 1999. "International Norms and Domestic Politics in Chile and Guatemala." In *The Power of Human Rights: International Norms and Domestic Change*, eds. Thomas Risse-Kappen, Stephen C. Ropp and Kathryn Sikkink. Cambridge: Cambridge University Press, 172–204. DOI:10.1017/CBO9780511598777.007.

Suominen, Kati. 2005. "Globalizing Regionalism: Harnessing Regional Organizations to Meet Global Threats." *UNU-CRIS Occasional Paper* 11: 1–24.

Tusk, Donald. 2019. "Remarks by President Donald Tusk after His Meeting with Taoiseach Leo Varadkar." February 6. www.consilium.europa.eu/en/press/press-releases/2019/02/06/remarks-by-president-donald-tusk-after-his-meeting-with-taoiseach-leo-varadkar/ (October 2, 2020).

United Nations. 2011. "The Role of Regional and Subregional Arrangements in Implementing the Responsibility to Protect." A/65/877 – S/2011/393. https://undocs.org/A/65/877 (February 18, 2020).

United Nations General Assembly. 2009. *Implementing the Responsibility to Protect. A/63/677.* https://undocs.org/A/63/677 (April 13, 2020).

Van Kersbergen, K. and B. Verbeek. 2007. "The Politics of International Norms: Subsidiarity and the Imperfect Competence Regime of the European Union." *European Journal of International Relations* 13 (2): 217–238. DOI:10.1177%2F1354066107076955.

Von der Leyen, Ursula. 2019. "A Union that Strives for More. My Agenda for Europe." https://ec.europa.eu/commission/sites/beta-political/files/political-guidelines-next-commission_en.pdf (October 2, 2020).

Welsh, Jennifer M. 2013. "Norm Contestation and the Responsibility to Protect." *Global Responsibility to Protect* 5 (4): 365–396. DOI:10.1163/1875984X-00504002.

Wiener, Antje. 2004. "Contested Compliance: Interventions on the Normative Structure of World Politics." *European Journal of International Relations* 10 (2): 189–234. DOI:10.1177%2F1354066104042934.

Wiener, Antje. 2008. *The Invisible Constitution of World Politics*. Cambridge: Cambridge University Press. DOI:10.1017/CBO9780511490408.

Wiener, Antje. 2009. "Enacting Meaning-in-Use: Qualitative Research on Norms and International Relations." *Review of International Studies* 35 (S1): 175–193. DOI:10.1017/S0260210509008377.

3 Contextual analysis

Regional approaches to security, sovereignty, and human rights

Introduction

This contextual chapter focuses on the way the European Union (EU) and the Economic Community of West African States (ECOWAS) have dealt with questions surrounding *security*, *sovereignty*, and *human rights and mass atrocity prevention/response* in the period between the founding of these regional organisations up to the adoption of the norm of the Responsibility to Protect (R2P) at the United Nations World Summit in 2005. Security, sovereignty, and human rights and mass atrocity prevention/response are seen as key principles and concepts underlying and relating to the norm of R2P. Security relates to R2P in the sense that R2P subscribes more to notions of human security, in which the security of people takes centre stage, than to traditional notions of national or state security (International Commission on Intervention and State Sovereignty et al. 2001; Christou 2014). Besides, situations of R2P concern, which involve the (imminent) commission of atrocity crimes, can relate to security breakdown in places. For instance, Islamic State (ISIS), was able to commit its war crimes and ethnic cleansing in Syria and Iraq because these states had lost grip on large parts of their territory. The same counts for the jihadist groups in Northern Mali. Sovereignty is a key concept relating to R2P, as underlying R2P was an attempt to shift the understanding of sovereignty from one of 'absolute sovereignty' to one of 'sovereignty as responsibility'. This reconceptualisation was first introduced by Deng et al. in the context of internally displaced people (1996). Basically, it means that R2P acknowledges and reinforces sovereignty, but that it makes this conditional on the responsible exercise of sovereignty, i.e. with respect for human rights (Deng et al. 1996). Human rights and mass atrocity prevention/response are key to R2P as the norm becomes activated in case of (imminent) mass atrocities.

Both the EU and ECOWAS were founded originally for economic purposes, although the European Community of Coal and Steel had a clear security dimension behind it, tying the fate of six European states to the pooling of resources essential for warfare at that time (European Union 2019). ECOWAS, however, was solely founded for the pursuit of economic prosperity and development in the West African region (ECOWAS 2019). It is interesting to see

DOI: 10.4324/9781003230731-3

how these regional organisations at different points had to face core questions surrounding security, sovereignty, and human rights. To truly understand how and to what extent the regional organisations under analysis have internalised the norm of R2P, it is crucial to zoom in on the era in which the underlying principles of the norm were already visible, yet latent and not yet concretised into a formal norm.

It is to this contextual analysis to which we will now turn. The first part of this chapter will analyse Europe's history of security, sovereignty, and human rights in the post-Second World War era up to 2005, when the norm of the Responsibility to Protect was adopted at the UN World Summit, and will address the EU's (and its predecessors' approach)[1] to these questions. The second part will do the same for ECOWAS, albeit the analysis here will focus mostly on the post-1975 era, as 1975 was the year in which ECOWAS was established with the Treaty of Lagos (ECOWAS 2019). The last part will sum up the findings of this chapter and set the stage for the empirical analysis.

From European Community of Coal and Steel to the European Union: Europe's approach to security, sovereignty, and human rights

Security

Europe from 1945 to 1989: an emphasis on (inter-)state security

When the Second World War ended, the European continent was in a precarious state. The destructive forces of fascism and National Socialism had raged over the continent and the Western-European states that had just been liberated by the Allies were in a poor condition (Judt 2005). The same counted for Eastern-Europe, in which the Soviets had defeated the forces of Nazi-Germany (Judt 2005). It was in this post-war context that the realisation started to emerge in Europe that, after centuries of competition between European states, it was time to start a project of cooperation. It was partly through the inner motivation of European states and their post-war elites to transcend the destructive era of two World Wars that in the late 1940s, the first steps were made towards European cooperation (European Union 2019).

Historians and political scientists have advanced multiple accounts for the move towards European cooperation and integration. Milward (1992) emphasises the economic explanations for European integration. He asserts that the post-war European states decided to give up limited areas of sovereignty based on economic necessities. The problems of the national political economies of the region necessitated complex answers in which the setting up of intergovernmental and supranational institutions could aid the nation-state in these efforts. Rather than undermining state power with new transnational organisations, those who founded regional integration defended and recast the traditional nation-states to new circumstances (Milward 1992). Etzioni (1963) argues that the European integration project has been successful because of the strategy that underpinned it. First, a small group of countries, which shared many background conditions and a commitment to unification started the integration project. Etzioni (1963) links this to the theory that the more homogenous a group of countries is, the more likely they are to form a union. Second, he sees a relationship between the level of ambition of various post-war European organisations and their degree of success. Paradoxically, the lower the level of ambition, the more successful the organisations have turned out to be. This would explain why the relatively modest European Coal and Steel Community (ECSC) turned out to be quite successful, whereas more ambitious projects such as the European Defence Community (EDC) failed. Etzioni (1963, 38) calls the step-by-step strategy, in which close targets are emphasised, and the adjustments and the loss of sovereignty the members have to endure are broken up in bits and stretched out, "the gradualist approach". Haas (1958) theorised that cooperation in one sector would logically spill over in other areas. The initial European cooperation in coal and steel soon extended to other areas as well. The close cooperation in various economic sectors may trigger the shifting of loyalties, interests, and expectations of different political, social, and economic actors from national levels towards a supranational institution. Besides these economic spill-overs, political actors, such as the European Commission would catalyse this spill-over process, as architects of European integration (Haas 1958).

This early European rapprochement culminated in the founding of the European Coal and Steel Community (ECSC) in 1951, in which Belgium, France, Germany, Italy, Luxemburg, and The Netherlands agreed to pool coal and steel – resources which were vital for warfare at that time (European Union 2019). The logic behind this first step of European integration was to "make war not only unthinkable but materially impossible", as French Foreign Minister Robert Schuman famously phrased it (Schuman 1950). The project was unique at the time as it meant bringing vital state resources under a supranational authority (European Union 2019). From a security perspective, this meant nothing less than a transformation of dominant security thinking among the founding members: for the first time in European history, security would not solely come from the state (through national defence and the national availability of war resources) but now also through a supranational organisation that was created by these states and that counter-intuitively provided security to its member states through pooling war resources, i.e. moving away these resources from the national level to the supranational level.

The founding of the ECSC was also remarkable as it brought former enemies together, with the Benelux states and France having been on one side of the Second World War, and Germany and Italy on the other (although the reality was of course more complex than this, with Vichy France actively collaborating with Nazi-Germany, whereas Italy had a strong resistance movement). The coming together of these states therefore also meant a transformation from past amity-enmity relations and state identities, most visibly signified by the Franco-German reconciliation. These two European states, which had been in conflict since the mid-19th century, were finally able to forge a lasting peace through the project of European cooperation (European Union 2019). For the Benelux states, starting this new project with Western-Germany was also a big step, with painful memories of wartime occupation still vivid. The ECSC was thus much more than only a material 'war-denying project' through the pooling of resources; it also marked a first positive step on the ideational level, in which former enemies came to see each other as partners with whom one could cooperate and work together towards common goods. From a security point of view, this meant that interstate threats would no longer realistically come from any of the states that formed part of this emerging European project.

Interstate security was, however, far from realised in post-Second World War Europe. While the end of the Second World War marked a definitive end to the threats that Nazi-Germany and fascist-Italy posed to the European continent, new rivalries readily formed. The Allies and the Soviet Union that had managed to cooperate during the Second World War came to be rivals with Europe partitioned between Western Europe under the sphere of influence of the Allies and Eastern Europe under the sphere of influence of the Soviets (Hanhimäki 2012). For the member states of the ECSC and later the European Community (EC), being part of the Western alliance and its security architecture, this meant that interstate threats came from the east, principally from the Soviet Union. The East-West rivalry would colour the European security experience for many decades until the Cold War came to an end in 1989 (Hanhimäki 2012).

In this period of time, important developments in European security integration took place as the ECSC members, partly at the instigation of the United States (US) in the face of the new Soviet threat, attempted to establish a European defence and security architecture. In the early 1950s, an attempt was made to create a European Defence Community (EDC). The EDC was to be a military organisation, but many also saw it as a further step in European integration. The new organisation would warrant not only a common army but also a common budget and common institutions (Urwin 1995, 63). Importantly, the EDC had been designed in a way to contain West German military power. West Germany would have all its military units placed under the integrated command structure, whereas the other EDC members (the Benelux states, France, and Italy) would only allocate a proportion of their armed forces to the European army. The EDC would be accompanied by a European Political Community (EPC), which was supposed to be the beginning of a comprehensive federation to which the ECSC and EDC would be subordinated. The EPC would have a complex and far-reaching institutional structure with a European Executive Council, a Council of National Ministers, a Court of Justice, and a popularly elected Parliament (Urwin 1995). The EPC stood or fell, though, with the ratification of the EDC. The EDC, however, was eliminated by a negative procedural vote in the French Assembly in 1954, as there were concerns over supranational elements of the EDC and West-German rearmament. The shelving of the EDC automatically also meant the end of the EPC, and therefore for far-reaching additional integration in the early years of the European project (Urwin 1995, 65; Van Meurs et al. 2018, 40).

With the failure of the EDC, the American insistence on a West German defence contribution or greater inputs from the other states, which was one of the driving external factors of the EDC, did not disappear. Hence, there was external pressure to find an alternative to the EDC. There was a convenient option readily available: the 1948 Treaty of Brussels. This was a collective defence alliance between Britain, France, and the Benelux states. The new British Conservative Prime Minister Eden took the lead in the process, as he suggested West Germany could rearm with the necessary level of supervision within NATO, which was founded in 1949, and that the Brussels Treaty could be expanded to include West Germany and Italy (Urwin 1995, 69; Van Meurs et al. 2018). The anti-German emphasis in the original treaty was replaced by a pro-European declaration. To meet French security concerns, Britain agreed to station troops in West Germany as part of its participation in the revamped body. The new body was to be called the Western European Union (WEU) and it was fundamentally intergovernmental in nature (Urwin 1995). The WEU did not achieve significant results, and in the 1950s it was only occasionally activated. It turned out to be a paper tiger. In the 1980s, the organisation was revived as it was used as a forum for a West European voice on defence issues, when it seemed that the US and the Soviet Union might actually come to an agreement on nuclear weapons that might neglect Western European interests (Urwin 1995, 71). The WEU also facilitated defence collaboration, such as when Germany provided naval cover in Western Europe when France and Britain sent ships to patrol in the Persian Gulf during the Persian Gulf crisis. The WEU's belated revival could, however, not do away with the fact that the role of the organisation in the process of European integration had been rather minimal (Urwin 1995).

In 1970, the European Political Cooperation (EPC) was kickstarted, which sought further political cooperation between the European Community (EC) member states through coordination of foreign policy (Urwin 1995, 148; Van Meurs et al. 2018, 89). The EPC was created outside the EC institutional framework and cooperation under the scheme was essentially intergovernmental, voluntary, and loosely institutionalised. The political cooperation was non-binding and aimed "to ensure a better mutual understanding of the major problems of international politics through regular information and consultation; . . . to promote the harmonisation of views and the coordination of positions; . . . to attempt to achieve a common approach to specific cases" (Urwin 1995, 149). The EPC enabled the EC states to speak with one voice in bodies such as GATT, and it proved instrumental in the negotiations during the Conference on Security and Cooperation in Europe in Helsinki in 1975. Although the EPC succeeded in increasing the level of cooperation, its general statements of policy were not always followed through, and when, for instance, sanctions were applied, it was not uncommon for one or more member states to break ranks. This shows again that the EPC remained "an essentially intergovernmental and voluntary operation" (Urwin 1995, 217). Its significance should not be understated though, as the EPC was the first scheme that aimed to foster foreign policy coordination among the EC-states with an actual degree of success.

It is important to remark that throughout this time period of the Cold War, security and security threats were predominantly conceived as 'traditional' in the sense that threats were seen to come from external (state-) actors (the Soviet Union and its allies) and that the state was seen as the referent object of security (i.e. the threats from the Soviet Union were seen as a matter of 'national security' – they were seen as threatening to Western states) (Buzan et al. 1998). This 'traditional security paradigm', which was the norm during the Cold War, did not, or only, marginally allowed elites 'to open the box' of security, i.e. moving conceptions of security beyond state security, which is so characteristic of the norm of R2P (probably the most notable exception to this is the adoption of the Common Agricultural Policy, which sought to secure sufficient food levels in Europe as a basic right for all and which could be seen as one of the first human security policies) (European Commission 2020). It was only after the end of Cold War that new security agendas found a window of opportunity to emerge.

Europe after 1989: the emergence of human security and the Responsibility to Protect

As addressed in the chapter, the 1990s was a decade in which new norms found currency in the international community, such as 'human security' and 'sovereignty as responsibility' (the latter will be covered in the discussion on sovereignty). For decades, the Cold War had 'frozen' the conception of security in the sense that security was a matter of the state and that foreign policy, when it came to 'high politics' (i.e. security), was often an expression of states' Cold War identity. States belonged to one of the two 'camps', predominantly expressed through membership of the collective defence organisations of NATO and the Warsaw Pact, or retained neutrality through joining the Non-Aligned Movement (Hanhimäki 2012). The end of the Cold War witnessed both the unpacking of the 'box of security' (e.g. the emergence of new security agendas that moved beyond 'national/state security') and the disappearance of the 'frozen international system', which had frozen state allegiances and their foreign policies (in high politics) for decades. The former included the widening (beyond military issues) and deepening (from the level of the state to societies and individuals) of security agendas, which will be further discussed in the next section on human security. The latter was first seen as something positive in the West: with the fall of the Berlin Wall, the only strategic competitor to the Western bloc had disappeared and there were high hopes of a more prosperous and safer world based on the principles of liberal democracy, the market economy, the rule of law and human rights (Fukuyama 1989). Under US unipolarity, the West would be uniquely positioned to create a world in its own image, a 'New World Order' as US President Bush senior called it (Bush 1990).

However, with the dissolution of the Soviet Union and the end of the bipolar world order, elements of stability and predictability in the international system also vanished. In practice, this meant that the post-Cold War era turned out much less peaceful than analysts had thought in the early years after 1989. Conflicts (mostly intra-state) broke out in various parts of Africa and Europe, with those in Yugoslavia and Rwanda, with their high incidence of mass atrocities, of particular concern to this book (the conflict of Yugoslavia will be discussed in the part on 'human rights/mass atrocities prevention/response') (Baker 2015; Thomson 2018). The increasing rate of intra-state conflicts, which often went together with instances of mass atrocities (i.e. ethnic cleansing, war crimes, crimes against humanity, and genocide), showed the vulnerability of individuals and societal groups (UNDP 1994). It was out of this perception of vulnerability of people that the human security agenda emerged (Liotta and Owen 2006).

Human security

The first explicit reference to human security within the UN was made by then Secretary General Boutros-Ghali in the 1992 Agenda for Peace report (Boutros-Ghali 1992). It was Special Advisor to United Nations Development Program (UNDP) Mahbub ul Haq who, together with his UNDP team, drew the world's attention to this idea of human security in the UN Human Development Report 1994 (UNDP 1994). The report problematised the narrow conception of security, i.e. the idea of seeing security as "security from external aggression, or as protection of national interests in foreign policy or as global security from the threat of a nuclear holocaust" (UNDP 1994, 22). For a long time, the focus had been too much on nation-states, and too little on people, too much on 'high politics events' (the Cold War, the independence struggle of developing states) and too little on the daily concerns of ordinary people. According to the UNDP report, these concerns include worries about unemployment, access to food, neighbourhood safety, but also risks of gender violence, religious or ethnic persecution, and the risk of torture by a repressive state. It was these daily concerns of people that would be a much more dominant source of their feelings of insecurity than "the dread of a cataclysmic world event" (UNDP 1994, 22). The report identified four "essential characteristics" of human security, namely that it was of *universal* concern (acknowledging that human security concerns are relevant to people everywhere), that its components were *interdependent* (acknowledging that sources and consequences of human insecurity easily travel the globe), that it was "*easier to ensure through early prevention than later intervention*" (acknowledging that prevention is often less costly than reaction), and that it is *people-centred* (UNDP 1994, 22–23, parentheses added).

Several middle powers emerged as key norm entrepreneurs of human security. States like Canada, Japan, and Norway made human security a foreign policy priority and engaged other states on the topic. Although emphasising different aspects of the human security agenda – Japan tended to emphasise the 'freedom from want' aspect, whereas Canada and Norway leaned more towards the 'freedom of fear' aspect of human security – all were critical in shaping the human security agenda (Behringer 2013). An example of this norm entrepreneurship is the creation of the Human Security Network by Canada and Norway in 1998, a multilateral arrangement which brought like-minded states together to work on human security issues (Behringer 2013, 22).

The concept gained popularity in the late 1990s and early 2000s, also in the EU. The EU engaged with human security in multiple ways. Most well-known are the 2003 European Security Strategy and the 2004 Barcelona Report of the Study Group on Europe's Security Capabilities, both driven by then EU High Representative for Common Foreign Policy, Javier Solana. The Barcelona report noted that the attacks of 9/11 and 11 March (Madrid) had revealed that national borders no longer offered sufficient protection to citizens and that threats no longer most likely come from foreign armies (Study Group on Europe's Security Capabilities 2004). Addressing human security needs across the globe would be a way "to make the world safer for Europeans" (Study Group on Europe's Security Capabilities 2004, 2). The report advocated a bottom-up approach to human security and focused on the 'freedom from fear' aspect of the concept. It called on the EU to be 'more active' and 'more capable' in the human security domain through "preventive engagement, a strategy of effective multilateralism and the extension of the international rule of law" (Study Group on Europe's Security Capabilities 2004, 3). According to the report, the EU ought to base its policies on human security instead of state security for moral reasons (the notion that all human beings are equal), legal reasons (the notion that human security and human rights are two sides of the same coin), and out of 'enlightened self-interest' (the understanding that addressing insecurities and instability around the world would benefit the EU's security needs) (Study Group on Europe's Security Capabilities 2004, 5; parentheses added).

Interestingly, the study group behind the Barcelona Report as driven by Solana was open to implementing human security partly through military means, as a 'human security battle group' of 15,000 men was proposed (Study Group on Europe's Security Capabilities 2004, 19). This proposal eventually did not make it as there was not enough support for it across the EU (Christou 2014, 370). Nor was everyone within the EU convinced about the concept of human security itself. The European Commission's development directorate DEVCO never integrated the term into its strategic narrative, for instance (Harnisch 2017). Some member states, such as France, the UK, and some CEE-states, were also sceptical about the fuzzy nature of the concept and its unclear operational consequences (Christou 2014). The fact, though, is that the 'human security-narrative' evidently penetrated high-level discourse at the time, as both Solana and EU Commissioner for External Relations and European Neighbourhood Policy, Benita Ferrero-Waldner (until 2009) actively endorsed the concept, both in speeches and in policy documents (Christou 2014). Among the member states, Finland,

Sweden, and the Human Security Network members Austria, Greece, Ireland, and the Netherlands were supportive of the concept (Harnisch 2017). This is relevant as this high-level EU support for human security occurred at the time that the norm of the Responsibility to Protect was emerging.

As noted earlier, the term 'Responsibility to Protect' first appeared in a report by the International Commission on Intervention and State Sovereignty et al. (2001), sponsored by Canada, and it was later endorsed by the UN High-level Panel on Threats, Challenges and Change (2004) and the UN Secretary General ("In larger freedom: towards development, security and human rights for all", 2005 Report). The 'twin-development' of the norms of human security and the responsibility to protect (R2P) should not come as a surprise, as R2P is seen by some as narrower, although closely related to human security (Christou 2014). Clearly, both norms are part of a broader normative movement in which the centrality of individuals in security is leading and state sovereignty is reconceptualised, although it has to be said that R2P, contrary to human security, is narrow in its application (limited to the occurrence of mass atrocity crimes). It is evident in any case, that in the pre-2005 World Summit period, the human security discourse was popular among at least some EU elites and that the emerging norm of R2P already seemed to make inroads in this discourse (e.g. the human security battle group proposal of Solana) (Christou 2014; Study Group on Europe's Security Capabilities 2004). Based on this observation, one can argue that the EU pre-2005 had some influential supporters of human security and R2P and that EU support for the new principle at the World Summit of 2005 therefore was in line with expectations.

Sovereignty

Sovereignty is a key component of the norm of the R2P, mostly as the norm attempts to reconceptualise sovereignty from 'absolute sovereignty' (in which the state is the highest authority, which by necessity means it is not accountable) towards a notion of 'sovereignty as responsibility' (in which sovereignty would be accountable) (International Commission on Intervention and State Sovereignty et al. 2001). This notion derives from UN Special Rapporteur on the Human Rights of Internally Displaced Persons Francis Deng's reconceptualization of 'sovereignty' towards 'sovereignty as responsibility', which he introduced in the 1990s (Deng et al. 1996). It is therefore important to analyse the history of sovereignty in the region in the time period under analysis and to see what the EU's approaches to sovereignty have been in this time period. It is to this analysis that we now turn.

The EU's experience with sovereignty in the post-Second World War era

The nascent European project soon had to deal with questions surrounding sovereignty. Pooling resources like coal and steel necessarily meant pooling sovereignty – an experience which was unique at that time (European

Union 2019). It was through the historical lesson of the recent past, however, that this was deemed an appropriate solution not only to security concerns on the continent but also to forge future economic prosperity and bring about a coming together of European nations. In the decades following the founding of the ECSC, the Community gradually deepened and widened, with task and membership expansion (European Union 2019).

With every new treaty, the cooperation of European states deepened. In 1957, the Treaty of Rome created the European Economic Community (EEC) (better known as the 'Common Market') (European Union 2019). In the 1960s, member states agreed on 'joint control over food production', initiated by the 1962 launch of the 'Common Agricultural Policy' (CAP). The dual aim of the CAP was a guaranteed supply of food for European citizens and socio-economic security for farmers (Van Meurs et al. 2018). France pushed for the CAP, as the country's large agricultural sector stood to benefit from the policy, while Germany, as net importer of agricultural products, had its hesitations, but finally conceded to it (Van Meurs et al. 2018, 74–75). In the 1970s, the first EU laws on the environment were adopted (European Union 2019). In the 1980s, the Single European Act (SEA) (1986) was signed, which created the 'Single Market'. The SEA made one Community out of the EEC with objectives beyond economy and trade (Van Meurs et al. 2018). It also introduced institutional reform, such as the extension of qualified majority voting in the Council of Ministers and an increase in the legislative competence of the EP (Urwin 1995, 232–233). According to Van Meurs et al. (2018, 138), the greatest significance of the SEA, however, was the improvement of relations among the member states and the renewed prevalence of beliefs in the added value of cooperation over going-it-alone approaches. The main theoretical accounts of European integration, neofunctionalism and liberal intergovernmentalism, have provided different explanations for the creation of the SEA. While neofunctionalism emphasises the supranational involvement on part of the Commission and EP with the support of European multinationals, liberal intergovernmentalism tends to consider the SEA as the product of converging German, French, and British economic interests (Van Meurs et al. 2018, 141).

In 1993, the Single Market was completed, as EU citizens came to enjoy the free movement of goods, services, people, and money (European Union 2019). The 1990s also witnessed the signing of the Maastricht Treaty (1992), in which the European Union was formally founded, and the Treaty of Amsterdam (1997). In 1995, the Schengen agreement became effective, gradually allowing people to travel without having their passports checked at the borders (European Union 2019). Finally, 2002 marked the introduction of the Euro, a new currency that was introduced in many EU member states (European Union 2019).

It is important to note, however, that integration has not been a linear and even process across all sectors. For instance, while there has been very significant integration in, for instance, trade and economics, this has been less the case for foreign policy, defence, and home affairs. The Maastricht Treaty

(1992) clearly reflects this process of uneven integration, as it created a pillar structure in which pillar I (economics and the common market) operated on the basis of the Community method (with qualified majority voting in the Council), whereas pillar II (foreign and security policy) and III (justice and home affairs) operated on the basis of intergovernmentalism (with unanimous voting in the Council) (European Union 1992). The pillar structure was abandoned with the Lisbon Treaty (2007), but the fact remains that integration has advanced much further in some areas than in others (European Union 2007). At the institutional level, there are also divergent views on sovereignty pooling, with the European Commission and the European Parliament often driving the integration process, while the member states occasionally pull the brakes in the European Council, when they perceive integration is proceeding too quickly (Milward 1992, 1; Haas 1958; 1961). EU member states have espoused divergent views on integration and their attitudes have also changed over time, which makes it impossible to speak of pro- and anti-integration member states during the entire course of European integration. To give just one example, some observers have asserted that The Netherlands has become more Eurosceptic since the 2000s, while it was historically seen as one of the strongest pro-European member states.[2] So, to sum up, integration has not been a linear and even process and divergent views on integration have been there since the start at both the EU institutional level and among the member states.

Despite these caveats, it is fair to argue that the EU member states have built a significant amount of experience in sovereignty pooling since the start of the European integration process. This becomes especially clear when comparing the EU to other regions in the world where states have much more strongly guarded their sovereignty, such as in Southeast Asia where ASEAN-member states have cooperated regionally almost exclusively on an intergovernmental basis. The experience that EU member states have built with pooling sovereignty gives rise to the expectation that they should be receptive to the R2P norm, as R2P shares this qualified understanding of sovereignty. This notion has also informed one of the factors outlined in the analytical framework and will be tested in the empirical analysis.

Human rights and mass atrocities prevention/response

In terms of human rights, the states that later formed the European Union signed up to a variety of human rights treaties, among which the European Convention on Human Rights (ECHR) 1950 is one of the most important (Council of Europe 1950). More recently, the Charter of Fundamental Rights of the European Union (2000) offers citizens of the European Union a broad range of human rights protection, which has later been incorporated into the Lisbon Treaty (European Union 2007). Relevant to the norm of R2P are the following articles of the Charter, which relate to the physical security of citizens: the right to human dignity (article 1), the right to life (article 2), prohibition of torture and inhuman or degrading treatment or punishment (article 4), prohibition of slavery and forced labour (article 5), right to liberty and security (article 6), protection in the event of removal, expulsion, or extradition (article 19), and the prohibition of abuse of rights (article 54) (European Union 2007). These rights collectively guarantee the physical safety of European Union citizens and therefore safeguard these citizens against the eventuality of mass atrocity crimes. These rights are further externally confirmed through the EU's conditionality mechanism: candidate member states can only join the union if they respect the rights enshrined in its founding treaties (Schimmelfennig et al. 2003). Through this principle, the EU ensures that the integrity of the collective of rights it ensures to its citizens remains intact over time and that they are automatically extended to new citizens in the case of membership growth. The importance of the Lisbon Treaty in ensuring and maintaining respect of human rights, through conditionality and collective adherence, was also mentioned by a European Commission official in an interview (European Commission official 2018).

A key convention in the field of mass atrocities is the 1948 Convention on the Prevention and Punishment of the Crime of Genocide. This convention recognised genocide as a crime under international law, and it came in direct response to the systematic and planned extermination of the Jewish people and other groups during the Holocaust (Budapest Centre 2018). It is important to note in this respect that the convention received strong support from European states that are now EU member states. This support was later strengthened and widened with the EU's backing of the International Criminal Court (ICC), which was established in 2002 (European Union 2006). The ICC has jurisdiction over the crimes that are covered by the norm of R2P, namely genocide, war crimes, and crimes against humanity (International Criminal Court 2019). The fourth crime that falls under the scope of the norm, ethnic cleansing, currently lacks a legal definition and is therefore not punishable through the ICC (United Nations Office on Genocide Prevention and the Responsibility to Protect 2019).

The crimes just mentioned came to the fore in Europe during the Bosnian civil war (1992–1995), which was part of the broader dissolution of Yugoslavia. The Bosnian civil war was characterised by bitter fighting between the Yugoslav Army units (which later transformed into the Army of Republika Srpska) in Bosnia on the one side and a coalition of Bosniaks (through the Army of the Republic of Bosnia and Herzegovina) and Croats (through the Croatian Defence Council) on the other side (Baker 2015). During the conflict, ethnic cleansing and, in some accounts, even genocide took place (ICTY 2004). In July 1995, more than 8000 Bosniaks, mostly internally displaced people, were trapped in the enclave of Srebrenica. In the months leading up to July, the Army of Republika Srpska and the Scorpions, a paramilitary unit from Serbia had strengthened their positions in the area, and in July 1995 they marched into the enclave. What followed was the killing of over 8000 Bosniak men and boys (Baker 2015). The enclave of Srebrenica was designated by the UN as "safe area", which in practice was not the case as the UN had failed to demilitarise the zone in the lead-up to the July 1995 tragedy (Baker 2015). UNPROFOR's Dutchbat soldiers who were stationed in the area to protect the residing population were unable to prevent the humanitarian tragedy as they were heavily outnumbered by the advancing Serbian force and their mandate belonged to the realm of traditional peacekeeping as opposed to peace enforcement, which meant that, in any case, they were only allowed to use force in self-defence (Daalder 1998).[3] Moreover, promised air support from the United States and the United Kingdom did not come when the time was there (Hartmann and Vulliamy 2015). The mass killing of July 1995 sent shockwaves around the world. United Nations Secretary General Kofi Annan would later call the events the worst crime on European soil since the Second World War that would "forever haunt the UN" (UN 2000). Later that summer, partly incited by the July 1995 killings, but in the first place part of a broader US strategy, allied bombings and successful negotiations by US representative Richard Holbrooke brought an end to the war in Bosnia (Daalder 1998).

During the Yugoslavian wars, the International Criminal Tribunal for the former Yugoslavia (ICTY) was established in The Hague to ensure accountability for war crimes committed during and after the conflicts. In *Prosecutor v. Krstić (2004)*, the Tribunal ruled that the events of July 1995 constituted genocide, a crime under international law.[4] This decision was later upheld by the International Court of Justice in 2007 (International Court of Justice 2007).[5]

Although international accountability was ensured through the ICTY, the response of the EU to the conflicts in Yugoslavia in general and to Srebrenica specifically was not very decisive. European states did not confront Serbian forces as some of their own forces had been taken hostage by Serbian forces in May 1995 (Daalder 1998). Partly, this 'passive stance' also resulted from UN insistence on "traditional peacekeeping principles" which made it impossible for UNPROFOR troops to enforce the peace, which would inherently entail taking sides (Daalder 1998). The main obstacle to an effective European response, however, stemmed from the fact that the Common Foreign and Security Policy (CFSP) was only in the making at the time. The Maastricht Treaty (1992) introduced the CFSP as successor to the EPC (European Union 1992). The CFSP became the second pillar of the EU's new three-pillar structure. In this second pillar, contrary to the first pillar which included internal market issues and agriculture, member states continued to dominate initiation and implementation of CFSP, and decision-making still required unanimity. The CFSP provided the EU with two legally binding instruments: Common Positions and Joint Actions (European Union 1992). Throughout the Bosnian war, the EU member states struggled, however, to find common ground, especially with regard to the use of force to stop the conflict (Gross 2007). This meant that the EU had to lean heavily on the US, both militarily and diplomatically during various phases of the Yugoslav conflict. The experience demonstrated that the EU and its member states were ill-prepared to respond to violent conflicts at the EU's borders (Gross 2007, 101). Moreover, the EU's incipient CFSP did not provide the tools to apply a mass atrocity prevention/response lens to the Bosnian civil war, as the conflict was addressed through a traditional conflict management approach by its member states (some of which sent troops to Bosnia in UN-formation and later NATO-formation). In addition, EU diplomatic and economic efforts were not tailored to preventing or stopping mass atrocities, but on economic support for Yugoslavia in the lead-up to the conflict and on conflict management and resolution in later stages of the conflict (Dover 2005).

The Yugoslav conflicts taught some important lessons to the EU. The EU's ineffectiveness throughout the conflict was one of the factors that led UK Prime Minister Blair and French President Chirac to promote closer EU defence cooperation in a wider European framework at the Anglo-French St. Malo Summit in 1998. Here, they issued a Joint Declaration on European Defence that called for the creation of autonomous capacities along with credible military force (Gross 2007). At the global level, the tragedy of the Yugoslav conflicts, and particularly the Srebrenica massacre, proved to be one of the lessons that resulted in the development of the norm of the Responsibility to Protect (Global Centre for the Responsibility to Protect 2020).

The Economic Community of West African States: West Africa's approach to security, sovereignty, and human rights

This section will analyse how the Economic Community of West African States (ECOWAS) engaged with questions of security, sovereignty, and human rights. Before commencing with this discussion, I will first provide some general information about the West African regional organisation.

ECOWAS was founded in 1975 with the Treaty of Lagos comprising 15 states in the West African region (ECOWAS 2019). Member states make use of three official languages (English, French, and Portuguese) based on their respective colonial heritages (ECOWAS 2019). The Treaty of Lagos was originally conceived as an economic initiative, fostering interstate economic cooperation, but security concerns forced the regional organisation to revise its Treaty in 1993 to broaden the mandate of ECOWAS into security affairs (ECOWAS 1993). Some steps into this direction had already been taken with the signing of the Protocol on Non-Aggression (PNA) in 1978 and the Protocol on Mutual Assistance in Defence (PMAD) in 1981, committing member states to "refrain from the threat and the use of force or aggression" against each other and to a collective defence treaty respectively (ECOWAS 1978; 1981). The signing of the 1993 Revised Treaty marked the start of a new era of institution-building in ECOWAS, mostly relating to regional security.

Security

West Africa has been a particularly conflict-prone region in the time period under analysis.

Civil wars took place in Nigeria, Senegal, Mauritania, Liberia, Mali, Sierra Leone, Guinea-Bissau, Ivory Coast, and Niger (Marc et al. 2015, 8). Some of these listed conflicts continue to the present day (2022), such as the Boko Haram uprising in Nigeria and the fighting between different armed groups in Mali (Council on Foreign Relations 2020; Human Rights Watch 2020).

The conflicts occurred in the first decades after the Second World War against a backdrop of national struggles for independence from colonial masters and the context of the Cold War. Concerning the former, anti-colonial struggles were waged across the African continent, to which West Africa was not an exception. These independence movements were initially met by opposition of various degrees from colonial powers in the region – the UK, France, and Portugal – but eventually they all succeeded (Goldberg 1986; Chabal 1981). Ghana was the first state in the region to gains its independence – from the UK – in 1957 and Western Sahara – from Spain – the last, in 1976 (Christopher 2002). The struggle against colonialism was a formative moment in the history of many West African states, as they had lived under colonial rule since the late 19th century (Hargreaves 1985). The various West African states regained their independence against the backdrop of the Cold War. Although West Africa was not the region in which the Cold War was most strongly experienced, it still played a role as West African states such as Guinea attempted to exploit the rivalries between the Eastern and the Western Bloc by seeking favours from both of them in turns – a strategy that was used by many developing states at the time (The New York Times 1964). It was against this backdrop of decolonisation processes and the Cold War that ECOWAS was founded in the 1970s. Although principally an initiative to develop the region economically, the organisation can also be seen as an expression of self-determination of the region against outside interference.

With the end of the Cold War in 1989, as discussed in the section on Europe, the frozen system of East-West allegiances disappeared, and this brought many tensions and rivalries to the fore in regions across the globe. West Africa was particularly affected by these developments, as evidenced by the strong increase in intrastate conflicts in the 1990s (UK Department for International Development, Ministry of Defence, Foreign & Commonwealth Office 2006, 22).

The quickly deteriorating security situation in the sub-region forced ECOWAS to transform itself from an economic sub-regional organisation to one with a security mandate as well (ECOWAS 1993). To this aim, ECOWAS revised its 1975 Founding Treaty in 1993 with the ECOWAS Revised Treaty (ECOWAS 1993). The relevant security provisions are outlined in articles 4, 22, and 58. Article 4 d) stipulates non-aggression between Member States, 4 e) maintenance of regional peace, stability, and security through the promotion and strengthening of good neighbourliness, 4 f) peaceful settlement of disputes among member states, active cooperation between neighbouring countries, and promotion of a peaceful environment as a prerequisite for economic development. Article 22 f) establishes a 'Political, Judicial and Legal Affairs, Regional Security and Immigration' technical commission, while Article 56 relates to cooperation of the signatory states to realise the objectives of the Protocol on Non-Aggression, the Protocol on Mutual Assistance on Defence, the Community Declaration of Political Principles, and the African Charter on Human and Peoples' Rights (ECOWAS 1993). Article 58, Regional Security, establishes the regional security mandate of ECOWAS, in which "Member States undertake to work to safeguard and consolidate relations conducive to the maintenance of peace, stability and security within the region" (ECOWAS 1993). With that comes a pledge for Member States to "cooperate with the Community in establishing and strengthening appropriate mechanisms for the timely prevention and resolution of intra-State and inter-State conflicts" (ECOWAS 1993).

Despite the adoption of the 1993 Revised Treaty, intra-state conflicts in the region spiked in the 1990s and the ECOWAS Cease-fire Monitoring Group (ECOMOG) – the Nigerian-led regional multilateral armed force which was later enshrined in the 1999 Mechanism – had to intervene in multiple conflicts (ECOWAS 1999). It first intervened on an ad hoc basis in the civil war in Liberia (1989–96) and later in Sierra Leone (1997) and Guinea Bissau (1999) (Olonisakin 2011). In Liberia, there had been "a breakdown of law and order" and the government led by President Doe was "on the verge of collapse" when ECOMOG intervened (Olonisakin 2011, 12). In Sierra Leone, the central government was challenged by the rebel Revolutionary United Front (RUF) and part of the military sided with the rebels. The precarious security situation led to over a million displaced persons and over 300,000 refugees that had to seek refuge in Guinea (Olonisakin 2011, 12–13). In Guinea Bissau, a military coup had taken place and help from Senegal and Guinea was not sufficient to confront the challenge. In Cote d'Ivoire, rebels had caused a precarious security situation which the central government was unable to manage on its own (Olonisakin 2011, 13). In all cases, ECOWAS launched peacebuilding missions through ECOMOG, with various degrees of success (Olonisakin 2011).

Assessments of ECOWAS' performance in the various operations vary widely. Especially its first involvement, in Liberia, incited a heated debate among scholars about "the role and mandate of the interventionist force" (Gberie 2003, 148). For Vogt (1992), this first intervention amounted to a "bold attempt at peacekeeping, offering strong lessons in regional conflict management in a world in which the international community had progressively disengaged from Africa". Sesay (1996), on the contrary, saw the intervention as "an ill-conceived and regionally divisive intervention exercised by autocratic leaders, with disastrous consequences for regional cohesion and sustainable democracy." Part of the criticism was that ECOMOG was operating on shaky legal grounds in its first intervention, as ECOMOG as such had not been enshrined in a treaty yet but was the result of ad hoc decisions by the region's Anglophone powers (Adebajo 2002). The legal recognition of ECOMOG would only happen in 1999, when the regional monitoring group was formally established by 'the Mechanism' (see below).

As intra-state conflicts spiked in the 1990s, West African leaders indeed came to realise that the 1993 Revised Treaty, although an important step in the right direction, still had its deficiencies in providing security to the sub-region.

Consequently, in 1999, ECOWAS member states adopted the 'Mechanism for Conflict Prevention, Management, Resolution, Peace-Keeping and Security' (better known as 'the Mechanism'), which established a mechanism for collective security and peace (ECOWAS 1999, 4). In the 'Mechanism', ECOWAS member states affirmed that they were "concerned about the proliferation of conflicts which constitute a threat to the peace and security in the African continent, and undermines efforts to improve the living standards of our peoples" and asserted that "good governance, the rule of law and sustainable development are essential for peace and conflict prevention" (ECOWAS 1999, 2). The 1999 Mechanisms outlined when ECOWAS could become involved in regional peace and security matters, defined in Article 25 ('Conditions for Application'):

> "In cases of aggression or conflict in any Member State or threat thereof; In case of conflict between two or several Member States; In case of internal conflict: a) that threatens to trigger a humanitarian disaster, or b) that poses a serious threat to peace and security in the sub-region; In event of serious and massive violation of human rights and the rule of law. In the event of an overthrow or attempted overthrow of a democratically elected government; Any other situation as may be decided by the Mediation and Security Council."
>
> Source: Article 25, ECOWAS 1999 Mechanism

The Mechanism can be activated by the Authority, the Mediation and Security Council, at the request of a Member State, on the initiative of the Executive Secretary and at the request of the African Union or the United Nations (Art. 26) (ECOWAS 1999). When a situation in a member state requires an intervention, the Mediation and Security Council "shall consider several options and decide on the most appropriate course of action to take in terms of intervention. Such options may include recourse to the Council of Elders, the dispatch of fact-finding missions, political and mediation missions or intervention by ECOMOG" (Art. 27) (ECOWAS 1999).

Crucial for the purpose of this book is to observe that some of the terminology that would eventually come to constitute the norm of R2P is already present in these ECOWAS Treaties. Especially Article 25 of the 1999 Mechanism resembles this, as it allows for intervention in cases of "humanitarian disaster" and "massive violations of human rights and the rule of law". It can be argued that the mass atrocity crimes specified in the R2P norm (i.e. ethnic cleansing, war crimes, crimes against humanity, and genocide) in fact boil down to the umbrella terms "humanitarian disasters" or "massive violations of human rights and the rule of law" and that what changed mostly is the level of specification of these disasters and violations, which were broadly phrased in the ECOWAS 1999 Mechanism and now specified in the R2P norm (ECOWAS 1999; UNGA 2005). This raises important questions about norm diffusion, i.e. whether one of the roots of R2P could possibly lie in West Africa. In an interview with an ECOWAS Commission policy officer, this notion was indeed confirmed, as the policy officer alluded to the fact that former UN Secretary General Annan was from the West African region (Ghana) and that he would never have been able to drive the R2P agenda on the global level "had he not come from the region" (ECOWAS Commission Policy Officer 2019). Gberie (2003, 147–148) concurs with this notion, stating that Annan's advocacy for a human security agenda (which is closely related to the norm of R2P) was

> "almost certainly influenced by events in West Africa, his home region, coming as they did shortly after Nigerian-led West African troops intervened in Sierra Leone following a highly destructive coup, unseated the military junta government and reinstated the democratically elected government that had been overthrown. It would appear from this that West Africa was, for once, shaping global policy, not just being a recipient of it."

West African actors thus actively contributed to the norm building of R2P through processes of local norm construction.

Sovereignty

Given its colonial history, West African states put a strong emphasis on their sovereignty in the post-colonial era. ECOWAS as a sub-regional organisation therefore also did not follow the track of EU integration: it limited regional cooperation to economic cooperation and regional trade for the first few decades of its existence and only moved into the area of security later and out of necessity (ECOWAS 2019; Boddy-Evans 2018). The architecture of ECOWAS has some supranational features, but most of them have only been added or strengthened in recent years, such as with the transformation of the ECOWAS Secretariat into the ECOWAS Commission in 2007 (ECOWAS 2019). This 'slow-track', limited regional integration process is of course understandable given the colonial legacies in the region: having been deprived of sovereignty during the colonial era, it would have been surprising to witness a sovereignty-pooling project like the EU only years after West African states had regained their sovereignty.

Söderbaum (2004, 426) argues along these lines by asserting that ECOWAS belongs to the "sovereignty-boosting" type of regional organisations, which he characterises as instances in which "political leaders and regimes are using regional governance to promote rather than to reduce absolute state sovereignty and its legitimacy." State actors and political leaders in this type of regional integration thus instrumentalise regionalism and regional governance "to bolster their regimes and governments" (Söderbaum 2004, 425). The author hereby problematises the dichotomy between sovereignty and functional regional integration, which is characteristic of theories focused on European integration, such as neofunctionalism (Söderbaum 2004, 425).

To understand (sub)regional projects in Africa, there is a need to move beyond these traditional understandings of regional integration. Concerning ECOWAS, Söderbaum (2004, 427) maintains that it "can be seen as a relatively informal governance and a collective intervention mechanism, whereby ruling governments pool sovereignty and power in order to strengthen their own and their neighbours' weak governments and regimes against domestic opposition and national disintegration". This seems to be an overtly pessimistic view of ECOWAS' regional security efforts though, especially in the light of more recent developments, in which ECOWAS has actively intervened in support of democratically elected governments in the region – a practice which is enshrined in its treaties, as was discussed in the security part of this section (BBC 2017; ECOWAS 1993; 1999).

The notion of sovereignty boosting is an interesting one, nevertheless, as it can indeed be argued that, in general, ECOWAS member states have moved fewer policy areas to the regional level than EU member states have, i.e. ECOWAS has gone less far in pooling sovereignty than the EU has. At the time of the establishment of ECOWAS most West African leaders were also careful in ensuring that regional cooperation should not encroach on state sovereignty (Piccolino 2016). Additionally, ECOWAS indeed seems to be used more for "sovereignty-boosting reasons" (such as providing West African elites with legitimacy) than the EU. On the contrary, EU member states like Hungary and Poland have in recent years vocalised their resistance against the EU to maintain popularity at home (Söderbaum 2004; Waller 2017).

Contrary to the above assertion are the more recent developments in the area of regional security in West Africa, in the sense that they allow for regional measures that are unconceivable on the European continent, of which military intervention is the best case in point (see also the discussion in the security section). One could make the argument that, at least in the area of security, the ECOWAS member states have gone much further than their EU counterparts in pooling sovereignty (with ECOMOG coming close to a West African standing force, something which the EU is now only aspiring too) and also allowing regional measures that could be very intrusive vis-à-vis sovereignty (all the way up to military intervention in case of serious breaches of democratic governance, massive human rights violations, and other breaches as listed in Article 25 of ECOWAS' 1999 'Mechanism') (ECOWAS 1999). This point has also been made by Piccolino (2016, 17), who argues that "in the peace and security domain, ECOWAS is arguably more, and not less, supranational than the EU." One can debate the underlying motives behind the regional interventions, with Söderbaum (2004) clearly adopting a sceptical view, whereas others are more positively inclined (see, for instance Vogt (1992)). However, the fact remains that the observation that these interventions are possible in the first place says something about sovereignty in the region, and most likely that a categorisation of ECOWAS' regional project as purely "sovereignty-boosting" misses some nuance. When comparing ECOWAS with the EU, one can conclude that the EU has gone further in sovereignty pooling in most areas, such as trade, economics, and judicial cooperation, while in the area of security, ECOWAS has exceeded the EU. This is reflective of the integration experience of both regions, where ECOWAS had to take some exceptional steps in regional security cooperation from the 1990s onwards, because of the precarious security situation in the West African region.

Human rights and mass atrocities prevention/response

It is hard to establish member state support for human rights in West Africa in the early years after the Second World War, as West African states were not UN members yet at the date of signing of the Universal Declaration of Human Rights in 1948. This was a result of the fact that West African states were still colonised at the time and thus lacked the sovereignty to sign. Africa also lacked a continental movement leading to a continental human rights treaty, as was witnessed on the European continent with the signing of the pan-European 'European Convention on Human Rights (ECHR)' in 1953. When ECOWAS was established in 1975, human rights language in its founding document was lacking. The document did make mention of economic freedoms, but these were "carefully couched to avoid any link with rights" (Ebobrah 2010, 3). In the decades that followed, only very rare and few references to human rights can be found, one of the exceptions being the 1979 Protocol relating to free movement, which establishes the "rights to enter, reside and establish".[6] Only in 1991, when ECOWAS still operated on the basis of the 1975 ECOWAS Treaty, the regional organisation first alludes to human rights as part of its adoption of the declaration on political principles. Here it makes mention of human rights under "universally recognised international instruments on human rights and in the African Charter on Human and Peoples' Rights".[7]

According to Ebobrah (2010), the 1993 Revised Treaty revolutionised "the perception and reception of human rights in the ECOWAS constitutional framework" as the Treaty "makes specific reference to human rights in its preamble", "and recognizes the "promotion and protection of human and peoples' rights in accordance with the African Charter on Human and Peoples' Rights" (African Charter) as one of the fundamental principles to which ECOWAS members states will adhere in the pursuit of ECOWAS objectives" (Ebobrah 2010, 4). In the Revised Treaty, ECOWAS member states also agree "to cooperate for the purpose of realising the objects" of the African Charter. In the post-1993 era, ECOWAS adopts further protocols that make "clear references to human rights instruments and use relatively unambiguous rights language" (Ebobrah 2010, 4). The author critically notes that mentioning of human rights does not imply that ECOWAS sees this as a goal for its organisation, as neither the 1975 Treaty nor the 1993 Revised Treaty "enumerate the promotion and protection of human rights as a purpose or function of the organisation" (Ebobrah 2010, 5). The fact though that human rights are mentioned in the 1993 Revised Treaty, but also in the 1999 Mechanism and the 2001 Protocol on Democracy and Good Governance, shows that ECOWAS has become not only cognisant of but also supportive of human rights in the post-1993 era, something which was not the case yet when ECOWAS was founded in 1975.

Having discussed the formal, legal aspect of ECOWAS' engagement with human rights, it is now time to shortly address practices, both the human rights situation in West African states and ECOWAS' approach to these situations. The operations conducted by ECOMOG that were discussed in the security part of this section were partly in response to human rights abuses in West African states. The civil wars in states like Liberia (1989–96), Sierra Leone (1997), and Guinea Bissau (1999) witnessed mass displacements of people and large refugee streams. During the Liberian civil war, tens of thousands of people died in a population of 2 million (Gberie 2003, 148). Traore (2016, 20) argues that ECOWAS launched its first intervention in Liberia in 1990 "to prevent further killing of civilians". Even though it was not explicitly stated at the time, "the intervention was to prevent state-sponsored mass atrocities during armed conflict" (Traore 2016, 20). ECOWAS' involvement in Sierra Leone in 1998 was motivated by similar reasons, this time to prevent mass killing by both state and non-state actors (Traore 2016, 20). The direct aim of ECOWAS involvement in these conflicts remained conflict management as it did not have a conflict prevention framework in place yet, let alone a mass atrocity prevention lens (Traore 2016, 20). It is noteworthy though that ECOWAS' interventions at the time seemed more informed by targeting mass atrocities than were the EU's measures during the Bosnian civil war. Part of this seems due to the effect of the treaty changes of the 1990s, enabling ECOWAS to be a more credible and effective security provider (and mass atrocity 'denier' in effect) in West Africa than the EU could be in Europe in that time period.

Differences in institutional mechanisms between the two regional organisations at the time certainly had a role to play. During the Yugoslav conflicts, the EU was transitioning from the EPC, which merely allowed for an exchange in and coordination of foreign policy positions, to the CFSP, which introduced room for common positions and joint actions. The Yugoslav conflicts were in full swing though when the CFSP was introduced and member states still had to familiarise themselves with the new policy. More importantly, procedurally, CFSP decisions required unanimity among member states, something which did not hamper ECOWAS in its decision-making, as the 1999 Mechanism allowed for majority voting on matters of peace and security (European Union 1992; ECOWAS 1999). The novelty of the CFSP along with its procedural constraints left the EU ill-equipped to address the tragedies unfolding in the former Yugoslavia. These were thus institutional obstacles to early EU engagement with mass atrocity prevention and response.

Concerning ECOWAS, while the regional organisation repositioned itself in the 1990s to become a regional security actor next to its economic mandate, it is important to note that the most significant changes in the end came at the end of the decade, when the 1999 Mechanism was adopted. Importantly, while expanding and fortifying ECOWAS' regional security mandate, the 1993 Revised Treaty did not include provisions on regional interventions. These were only introduced in the 1999 Mechanism. So, the fact that ECOWAS appeared to be a more credible and effective security provider in its region than the EU in Europe in the 1990s cannot be simply explained by differences in institutional mechanisms relating to regional security. More importantly, it was regional security practices that made the difference. It was the willingness of certain member states, first and foremost Nigeria, to go *beyond* what ECOWAS' treaty and protocols allowed for at the time that a practice of regional intervention emerged in the late 1980s and 1990s. One should not forget that ECOMOG, the region's multilateral armed force, lacked a constitutional basis when it intervened first in Liberia and then in Sierra Leone. This nevertheless did not prevent Nigeria and several other member states to employ it to put a lid on civil wars and the commission of atrocities in the region. Nigeria's leadership on these issues is in line with hegemonic stability thesis, as captured in the regional factor on hegemonic regional systems.

Conclusion

This contextual chapter has provided a historical overview of questions surrounding security, sovereignty, and human rights in Europe and West Africa and has showed how the EU and ECOWAS have approached these questions. For the EU, its security experience after the Second World War was heavily influenced by the Cold War and notions of human security only came up after this time period. Under Solana, the EU became an important driver of the human security agenda, which resonates with the norm of R2P. Given support for the human security agenda from a significant number of member states and EU elites in the pre-World Summit period, R2P hit fertile ground in the EU when it was adopted at the UN in 2005. In terms of sovereignty, EU member states built up decades of experience with pooling sovereignty. This qualified notion of sovereignty should make the EU receptive to the norm of R2P, which understands sovereignty not as absolute sovereignty but as 'sovereignty as responsibility'. The EU has an elaborate human rights architecture, of which the Charter of Fundamental Rights of the European Union (2000) is the principal one, enshrining the rights of EU citizens. The conflicts in Yugoslavia, and the Bosnian Civil War in particular, posed an important challenge to the EU as it had to confront a conflict and mass atrocities at a time when its CFSP was still in the making. The analysis showed that the EU lacked a mass atrocity lens in responding to Srebrenica and the wider Bosnian Civil War and it struggled to play a decisive role as the UN, NATO, and the US were also engaged with the crises. The Yugoslav conflicts provided an impetus for EU initiatives in foreign policy and defence, of which the 1998 St. Malo Summit was the first visible expression, while the Srebrenica massacre was one of the main events that contributed to the development of the norm of R2P (Global Centre for the Responsibility to Protect 2020; UN News 2015).

ECOWAS was originally founded for economic purposes, but the quickly deteriorating security situation in West Africa after the end of the Cold War forced the organisation to adopt a security mandate. A treaty change and the adoption of various mechanisms and protocols in the 1990s and 2000s allowed ECOWAS to move into the field of security. The organisation was soon put to the test as multiple civil wars in the 1990s necessitated ECOWAS to intervene through the ECOWAS Cease-fire Monitoring Group (ECOMOG). ECOMOG was first set up on an ad hoc basis by the region's Anglophone powers but was later formally institutionalised in the 1999 Mechanism (ECOWAS 1999). In terms of sovereignty, West African states have generally moved fewer policy areas to the regional level than EU member states have, but in the field of security, they have gone arguably further. The 1999 Mechanism allows ECOWAS to intervene in member states under certain conditions, which is not conceivable in the EU. Interestingly, the language of Article 25 of the 1999 Mechanism, which specifies when ECOWAS can intervene in member states, resembles and has possibly inspired the norm of R2P, as it allows for intervention in cases of "humanitarian disaster" and "massive violations of human rights and the rule of law" (ECOWAS 1999). The civil wars of the 1990s in the West African region witnessed large-scale human rights abuses and some authors have argued this was at least part of the reason for ECOWAS to intervene in these cases (Traore 2016). These interventions would thus represent an early application of the responsibility to react in the pre-World Summit era. The main motivation to become involved at that time was still conflict management, though, as neither a conflict prevention framework nor a specific mass atrocity lens was in place yet (Traore 2016). Nigeria's leading role in these interventions is significant in light of this book. The regional hegemonic factor in the analytical framework assessed the important role the hegemon can play in institutionalising norms in a regional hegemonic stability system. It seems that Nigeria has indeed played this role within ECOWAS, through innovating with its intervention practice that has strong resonance with R2P. This finding will be further assessed in the empirical chapter on ECOWAS.

Notes

1 The European project started with the European Coal and Steel Community (ECSC) in 1952. In 1957, the Treaty of Rome created the European Community (EC), which included three economic associations: the European Economic Community (EEC), the European Coal and Steel Community (ECSC), and the European Atomic Energy Community. In 1993, when the Maastricht Treaty came into effect, the European Community was replaced by the European Union (EU) (European Union 2019). When discussing different historical periods in this contextual chapter, I will refer to the European organisation that existed in that time period.

2 For a nuanced historical account of the Dutch position towards EU-integration, see Vollaard (2012).

3 The Dutch Supreme Court ruled in July 2019 that the Dutch State bears very limited liability in the 'Mothers of Srebrenica' case. The liability was limited to 10 percent of the damages suffered by the surviving relatives of approximately 350 victims (for information on the judgment, see Rechtspraak (2019). In response to the Supreme Court judgment, The Mothers of Srebrenica war victims' association filed a complaint against the Netherlands at the European Court for Human Rights, alleging that "in July 1995, the Netherlands failed to take the measures within its power to protect the men and boys in the safe area Srebrenica" (Brkanic 2020).

4 "Prosecutor vs Krstic, Appeals Chamber Judgement" (PDF). ICTY. 19 April 2004. para. 37. Retrieved 5 May 2019.
5 International Court of Justice (26 February 2007). "Application of the Convention on the Prevention and Punishment of the Crime of Genocide (Bosnia and Herzegovina v. Serbia and Montenegro), Judgment" (PDF). p. 166 § 297. General List No. 91. "The Court concludes that the acts committed at Srebrenica falling within Article II (a) and (b) of the Convention were committed with the specific intent to destroy in part the group of the Muslims of Bosnia and Herzegovina as such; and accordingly that these were acts of genocide, committed by members of the VRS in and around Srebrenica from about 13 July 1995".
6 Art. 2 of ECOWAS Protocol A/P.l/5/79 Relating to Free Movement of Persons, Residence and Establishment (ECOWAS 1979).
7 Declaration A/DCL.1/7/91 of Political Principles of the Economic Community of West African States (ECOWAS 1991).

Bibliography

Adebajo, Adekeye. 2002. *Liberia's Civil War: Nigeria, ECOMOG, and Regional Security in West Africa*. London: Lynne Rienner Publishers, Inc.

Baker, Catherine. 2015. *The Yugoslav Wars of the 1990s*. Basingstoke: Palgrave Macmillan.

BBC. 2017. "Gambia Crisis: Senegal Sends in Troops to Back Elected Leader." *BBC*. January 19. www.bbc.com/news/world-africa-38682184 (May 5, 2019).

Behringer, Ronald M. 2013. "The Dynamics of Middlepowermanship." *Seton Hall Journal of Diplomacy and International Relations* 14 (2): 9–22.

Boddy-Evans, Alistair. 2018. "What is the Economic Community of West African States (ECOWAS)?" *ThoughtCo*. April 15. www.thoughtco.com/economic-community-west-african-states-ecowas-43900 (May 5, 2019).

Boutros-Ghali, Boutros. 1992. *An Agenda for Peace: Preventive Diplomacy, Peacemaking, and Peace-keeping: Report of the Secretary-General Pursuant to the Statement Adopted by the Summit Meeting of the Security Council on 31 January 1992*. New York: United Nations.

Brkanic, Dzana. 2020. "'Mothers of Srebrenica' File Euro Court Complaint against Netherlands." *BalkanInsight*. January 21. https://balkaninsight.com/2020/01/21/mothers-of-srebrenica-file-european-court-complaint-against-netherlands/ (May 24, 2020).

Budapest Centre for Mass Atrocities Prevention. 2018. "Statement for the 70th Anniversary of the Adoption of the UN Convention on the Prevention of Genocide." December 7. www.genocideprevention.eu/statement-for-the-70th-anniversary-of-the-adoption-of-the-un-convention-on-the-prevention-of-genocide/ (May 3, 2019).

Bush, George H.W. 1990. "Toward a New World Order." *National Archives*. September 11. (Records of the United States House of Representatives).

Buzan, Barry, Waever, Ole and de Wilde, Jaap. 1998. *Security: A New Framework for Analysis*. Boulder: Lynne Rienner.

Chabal, Patrick. 1981. "National Liberation in Portuguese Guinea, 1956–1974." *African Affairs* 80 (January): 75–99. DOI:10.1093/oxfordjournals.afraf.a097302l.

Christopher, A.J. 2002. "Decolonisation without Independence." *GeoJournal* 56 (3): 213–224. DOI:10.1023/A:1025165118672.

Christou, George. 2014. "The European Union's Human Security Discourse: Where Are We Now?" *European Security* 23 (3): 364–381. DOI:10.1080/09662839.2014.884075.

Council of Europe. 1950. European Convention for the Protection of Human Rights and Fundamental Freedoms, as amended by Protocols Nos. 11 and 14, November 4, 1950.

Council on Foreign Relations. 2020. "Boko Haram in Nigeria." www.cfr.org/global-conflict-tracker/conflict/boko-haram-nigeria (October 2, 2020).

Daalder, Ivo. 1998. "Decision to Intervene: How the War in Bosnia Ended." *Brookings*. December 1. www.brookings.edu/articles/decision-to-intervene-how-the-war-in-bosnia-ended/(May 1, 2019).

Deng, Francis M., Sadikiel Kimaro, Terrence Lyons, Donald Rothchild and William Zartman. 1996. *Sovereignty as Responsibility: Conflict Management in Africa*. Washington, DC: Brookings Institution Press.

Dover, Robert. 2005. "The EU and the Bosnian Civil War 1992–95: The Capabilities – Expectations Gap at the Heart of EU Foreign Policy." *European Security* 14 (3): 297–318. DOI:10.1080/09662830500407770.

Ebobrah, Solomon. 2010. "Critical Issues in the Human Rights Mandate of the ECOWAS Court of Justice." *Journal of African Law* 54 (1): 1–25. DOI:10.1017/S0021855309990143.

ECOWAS. 1978. *Protocol on Non-Aggression*. Abuja: ECOWAS.

ECOWAS. 1979. *Protocol Relating to Free Movement of Persons, Residence and Establishment*. Abuja: ECOWAS.

ECOWAS. 1981. *Protocol Relating to Mutual Assistance on Defence*. Abuja: ECOWAS.

ECOWAS. 1991. *Declaration of Political Principles of the Economic Community of West African States*. Abuja: ECOWAS.

ECOWAS. 1993. *Revised Treaty of ECOWAS*. Abuja: ECOWAS.

ECOWAS. 1999. *Mechanism for Conflict Prevention, Management, Resolution, Peace-Keeping and Security*. Abuja: ECOWAS.

ECOWAS. 2019. "History." www.ecowas.int/about-ecowas/history/ (May 5, 2019).

ECOWAS Commission Policy Officer. 2019. Interviewed by Jochem Rietveld, Skype, April 2019.

Etzioni, Amitai. 1963. "European Unification. A Strategy of Change." *World Politics* 16 (1): 32–51.

European Commission. 2020. "The Common Agricultural Policy at a Glance." https://ec.europa.eu/info/food-farming-fisheries/key-policies/common-agricultural-policy/cap-glance_en (April 20, 2020).

European Commission Official. 2018. Interviewed by Jochem Rietveld, Brussels, June 2018.

European Union. 1992. "Treaty on European Union (Consolidated Version), Treaty of Maastricht, 7 February 1992." *Official Journal of the European Communities C 325/5*, 24 December 2002.

European Union. 2000. "Charter of Fundamental Rights of the European Union." 2000/C 364/01. *Official Journal of the European Communities*. www.europarl.europa.eu/charter/pdf/text_en.pdf (May 5, 2019).

European Union. 2006. "Agreement between the International Criminal Court and the European Union on cooperation and assistance." L115, 28/04/2006, 50. https://eur-lex.europa.eu/legal-content/EN/TXT/?uri=CELEX%3A52016IP0051 (May 5, 2019).

European Union. 2007. "Treaty of Lisbon. Amending the Treaty on European Union and the Treaty Establishing the European Community." 2007/C 306/01. *Official Journal of the European Union*. https://eur-lex.europa.eu/legal-content/EN/TXT/?uri=celex%3A12007L%2FTXT (May 5, 2019).

European Union. 2019. "The history of the European Union." https://europa.eu/european-union/about-eu/history_en (May 1, 2019).

Fukuyama, Francis. 1989. "The End of History." *The National Interest* 16 (Summer): 3–18.

Gberie, Lansana. 2003. "Review: ECOMOG: The Story of an Heroic Failure." *African Affairs* 102 (January): 147–154.

Global Centre for the Responsibility to Protect. 2020. "Statement on the 25th Anniversary of the Genocide in Srebrenica." July 10. www.globalr2p.org/publications/statement-on-the-25th-anniversary-of-the-genocide-in-srebrenica/ (June 9, 2022).

Goldberg, Melvin. 1986. "Decolonisation and Political Socialisation with Reference to West Africa." *The Journal of Modern African Studies* 24 (December): 663–677.

Gross, Eva. 2007. "European Union Foreign Policy towards the Balkans." In *European Foreign Policy in an Evolving International System*, eds. Nicola Casarini and Costanza Musu. Basingstoke: Palgrave Macmillan, 97–111. DOI:10.1057/9780230593145_7.

Haas, Ernst. 1958. *The Uniting of Europe: Political, Social, and Economical Forces, 1950–1957*. Notre Dame: University of Notre Dame Press.

Haas, Ernst. 1961. "International Integration: The European and the Universal Process." *International Organization* 15 (3): 366–392.

Hanhimäki, Jussi. 2012. "Europe's Cold War." In *The Oxford Handbook of Postwar European History*, ed. Dan Stone. Oxford: Oxford University Press, 283–298. DOI:10.1093/oxfordhb/9780199560981.013.0014.

Hargreaves, John D. 1985. *West Africa Partitioned. Volume II. The Elephants and the Grass*. Basingstoke: MacMillan Press. DOI:10.1007/978-1-349-02825-2.

Harnisch, Sebastian. 2017. "Theory and Practice of Human Security concerns in EU-Japan relations: the EU perspective." *EU-Japan Security Cooperation: Challenges and Opportunities* (Spring/Summer): 1–11.

Hartmann, Florence and Ed Vulliamy. 2015. "How Britain and the US decided to abandon Srebrenica to its fate." *The Guardian*. July 4. www.theguardian.com/world/2015/jul/04/how-britain-and-us-abandoned-srebrenica-massacre-1995 (May 5, 2019).

Human Rights Watch. 2020. "Mali. Events of 2019." www.hrw.org/world-report/2020/country-chapters/mali (October 2, 2020).

International Commission on Intervention and State Sovereignty, Gareth J. Evans, and Mohamed Sahnoun. 2001. *The Responsibility to Protect: Report of the International Commission on Intervention and State Sovereignty*. Ottawa: International Development Research Centre.

International Court of Justice. 2007. "Application of the Convention on the Prevention and Punishment of the Crime of Genocide (Bosnia and Herzegovina v. Serbia and Montenegro), Judgment." February 26. p. 166 § 297. General List No. 91.

International Criminal Court. 2019. "How the Court works. The Crimes." www.icc-cpi.int/about/how-the-court-works (May 5, 2019).

International Criminal Tribunal for the former Yugoslavia. 2004. "Prosecutor v. Krstić." Case No: IT-98–33-A.

Judt, Tony. 2005. *Post War. A History of Europe since 1945*. New York: The Penguin Press.

Liotta, P.H. and Owen, T. 2006. "Why Human Security?" *The Whitehead Journal of Diplomacy and International Relations* 43 (Winter/Spring): 37–54.

Marc, Alexandre, Neelam Verjee, and Stephen Mogaka. 2015. *The Challenge of Stability and Security in West Africa*. Washington, DC: The World Bank.

Milward, Alan. 1992. *The European Rescue of the Nation-State*, 2nd ed. London: Routledge.

Olonisakin, Oluwafunmilayo. 2011. "ECOWAS from Economic Integration to Peacebuilding." In *ECOWAS and the Dynamic of Conflict and Peace-building in West Africa*, eds. T. Jaye, D. Garuba and S. Amadi. Dakar: Council for the Development of Social Science Research in Africa, 11–26.

Piccolino, Giulia. 2016. "International Diffusion and the Puzzle of African Regionalism: Insights from West Africa. *UNU-CRIS Working Papers 2016/1* 1–32.

Rechtspraak. 2019. "Dutch State Bears Very Limited Liability in 'Mothers of Srebrenica' Case."July 19. www.rechtspraak.nl/Organisatie-en-contact/Organisatie/Hoge-Raad-der-Nederlanden/Nieuws/Paginas/Dutch-State-bears-very-limited-liability-in-Mothers-of-Srebenica-case.aspx (May 24, 2020).

Schimmelfennig, Frank, Stefan Engert and Heiko Knobel. 2003. "Costs, Commitment and Compliance: The Impact of EU Democratic Conditionality on Latvia, Slovakia and Turkey." *Journal of Common Market Studies* 41 (3): 495–518. DOI:10.1111/1468-5965.00432.

Schuman, Robert. 1950. "The Schuman Declaration-9 May 1950." https://europa.eu/european-union/about-eu/symbols/europe-day/schuman-declaration_en (May 5, 2019).

Sesay, Max. 1996. "Civil War and Collective Intervention in Liberia: A Strange Case of Peace-keeping in West Africa." *Review of African Political Economy* 23 (March): 35–52. DOI:10.1080/03056249608704176.

Söderbaum, Fredrik. 2004. "Modes of Regional Governance in Africa: Neoliberalism, Sovereignty Boosting, and Shadow Networks." *Global Governance* 10 (4): 419–436.

Study Group on Europe's Security Capabilities. 2004. *A Human Security Doctrine for Europe. The Barcelona Report of the Study Group on Europe's Security Capabilities*. Barcelona: Study Group on Europe's Security Capabilities.

The New York Times. 1964. "East and West Reach a Cold War Truce in Guinea." *The New York Times*. July 24. www.nytimes.com/1964/07/24/archives/east-and-west-reach-a-cold-war-truce-in-guinea.html) (May 5, 2019).

Thomson, Susan. 2018. *Rwanda: From Genocide to Precarious Peace*. New Haven: Yale University Press.

Traore, Oury. 2016. "Annex. Economic Community of West African States (ECOWAS)." In *African Regional Communities and the Prevention of Mass Atrocities*, ed. African Task Force on the Prevention of Mass Atrocities. Budapest: Foundation for the International Prevention of Genocide and Mass Atrocities, 1–28.

UK Department for International Development, Ministry of Defence, Foreign & Commonwealth Office. 2006. *Conflict Trends in Africa, 1946–2004. A Macro-Comparative Perspective*. London: Department for International Development.

UN News. 2015. "Recalling 'Responsibility to Protect' UN Pays Tribute to Victims of Srebrenica Genocide." July 1. https://news.un.org/en/story/2015/07/503292-recalling-responsibility-protect-un-pays-tribute-victims-srebrenica-genocide (June 9, 2022).

United Nations. 2000. "Srebrenica Tragedy Will Forever Haunt United Nations History, Says Secretary-General On Fifth Anniversary of City's Fall." Press Release SG/SM/7489. July 10. www.un.org/press/en/2000/20000710.sgsm7489.doc.html (May 5, 2019).

United Nations Development Programme. 1994. *Human Development Report*. New York/Oxford: Oxford University Press.

United Nations General Assembly. 2005. *2005 World Summit Outcome. Resolution 60/1* (GA/RES/60/1). London: United Nations General Assembly.

United Nations Office on Genocide Prevention and the Responsibility to Protect. 2019. "Ethnic Cleansing." www.un.org/en/genocideprevention/ethnic-cleansing.shtml (May 5, 2019).

Urwin, Derek. 1995. *The Community of Europe: A History of European Integration since 1945*. 2nd ed. London: Routledge.

Van Meurs, Wim, Robin de Bruin, Liesbeth van de Grift, Carla Hoetink, Karin van Leeuwen and Carlos Reijne. 2018. *The Unfinished History of European Integration*. Amsterdam: Amsterdam University Press. DOI:10.5117/9789462988149.

Vogt, Margaret. 1992. *The Liberian Crisis and ECOMOG: A Bold Attempt at Regional Peace-Keeping*. Lagos: Gabumo Publishing Co.

Vollaard, Hans. 2012. "The Netherlands is Euro-pragmatic Rather than Eurosceptic." *EURACTIV*. August 17. www.euractiv.com/section/elections/opinion/the-netherlands-is-euro-pragmatic-rather-than-eurosceptic/ (April 13, 2020).

Waller, Luke. 2017. "Viktor Orbán. The Conservative Subversive." *POLITICO*. www.politico.eu/list/politico-28/viktor-orban/ (May 5, 2019).

4 The EU and R2P

From public endorsements to implementation?

Introduction

This empirical chapter will assess how and to what extent the EU has internalised the norm of the Responsibility to Protect (R2P) since the norm's adoption at the UN in 2005. This chapter thus aims to provide answers to the research question for the case of the EU, where the next chapter will do so for ECOWAS.

The first section discusses what the normative status quo in the EU looked like when R2P emerged and what this implied for norm entrepreneurs and antipreneurs of R2P. Subsequently, it will be discussed how the norm of R2P has generally been received in the EU since 2005. Providing this context is important as it will set the stage for the cases that will be analysed in the third section of the chapter, which will focus on four cases that are relevant for assessing the internalisation of R2P in the EU: the crises in Libya and Syria, the European refugee crisis, and the Rohingya crisis in Myanmar. The cases include both external and internal crises and they ensure variance in the EU's R2P response: while in the Syrian and Rohingya crises, measures stayed limited to the application of sanctions, in the case of Libya, a few EU member states intervened. The subsequent section offers some case reflections and case comparisons. The cases and reflections together will demonstrate how and to what extent the EU and its member states have internalised the norm of R2P in practice and how different European actors have operated during crises. In these sections, I will assess the different aspects of internalisation of R2P, ranging from formal support to measures consistent with the responsibility to rebuild. Finally, based on the way the EU and its member states have responded to the norm of R2P, both generally and in concrete cases, it will be assessed to what extent they have internalised the norm. The concepts of absorption, accommodation, and transformation from the Europeanisation literature will be used to assess the depths of change.

Before offering some concluding remarks, the chapter will revisit and systematically assess the regional factors that were identified in the theory chapter of this book. References to the regional factors are made throughout the chapter, but it is in this penultimate section that they are systematically assessed based on the chapter's findings.

The final section will offer some concluding remarks.

DOI: 10.4324/9781003230731-4

The normative status quo in the EU pre-2005

As was discussed in the contextual chapter, traditional notions of sovereignty were far from entrenched in the EU in the early 2000s, when the norm of R2P first emerged and negotiations around it started. The EU had already accumulated extensive experience with sovereignty-pooling and concepts like human security, which subscribe to a qualified understanding of sovereignty, had gained, although with some exceptions, high-level popularity in the EU at the time. One can thus assert that rather than enjoying an entrenched status, sovereignty's normative status quo in the EU was already unstable in the period when R2P as a norm emerged. Analysing the normative context was the first necessary step identified in the analytical framework of this book. The 'unstable normative status quo' of sovereignty in the EU comes with a number of expectations. First, in the context of an unstable status quo, entrepreneurs are expected to be advantaged over antipreneurs. In the case at hand, one should expect R2P norm entrepreneurs to be well positioned to seize the opportunity produced by the unstable normative status quo to problematise the status quo and advocate for a new norm to address the problem. In the case of the EU, it seems worthwhile to ask the question whether sovereignty can even be seen as representing the (clearly unstable) normative status quo. It might be more accurate to assume 'qualified sovereignty' as the normative status quo in the EU. The next question then becomes how much 'problematising' there was truly to do for the R2P norm entrepreneurs, as R2P resonates strongly with qualified notions of sovereignty. Evidence for this is that there were no European actors really pushing back against the 2005 World Summit Consensus and that EU member states all signed up to R2P and subsequently endorsed the norm in multilateral fora (Stefan and Newman 2020).

Under conditions of an unstable status quo, antipreneurs are expected to be less successful in exploiting blocking opportunities. Given sovereignty's contested status in the EU, it will be difficult for norm antipreneurs to defend traditional notions of sovereignty in the advent of the norm of R2P. The first blocking opportunity they have, to maintain there are no problems with the current status quo, will thus be difficult to seize. There has been no documentation of norm antipreneurship from EU member states around the World Summit negotiations. In more recent years, the position of the Visegrad states during the refugee crisis, in which many of them refused to take in refugees and emphasised their sovereignty against perceived EU interference concerning refugee quota, etc., is indicative of R2P norm antipreneurship, though. This will be further discussed in the section on the European refugee crisis.

There have been a few structural factors at the EU level that have operated against a rapid regional internalisation of R2P. The first is that the EU lacks a clear hegemon and instead has several leading member states. These leading member states have not always seen eye to eye on R2P, though, which has prevented collective normative leadership on the issue. The second factor is the unanimity rule that applies to CFSP decision-making processes. According to an ALDE-MEP at the time, this is the main obstacle to really move forward and develop a truly consensual European position on R2P, especially concerning the question when the use of force is appropriate (ALDE-MEP 2018).

In terms of European leaders and prominent individuals, a few people stand out when assessing regional R2P norm entrepreneurship. In the R2P literature, the names of former UK Prime Minister Tony Blair, former French Foreign Minister and humanitarian Bernard Kouchner, and former German Foreign Minister Joschka Fischer are frequently mentioned (Bellamy 2009; Brockmeier et al. 2014; Crossley 2016). Former UK Prime Minister Tony Blair is widely seen as an advocate of some of the underlying principles of R2P through his support for liberal internationalism. Importantly, Blair justified the 1999 Kosovo intervention on humanitarian grounds, providing a set of criteria that laid out when it was right to intervene in his 'Chicago speech'. Many of these criteria have their roots in 'Just War Theory' originating from the works of Augustine and Thomas Aquinas (Vorster 2015). According to Bellamy (2009, 81), with his speech, "Blair anchored sovereignty as responsibility into the changing nature of international order", while the intervention criteria he formulated were revisited in the 2001 ICISS Report (Crossley 2016). Critics, however, have argued that Blair damaged the reputation of the nascent R2P norm through association with the Iraq war, in which the promotion of democracy and the defence of human rights was used discursively to justify the unauthorised intervention (Crossley 2016, 83–84).

French humanitarian Bernard Kouchner, who co-founded Médecins Sans Frontières (MSF) and later served as Foreign Minister under President Sarkozy, is another influential individual who advocated for precursors of the R2P norm. Kouchner co-founded MSF in 1971, subscribing to the notion of '*le droit d'ingérence*', "the right or duty to intervene or to interfere in humanitarian crises" (Crossley 2016, 49). This reflected a key development in an important debate in the French humanitarian community. This debate centred around the question if the traditional principles of impartiality, neutrality, and independence should be observed by aid workers in cases where a government's refusal to let in aid workers could worsen human suffering. Kouchner and his colleagues argued these traditional principles could not be observed in these cases if human rights had anything to mean in practice and they thus deviated from a strict line of neutrality. In practice, this opened the door to the provision of humanitarian relief without government consent. The R2P literature has generally recognised this shift as a key event in the history of humanitarianism, "as it signalled a departure from a traditional understanding of state sovereignty" (Crossley 2016, 49). '*Le droit d'ingérence*' can therefore be seen as an important French, and in the context of this book, European, precursor of R2P. Kouchner later endorsed R2P, as it would capture the same spirit as '*le droit d'ingérence*' (Crossley 2016).

Finally, former German Foreign Minister Joschka Fischer can be seen as an early R2P norm entrepreneur, as he defended German participation in the 1999 NATO operations against the Former Yugoslavia. He effectively argued that Germany had a special responsibility to protect people against genocide given its own history. This constituted a re-interpretation of Germany's lessons from the Second World War, which had usually defaulted to the non-use of force abroad. Fischer's advocacy is all the more significant as he was a Green politician, and it was the first time since the Second World War German soldiers participated in an active combat mission (Brockmeier et al. 2014, 434).

Although there are more R2P norm entrepreneurs in the EU, these are the most widely mentioned in the R2P literature.

When relating the above discussion back to the process of local norm construction, there are a few things that stand out. First, the European norm entrepreneurs focused on localities where there was a clear threat of atrocities or where atrocities were already taking place. This means that the approaches they were suggesting should at least in theory be able to speak to other 'at risk localities' as well. The second facilitating factor was that the local norm should have a degree of success. The local norm or principle the European norm entrepreneurs have argued for seems to have been a precursor of the 'robust application of R2P'. Whether this had success cannot be uniformly answered. Some would argue that the Kosovo intervention for which Fischer (and Blair) argued represented a historical moment in which human rights concerns overrode sovereignty concerns and where an intervention aimed to put a halt to the commission of atrocities (Roberts 1999). Blair's humanitarian discourse in his justification of the Iraq war, on the contrary, has most likely done more damage than good to the incipient R2P norm. Third, it was argued that local norm construction was facilitated if some local actors emerged as global norm entrepreneurs. Blair is probably the most well-known of the three mentioned European norm entrepreneurs, but, as discussed, his support for (precursors of) R2P came at a cost for the R2P norm through association with the unmandated Iraq War.

The norm of R2P and the EU

Having assessed the normative status quo in the EU when the R2P norm emerged, it is now time to discuss how the norm of R2P has been generally received by the EU and its member states. This is important to get an overall impression of internalisation of R2P, before discussing this in relation to the cases. Overall, it can be argued that the EU has positively received R2P. In 2005, all EU member states supported R2P at the UN World Summit (UNGA 2005). The European Parliament (EP) endorsed the new norm as well in a resolution adopted after the World Summit in which it welcomed "the recognition of the international community's responsibility to protect populations from genocide, war crimes, ethnic cleansing and crimes against humanity, as well as the clear responsibility of each individual state to protect their own citizens from these crimes, including by means of the prevention of such crimes." The EP further underlined "the importance of the International Criminal Court as an essential body in the task of prosecuting the perpetrators of any such crimes"

(European Parliament 2005). In the European Consensus on Development, adopted in 2006, the EP, the Council, and Commission jointly expressed support for the norm of R2P: "The EU also strongly supports the responsibility to protect. We cannot stand by, as genocide, war crimes, ethnic cleansing or other gross violations of international humanitarian law and human rights are committed. The EU will support a strengthened role for the regional and sub-regional organisations in the process of enhancing international peace and security, including their capacity to coordinate donor support in the area of conflict prevention" (European Parliament, Council, Commission 2006, Art. 37). The norm subsequently found its way in the 2008 update to the 2003 European Security Strategy, called "Providing Security In A Changing World": "Sovereign governments must take responsibility for the consequences of their actions and hold a shared responsibility to protect populations from genocide, war crimes, ethnic cleansing and crimes against humanity" (European Union 2008, 2). The document also included a call upon the EU to continue to advance R2P (European Union 2008, 12).

The EP has been a major advocate of R2P within the EU. The institution endorsed the norm in a resolution shortly after the 2005 World Summit, and it made its first case-specific reference to the norm in a resolution aimed at the situation in Sudan in early 2006. The EP also played an important role in promoting R2P as a reason to intervene in the Libyan conflict. Early March 2011, the EP adopted a resolution that mentioned explicitly that "the EU and its member states must honour their Responsibility to Protect, in order to save Libyan civilians from large-scale armed attacks" (Stavridis 2016, 191). The resolution in question was passed with overwhelming support. In April 2013, when the dust of the intervention in Libya had settled, the EP adopted a recommendation to the Council concerning R2P. It recommended, among others, to adopt an inter-institutional 'Consensus on R2P', to integrate the R2P principle in the EU's development assistance, to identify an EU Focal Point for R2P in the EEAS, to strengthen cooperation with regional and sub-regional organisations in relation to R2P, and to focus on the prevention component of R2P. Besides, it encouraged to promote the R2P principle at the UN and to propose to the P5 of the Security Council a voluntary code of conduct which would limit the use of the right of veto in cases of mass atrocity crimes (European Parliament 2013a). Newman and Stefan (2020, 5) call the EP's recommendation "the most substantive European statement on R2P to date". Although the EP asked for "a concrete plan of action" on the follow-up of its proposals within six months, it took longer before a follow-up actually materialised. The reason for this delay has not been addressed in the existing literature on EU and R2P. Then Executive Director Dr. Simon Adams of The Global Centre for the Responsibility to Protect (GCR2P) indicated in an interview that one of the reasons might be that in these years the EU believed it was already 'doing R2P' – just by a different name in existing programs, such as early warning and human rights mechanisms. The necessity to create specific R2P policies was thus initially not seen (Adams 2018).

In July 2017, the EP adopted a resolution specifically addressing human rights violations in the context of mass atrocity crimes. Through the resolution, the EP called on the EU to integrate "the necessary tools for identifying and preventing any atrocity crime at an early stage" into its comprehensive approach to external conflicts and crises (European Parliament 2017a). The Framework of Analysis for Atrocity Crimes created by the relevant UN offices was cited as an example in this regard. The EP also called on the EU and its member states to "always adopt a strong stance in cases where crimes appear imminent and . . . use all peaceful instruments at their disposal" (European Parliament 2017a). The EP furthermore urged the Vice-President/High Representative (VP/HR) "to ensure that EU Special Representatives uphold the Responsibility to Protect (R2P) whenever necessary and broaden the mandate of the EU Special Representative on Human Rights to include R2P issues", "to further support the EU Focal Point for R2P in the EEAS in the context of the existing structures and resources" and to encourage the establishment of national focal points for R2P in the member states (European Parliament 2017a). At least a number of these recommendations have been followed up on, most notably through the development of the EU Atrocity Prevention Framework that was launched in early 2019 (Stefan and Newman 2020).

The actions and statements of the EP make it a critical norm entrepreneur of R2P in the EU. In terms of norm diffusion, its persistent focus on R2P through the years has ensured that the norm stayed on the political agenda in Brussels and has not lost momentum. In the language of the norms life cycle model of Finnemore and Sikkink (1998), the EP has ensured the cascade of the norm of R2P in the EU. In terms of norm internalisation, the EP scores very high on the first aspect of internalisation, concerning formal support. This aspect entails that mentioning of R2P in formal documents or speeches could be an indication of norm internalisation of R2P. It specifies a number of conditions under which formal support could count as norm internalisation of R2P, namely the authority of the actor, the importance of the document, the position on R2P it takes (positive/neutral/negative), and the number of references to the norm in a single document. The authority of the EP is high in the sense that it is the legislative body of the EU that has received a mandate from voters of all EU member states; resolutions are the most important instruments the EP can adopt; the position of the EP on R2P in its resolutions are without exception positive and, generally speaking, every resolution that contains R2P at least refers to it a number of times. One caveat that needs to be mentioned is that the EP's relative power to act and take decisions on R2P is limited, as it does not have any executive powers like the European Commission and the Council. Its advocacy nevertheless makes the EP a critical formal supporter of R2P within the EU.

2016 was the year in which the EU's Global Strategy was published. The strategy referred to R2P once. In the section "Global Governance for the 21st Century", the report states that "the EU will also promote the responsibility to protect, international humanitarian law, international human rights law and international criminal law" (European Union 2016, 41–42). It was framed more broadly in the context of the EU's support for widening the reach of international norms, regimes, and institutions (European Union 2016). The fact that R2P is mentioned in an enumeration of different bodies of international law seems to suggest that, at least in its Global Strategy, the EU views R2P through a legal lens, i.e. as an instrument of or strengthening existing international law. The reference to R2P indicates continued EU support for the norm but it remains vague on implementation. The fact that it is only mentioned once also gives the impression it was not high on the list of priorities. Smith (2018, 4), while reflecting on the EU's R2P track record mid-2018, observes "there is still no clear high-level declaration regarding the EU's commitment to mass atrocity prevention or R2P."

All the same, the EU has taken practical steps towards the implementation of R2P, of which the appointment of Christian Leffler as R2P regional focal point in 2016 is one example. In January 2017, the PRISM (Prevention of conflicts, Rule of Law/Security Sector Reform, Integrated Approach, Stabilization and Mediation) division was set up in the EEAS. The division helps "the delivery of an integrated EU response in fragile and conflict/crisis-affected areas" and has R2P as one of its focus areas (Newman and Stefan 2020, 7). Together with their colleagues from the EEAS' Global Division, the PRISM policy officers support the EU R2P focal point (in March 2019, PRISM changed into the Directorate Integrated Approach for Security & Peace, or ISP). In January 2019, the EEAS launched the *Atrocity Prevention Toolkit*. According to Newman and Stefan (2020), the toolkit is designed to support EU practitioners, through specific hands-on knowledge on how they can contribute to atrocity prevention through existing work strands, such as political reporting, or project design and implementation. The *Toolkit* includes structural risk indicators and imminent warning signs that atrocities may occur. It also provides guidance as to how the EU should respond in these situations (Newman and Stefan 2020, 9).

The focus of the toolkit is on prevention, which fits in with the extensive experience the EU has built up in conflict prevention over the years. This preventive emphasis allows it to consider how issues like development and governance all have a role to play in reducing the risk of atrocities occurring. The EEAS has ensured the toolkit is institutionally embedded, as it links atrocity prevention to existing bodies and programmes, such as the EEAS Crisis Response Mechanism, PRISM (now: ISP), and the R2P Focal Point office (Newman and Stefan 2020, 9). The toolkit's explicit focus on mass atrocities could address concerns voiced earlier in the academic community that the EU tends to conflate mass atrocity prevention with its more general conflict prevention approach (De Franco et al. 2016). According to Schmidt (2019, 321), R2P now forms one of the dimensions of the EU Conflict Early Warning System through the inclusion of indicators for atrocity prevention and it is part of the whole conflict response cycle. The prevention of atrocities has now also been integrated into the EU's Common Security and Defence Policy (CSDP) missions and operations and into the EU's capacity-building programmes, based on the *New European Consensus on Development* (Schmidt 2019, 321).

This specific attention for atrocity prevention is important for the implementation of R2P, as it enables the EU to detect early warning signals of atrocities in a way that was much more challenging under its more general conflict prevention approach. In terms of norm internalisation of R2P, the sophistication of mass atrocity prevention tools has important repercussions for especially the responsibility to prevent. Having accurate instruments to detect potential mass atrocity cases is crucial to be able to use direct prevention and/or early reaction. The Atrocity Prevention Toolkit therefore allows the EU to internalise the responsibility to prevent, which involves engaging in preventive efforts in R2P cases that are in line with actions prescribed by the R2P norm. In terms of types of internalisation, the recent policy efforts of the EU seem to indicate norm accommodation, in which existing processes, policies, and institutions have been adapted without changing their essential features and the underlying collective understandings attached to them (Börzel and Risse 2003). This is evidenced by the fact that R2P has now been integrated in existing policies such as the EU Conflict Early Warning System and the CSDP, rather than replacing them or fundamentally altering their essential features. This observation offers support for the third regional factor, which hypothesises that regional organisations will choose internalisation means that are in line with previous institutional and policy strengths and preferences, which for the EU lie in development, capacity-building, and conflict prevention. Furthermore, the institutional response of the EU to the norm of R2P offers support for the fourth regional factor, which holds that highly institutionalised regional organisations tend to react with institutional responses to global normative pressures, rather than with ad hoc, or case-by-case approaches.

One final observation made by De Franco et al. (2016) is that the EU seems to have chosen to implement R2P through external rather than internal policies (focusing on protecting populations in non-EU countries, potentially to avoid sensitive internal political debate), which is among others evidenced by mandating the EEAS to lead on the file. This extra-regional focus of the EU is not obvious as the UN has emphasised the important role for regional organisation in the implementation of R2P *inside* their respective regions (UN 2011). In terms of norm internalisation of R2P, this means that prevention, reaction, and rebuilding will mostly take place outside the EU. Apart from prevention, this focus makes sense, as it is currently inconceivable that any form of reaction and subsequent rebuilding would be warranted *within* the EU in the foreseeable future.

When it comes to member states, several important norm entrepreneurs can be identified. The GCR2P mentioned Denmark, The Netherlands, and Slovenia in particular (Adams 2018). Reasons for this norm entrepreneurship vary. One of the reasons for Slovenia's advocacy, for instance, is its national history, in which it witnessed the commission of atrocities in its 'backyard' during the Yugoslav wars, whereas one of the driving factors behind the advocacy of The Netherlands is its constitution, which commits it "to promote the development of the international legal order" (Republic of Slovenia 2013; Advisory Council on International Affairs 2010). These motivations for R2P advocacy and internalisation thus strongly reflect the self-images of these countries, a factor that was captured in the second regional factor as outlined in the analytical framework of this book. The self-image of these EU member states thus made them well positioned to become important EU R2P norm entrepreneurs.

Denmark has been an important norm entrepreneur as it set up the R2P Focal Point Network initiative in collaboration with Ghana and the GCR2P in 2010. This created a norm cascade, as through its initiative many other EU member states appointed national R2P focal points. Denmark thus aided the diffusion of R2P within the EU and provided a way to internalise it as well, as the appointment of a national R2P focal point represents an institutional response to the norm. Next to that, it should help states in creating 'R2P policies' and streamlining governmental efforts in the area. The state also engaged in project activities with the aim of advancing the R2P norm. An example is the funding Denmark provided to the Ghana-based West African Peacebuilding Network (WANEP) to assess the institutional capacities for the implementation of R2P in which Ghana served as a case study (WANEP 2016). The Netherlands played an active role in the negotiations on the World Summit Outcome Document in 2005 and has supported R2P since, among others, by co-chairing the Group of Friends of R2P in New York. It committed itself to operationalising R2P in its 2007 Human Rights Strategy. In a 2011 Memorandum to the Strategy it forecast that the future of R2P would lie to a large degree at the regional level (Fiott and Vincent 2013, 205). Slovenia has supported R2P from the start, appointing a national R2P Focal Point early on, supporting the Global Centre for the Responsibility to Protect and being an active member of the Group of Friends of R2P. It was the first host of a European regional meeting of National Focal Points in 2013 and it organised the meeting in 2015 and 2017 as well. In 2015, Slovenia made R2P a foreign policy priority. It is also member of the ACT Group, which, among others, aims to limit the use of the veto at the UN Security Council when atrocity cases are being considered (Republic of Slovenia, Ministry of Foreign Affairs 2019).

In an interview, Dr. Gerrit Kurtz, a research fellow at the German Council of Foreign Relations and academic expert on R2P, mentioned that EU member states were instrumental in 2009, when the first discussion of R2P in the UN General Assembly since the norm's adoption in 2005 was going to take place. At the time, there were some concerns about a backlash from a vocal minority of states, such as Venezuela, Nicaragua, and Pakistan, which had never really bought into the R2P principle. According to Dr. Kurtz, EU member states (specific states were not mentioned) made an 'outreach division of labour' towards the sceptics, i.e. an agreement about which different member states would approach which 'sceptics', to pre-empt a backlash against the norm (Kurtz 2019; Brockmeier et al. 2014, 444).

Given the way that and the extent to which R2P has been institutionalised within the EU, one can come up with some expectations of how the EU will likely respond to cases. The Atrocity Prevention Toolkit's emphasis on prevention, and the inclusion of R2P and atrocity prevention in the EU Conflict Early Warning System, CSDP missions, and the EU's capacity-building programmes create the expectation of a strong engagement through the responsibility to prevent. Concerning the responsibility to react, one can expect the application of sanctions, as the EU has done so for many years in crisis situations. Regarding the use of force, the other application of the responsibility to react, much more contestation is expected. The use of force is generally a hotly contested issue within the EU, and it is something that still falls squarely within the remit of member states. This will make it difficult for the EEAS, where the division working on R2P is located, to play a meaningful role in these types of crises. Concerning the responsibility to rebuild, many of the relevant measures have a clear prevention component to them, so this could play to the strengths of the EU.

The 2011 Libyan crisis

The first real test for the EU's support for R2P came with the crisis in Libya early-2011. The Libyan people took to the streets to protest against their government as part of the wider 'Arab Spring' movement. The Gaddafi government responded with a crackdown and the situation soon descended into a full-blown civil war. The EU's initial response was one of unity. On 23 February 2011, EU High Representative Ashton made a declaration in which she condemned the violence and the use of force against civilians. She also welcomed the UN Security Council statement of 22 February 2011, "which calls on the Government of Libya to meet its responsibility to protect its population (. . .)" Finally, Ashton stressed accountability for those responsible for aggression and violence against civilians and announced the EU decision to suspend negotiations with Libya on the EU-Libya Framework Agreement (European Union 2011). On 28 February 2011, the European Council adopted a decision implementing S/RES/1970 (2011), which included an arms embargo, visa bans, and asset freezes (UN Security Council 2011a). The Council went a step further than the UN measures as it "also prohibited trade with Libya in equipment which might be used for internal repression" and it imposed visa bans and asset freezes on additional individuals that were not targeted in S/RES/1970 (2011) (Council of the European Union 2011). On 10 March 2011, the European Parliament (EP) adopted a resolution in which it called on the EU "to establish relations with the [Libyan] Interim Transitional Council and to start the process of making them official." It also stressed that "the EU and its Member States must honour their Responsibility to Protect, in order to save Libyan civilians from large-scale armed attacks;" it pointed out "that no option provided for in the UN Charter can therefore be ruled out;" and it called "on the High Representative and the Member States to stand ready for a UNSC decision on further measures, including the possibility of a no-fly zone aimed at preventing the regime from targeting the civilian population" (European Parliament 2011a). The framing that the EP used in the Libyan crisis was thus one of a 'robust R2P', in which the use of force should be on the table to protect Libyan civilians.

The initial European unity in the Libyan crisis came under pressure when more forceful measures against Libya started to be considered. The Libyan government did not back down after the adoption of S/RES/1970 (2011). On the contrary, Colonel Gaddafi escalated his rhetoric and his army posed an imminent threat to the population of Benghazi (Kirkpatrick and Fahim 2011). In this context, the UN Security Council adopted Resolution 1973 on 17 March 2011, authorising all necessary measures to protect civilians under threat of attack in the country. The resolution imposed a no-fly zone and tightened sanctions on the Gaddafi government and its supporters (UN Security Council 2011b). S/RES/1973 (2011) divided European states, as France and the UK had led the efforts for the resolution to get passed, using considerable diplomatic skill in the process, while Germany abstained from voting (Adler-Nissen and Pouliot 2014).

In France, opinion had soon shifted towards intervention. In an analysis of national newspaper coverage of the Libyan crisis, Bucher et al. (2013) show that French newspaper articles were dominated by pro-intervention arguments, whereas counterarguments received only marginal treatment. The dominance of pro-intervention arguments in articles only increased in the lead-up to Resolution 1973. When comparing France to Germany, the other case in the article, what stands out is that much fewer arguments against intervention were used in France. So, counterarguments were not only numerically in the minority in newspaper coverage France, the range of different counterarguments that was used was also much narrower than in the German press (Bucher et al. 2013, 532). Several factors have been linked to France's intervention position: France's active leadership early in the Libyan crisis implicated its prestige, it wanted to maintain access to Libyan oil and minimise the terrorist threat from Libya (Davidson 2013). The repercussions of what happens in Libya for French strategic interests in the Sahel are also generally important in France's foreign policy making (Louw-Vaudran 2015). The need to maintain access to Libyan oil and to minimise the terrorist threat from Libya could have arguably been arranged through a deal with the Gadhafi regime. However, as this path had been cut off through Paris's distancing from the regime early on in the Libyan crisis, ensuring a victory for the Libyan opposition seemed to be now in Paris's best interest. The French public and the opposition were overwhelmingly supportive of the intervention: a poll showed two-thirds of the French public were in favour of the intervention and the Socialist Party announced its support for a no-fly zone (Davidson 2013, 320). Hence, there was no strong sense of domestic political contestation around the Libyan intervention within France.

In the UK, the Cameron government was initially reluctant to act on the Libyan crisis. Soon, however, an understanding started to take hold that the Gaddafi regime's human rights violations crossed a line. A strong perception started to develop at the top of government that "Benghazi could very easily become the Srebrenica of our watch" (Brockmeier et al. 2014, 446). The refugee threat from the Libyan crisis, the state's potential to become a source of terrorism, and endangered British and European economic interests in the region also meant that the Libyan crisis came to be viewed as a threat to British interests (Davidson 2013). British prestige became implicated from the moment that the British government took a leadership role in the Libyan crisis at the end of February 2011, when it successfully pushed for Libya's removal from the UN Human Rights Council. This international prestige could have suffered if the government would have parted with its assertive stance. In terms of domestic struggles, the British public showed a lack of appetite for an intervention. Political contestation, however, was limited as the opposition party Labour supported the government's decision to intervene. This prevented the issue from becoming an electoral tool (Davidson 2013, 325).

On 10 March 2011, Prime Minister Cameron and President Sarkozy wrote a joint letter to EU Council President Van Rompuy. In the letter, they condemned the use of military force against civilians and asserted "these acts may amount to crimes against humanity", thereby defining the Libyan crisis as an 'R2P crisis' (crimes against humanity are one of the atrocity crimes covered by R2P) (Cameron and Sarkozy 2011). Gaddafi's use of force against his own people led France and the UK to conclude that "the regime has lost any legitimacy it may have once had." Interestingly, the leaders also stated that "France and the UK are committed to the sovereignty, independence, territorial integrity and national unity of Libya" (Cameron and Sarkozy 2011). In a subsequent part of their speech, they added: "We support continued planning to be ready to provide support for all possible contingencies as the situation evolves on the basis of demonstrable need, a clear legal basis and firm regional support. This could include a no-fly zone or other options against air attacks, working with Allies and partners, especially those in the region. We are working together on elements of an appropriate UNSCR" (Cameron and Sarkozy 2011). The framing by Sarkozy and Cameron of the Libyan crisis is very interesting. They start with bringing the world's attention to Gaddafi's use of force against civilians that likely amount to crimes against humanity, thereby making it a case of R2P concern. The conclusion they make is that Gaddafi's regime has delegitimised itself through its actions. In R2P terms, the Libyan regime has failed to uphold its primary responsibility to protect. Then there is a coexistence of a commitment to "the sovereignty, independence, territorial integrity and national unity of Libya" and a readiness to consider all possible means to respond to the crisis. The latter is arguably in tension with the former. Sarkozy and Cameron seem to employ a discursive tool in which their words seem to suggest respect for Libya's sovereignty, while the actions they contemplate would infringe upon it. Their wording may be a way of making the application of the robust aspect of R2P (the application of the use of force as part of the responsibility to react) look less intrusive.

Brockmeier (2013) argues that the abstention vote of Germany on the Security Council on Resolution 1973 was partly due to a Bundestag debate on the topic that was based on outdated information. The debate among German lawmakers took place with the understanding that the United States (US) was reluctant about an intervention in Libya and would not support a resolution calling for it. The Bundestag members were unaware that the US government had changed its position on intervention as late as the night before, as Washington had not yet informed Berlin of the matter (Brockmeier 2013). When the news broke the US had changed its position, it became very difficult for the German government to change course. Chancellor Merkel was also guided by the impression that the German public was not enthusiastic about a possible intervention while on the campaign trail for regional elections. Foreign Minister Westerwelle subsequently assumed that non-participation of Germany in the intervention would logically mean an abstention on the Security Council, an assumption that was later contested by some of his colleagues and German lawmakers (Brockmeier 2013). The unfolding of events eventually resulted in Germany's abstention on S/RES/1973. Diplomats and politicians have confirmed that a consideration of R2P played no major role in the German decision-making process (Brockmeier 2013, 68). Apart from the problems with the information flow that played a role in the Bundestag vote, it is important to highlight that the Bundestag has been traditionally anti-interventionist, due to Germany's war past. So, although Germany feared atrocities in Benghazi as much as its European allies, its 'culture of restraint' made it more sceptical about the chances for success and wary of the dangers of a military mission in Libya (Brockmeier et al. 2014, 446). This was a key variable in bringing about the negative vote in the Bundestag and the German abstention at the Security Council on Resolution 1973 (Brockmeier et al. 2014).

Brockmeier et al. (2014, 445) argue that the discord over how to respond to the Libyan crisis showed "the extent of disagreement between major European governments about R2P, and the resulting paralysis of the European Union as a whole to support or implement R2P in practice." It is important to note though that the EU was initially united in condemning the violence against civilians in Libya and in adopting sanctions against the Libyan regime. The language used in S/RES/1970 (2011), as supported by EU member states on the Council, and the statement of the European Council on the implementation of UN sanctions and EU autonomous sanctions against Libya also contained 'R2P language', either explicitly or implicitly, so R2P was named as one of the reasons to become involved.

In S/RES/1973, R2P language is explicitly used as the Security Council reiterates "the responsibility of the Libyan authorities to protect the Libyan population," it condemns the "gross and systematic violation of human rights," it considers the widespread and systematic attacks against the civilian population may amount to crimes against humanity (UN Security Council 2011b). It authorises member states "to take all necessary measures, . . ., to protect civilians and civilian populated areas under threat of attack in the Libyan Arab Jamahiriya, including Benghazi" (UN Security Council 2011b). It is important to note that the European Council's resolutions are more implicit when it comes to R2P: it imposes sanctions on "those responsible for the violent crackdown on the civilian population" and it strongly condemns the violence and use of force against civilians (Council of the European Union 2011). The

Libyan government's primary responsibility to protect the Libyan population is not directly mentioned, however. During the Libyan crisis, the EP is the only EU-institutional actor that directly frames the crisis in R2P terms and that is willing to push for forceful action if needed.

Concerning the nature of the sanctions that were issued during the Libyan crisis, they seem to a large extent tailored towards R2P ends. The arms embargo and asset freezes directly impact the Libyan authorities' capacities to inflict atrocity crimes upon the civilian population. The sanctions are also serious: measures such as an arms embargo, asset freezes, and travel bans are about as far as the Security Council can go short of authorising a Chapter-VII mandate, which allows for the use of military means. When it turned out that the sanctions adopted under S/RES/1970 (2011) left the Gaddafi regime undeterred, the Council was forced to adopt forceful measures in S/RES/1973 (2011). Concerning the application of sanctions, the EU shows signs of internalisation of this aspect of R2P in the case of Libya: it applied sanctions in an R2P case, with (implicit) R2P references to become involved and the sanctions were serious enough to potentially change the calculus of the target state.

An element that is sometimes forgotten in discussions about the Libyan crisis is that of rebuilding. Rebuilding was not highest on the list of priorities of the intervening states in Libya, which is for instance evidenced by the fact that the UK spent less than half of its spending on the intervention on reconstruction in Libya (Keranen 2016). Libya's current state, one of chaos and disorder, can to some at least be partially attributed to a lack of significant rebuilding and reconstruction efforts in the post-intervention period (Keranen 2016). To be fair, the 'responsibility to rebuild' only featured in the 2001 ICISS report and never made it into the 2005 World Summit Outcome Document. However, if one is to hold that the responsibility to rebuild is an integral part of R2P, it seems evident that the intervening states, among which EU member states France and the UK, have fallen short of putting that component of R2P into practice in the case of Libya. More problematically, some EU member states, and France in particular, have contributed to the state of chaos Libya is currently in. France has provided support to General Haftar, who started an armed campaign in 2019 to conquer Libya and who has since been accused of committing war crimes (BBC 2019a; Cohen and Berlinger 2019; Assad 2019). Given this French involvement, this raises serious questions about the country's previous commitment to R2P in 2011. If it had all been about R2P from the start, one would have expected France to stay committed to the aim of minimising the risk of atrocity crimes throughout the conflict. Arming a general who is being accused of committing war crimes is obviously a far cry from that.

The EU itself has engaged in rebuilding efforts in Libya since the ousting of Gaddafi. It has, for instance, supported organisations as the Danish Demining Group that demine areas, such as farms, which allows Libyans to recover their normal lives and make a living again. Besides, the EU has contributed to the reopening of hospitals and schools (European External Action Service 2018). It has also worked towards implementing projects aimed at rebuilding infrastructure (Government Europa 2019). These rebuilding efforts make a positive contribution to conditions in Libya, although the question is to what extent they address R2P concerns, i.e. the prevention of future atrocity crimes. Some of the EU's efforts in Libya seem to fit in more with its migration agenda, in which it tries to reduce the number of migrants leaving for Europe (European Commission 2019a). The GCR2P also noted that there was a lack of rebuilding and reconstruction in Libya by the intervening parties. The mindset seems to have been: "let's do it quickly and get out of the way" (Adams 2018).

To conclude, Brockmeier et al.'s (2014) observation of EU paralysis on R2P seems limited to the 'robust application' of R2P, in which divisions indeed came to the fore in Libya: while France and the UK pushed for an intervention and non-permanent member Portugal supported this on the Security Council, Germany abstained from voting. The Libyan case therefore shows a partial internalisation of R2P at the European level: the EU's diplomatic steps and the adoption of sanctions in the Libyan case conformed to R2P expectations (consistent with the responsibility to prevent and the sanctions component of the responsibility to react), but disagreements over the use of force demonstrated that the robust application of R2P (the military component of the responsibility to react) has not fully been internalised at the European level and will likely remain a controversial topic in the future. An ALDE-MEP at the time mentioned in an interview that the decision-making process for the CFSP, based on unanimity in the Council of the EU, is the main obstacle to really move forward and develop a truly consensual European position on R2P, especially concerning the question when the use of force is appropriate (ALDE-MEP 2018). The limited rebuilding efforts in the post-intervention period merit the question whether the EU has internalised the rebuilding aspect of R2P, although it was acknowledged that the 'responsibility to rebuild' did not feature in the 2005 World State Outcome Document's paragraphs on R2P. The crisis also demonstrated that when it comes to 'high-politics crises', it is still very much the member states through the Council who dominate the decision-making process. The High Representative (HR) and the president of the Commission played only a limited role. This also limited their opportunity to engage with R2P during the crisis. The HR was actually criticised by EU and NATO diplomats for being too slow in developing a common position on the reconstruction of Libya, which clearly relates to the responsibility to rebuild (Fabbrini 2014, 188). In this case, the HR could have contributed to the internalisation of this aspect of R2P had she been more vigorous. It must be noted though that the EEAS was still being built up in this time, so the HR lacked administrative support in this period (Fabbrini 2014, 188).

The 2011 Syrian crisis

The unrest in Syria started in March 2011 as part of the wider Arab uprisings. Syrian protesters took to the streets in a few major cities to demand the release of political prisoners (Abboud 2016). The Assad regime cracked down on the protests and the situation soon escalated with increasing violence on both sides. By the end of 2011, Syria had transgressed in a full-scale civil war (Abboud 2016; Hinnebusch and Imady 2018). The situation in Syria forced the EU to reassess its policy of constructive engagement in the region which had been leading in the period before the Arab uprisings (Cavatorta and Turcotte 2019). The EU quickly marginalised the regime in the hope of its resignation. The first sanctions since 2005, when the EU adopted sanctions against Syria because it was implicated in the murder of Lebanese Prime Minister Hariri, were adopted in May 2011 and they were unilateral, which is quite unique as EU sanctions are usually the result of EU implementation of UN sanctions (Cavatorta and Turcotte 2019, 268; EU Sanctions 2020). The decision to declare that the Syrian regime no longer had any political legitimacy, as announced by High Representative Ashton in August 2011, was not undisputed. Bulgaria and Romania, given their historical ties with the Assads, had strong reservations, whereas the Czech Republic, Sweden, Poland, Finland, and Austria expressed doubts as well (Trombetta 2014, 32). Disagreements between member states over Syria also came to the fore when the EU considered to lift the arms embargo on Syria to arm rebels, when it had to respond to the 2013 chemical attacks, when it had to confront the rise of extremist groups in Syria and during the refugee crisis (Cavatorta and Turcotte 2019).

The European Parliament referred to R2P multiple times in resolutions on Syria. In July 2011, it called "on the EU Member States and the VP/HR to continue working with their international partners to secure the involvement of the UNSC in the situation in Syria and the implementation by the Syrian authorities of their responsibility to protect the Syrian population" thereby reiterating the Syria's government's primary responsibility to protect (European Parliament 2011b). In September 2012, it stressed that the EU should "continue to explore within the UNSC all options within the Responsibility to Protect (RtoP) framework, in close cooperation with the US, Turkey and the League of Arab States in order to assist the Syrian people and to halt the bloodshed" (European Parliament 2012). In a resolution in October 2013, the EP called upon the EU and the international community to react strongly to the use of chemical weapons in Syria "in order to fulfil their responsibility to protect civilians in Syria" (European Parliament 2013b). In November 2016, the EP reminded the Syrian government of its primary responsibility to protect the Syrian population in a resolution addressing the bombing and indiscriminate attacks on civilians in the country (European Parliament 2016). Unlike in Libya, however, the EP's calls for exploring all R2P options seemed to have fallen on deaf ears as any resolution even hinting on R2P was vetoed by Russia and China in the Security Council. The legacy of the Libyan intervention was quite visible here: Russia and China feared that another 'protection of civilians' mandate would again be a slippery slope towards regime change. Hence, they blocked any resolution coming even close to that (Gifkins 2012).

The EU's biggest member states also faced limitations in responding to the Syrian crisis. For France, a Libya-style intervention in Syria was for multiple reasons not a serious option. One of the reasons President Sarkozy had advocated for a forceful response to the Libyan crisis was that he wanted to take away the dominant impression in France that he was (too) close to the region's autocrats (Theron 2019). Theron (2019) estimates that the Libyan intervention was deemed sufficient to deal with this criticism, so this rationale no longer applied to the Syrian crisis. Second, Paris' heavy involvement in the Libyan crisis made it difficult to start yet another campaign in Syria. Besides, as mentioned, the legal and diplomatic context had changed completely, as Russia was strongly displeased with NATO's actions in Libya and was determined to prevent any action of the kind in Syria, where it had many more interests at stake (Theron 2019, 222).

The UK adopted an early position that Assad had to go. In 2012, Prime Minister (PM) Cameron even proposed a safe passage for Assad if this could facilitate a political transition in the state. Although Cameron preferred Assad to be held to account for his actions, his biggest priority was to end the conflict, and if a safe passage for Assad could enable that, in his view it was a price worth paying (Daily Express 2012). In 2013, in the aftermath of the Ghouta sarin attacks, Cameron stated that there was a responsibility to protect to prevent further humanitarian catastrophe in Syria (Kirkup 2013). The strikes that the US, the UK, and France considered as retribution for the sarin attacks were eventually called off, though, among others because PM Cameron lost a vote on the strikes in the House of Commons (BBC 2013). There was strong domestic and parliamentary contestation in Britain on the question of intervention. PM Cameron and Defence Secretary Hammond were disappointed by the result of the vote and former Liberal Democrat leader Lord Ashdown, whose party was a coalition partner of the Conservatives at the time, stated that in "50 years trying to serve my country I have never felt so depressed [or] ashamed" (BBC 2013). He argued that by doing nothing, Assad would not be deterred from using chemical weapons in the future and they could become more commonplace in the Middle East. Labour leader Milliband, on the contrary, welcomed the vote's outcome, as he believed the British people wanted its lawmakers to learn the lessons of Iraq and they did not want a rush to war (BBC 2013). The debates around the use of force in Syria show strong domestic contestation around the robust application of the responsibility to protect in Syria. Some analysts, however, have raised the question whether strikes would not have had as primary aim to defend the norm against the use of chemical weapons rather than to uphold the responsibility to protect (Weller 2018). The EP resolution and an interview with EEAS-policy officers seem to indicate, though, that some EU elites see strong responses to the use of chemical weapons as an integral part of the accountability aspect of R2P, and thus part of the responsibility to react (European Parliament 2013b; EEAS policy officer 2018).

In August 2011, in a joint statement with her French and British counterparts, German Chancellor Merkel backed the call for Assad to step down as he would have lost all legitimacy and could no longer claim to lead Syria (McGreal and Chulov 2011). It is important to note though that, as in the case of Libya, Germany was much more cautious than France and the UK about escalating the response to the Syrian regime. It strongly opposed the proposal by France and the UK to lift the EU arms embargo on the Syrian rebels in the spring of 2013 (Cavatorta and Turcotte 2019, 271). Second, when the UK and France prepared for strikes against the Syrian regime after the sarin attacks in the same year, German Foreign Minister Westerwelle ruled out taking part, stating that "such participation has not been sought nor is it being considered by us" (BBC 2013). This consistent German position of non-escalation and aversion of the use of force throughout the Arab uprisings seems to confirm the notion that it prefers non-coercive ways to internalise and implement R2P (Brockmeier et al. 2014).

Concerning internalisation of the R2P norm at the European level, the Syrian case seems to give a damning verdict. The civil war has entered its second decade at the time of writing and fighting and atrocities go unabated. The international community at large and the European Union have failed to offer meaningful protection to the Syrian people throughout the conflict. However, if one assesses the different aspects of norm internalisation of R2P as presented in the analytical framework of this book, the picture seems to be a little bit more nuanced than that. European leaders, such as British Prime Minister Cameron and EU High Representative Ashton, did express formal support for R2P, as they referred to the norm in statements on the Syrian crisis, which is a sign of internalisation of the formal support for R2P. The EU and its member states also took a number of diplomatic steps against the Syrian regime in response to atrocities: EU officials and heads of state condemned the repression and the use of force against civilians, they withdrew their ambassadors from Damascus and they expelled Syrian diplomats from their capitals (Black and McGreal 2012). European governments also sent arms to rebels in Syria, including to what later turned out to be jihadist groups. Quite decisive was the armament of the Kurdish Peshmerga, who were critical in the fight against Islamic State (Rettman 2014; Goldman 2019). Islamic State became a significant player later in the Syrian conflict and conquered great parts of Iraq and Syria in 2014 and 2015. Islamic State fighters committed many atrocity crimes, including (attempted) genocide on the Yezidi in 2014. A bombing campaign by the US and its allies and fighting on the ground, predominantly by the Kurdish Peshmerga, brought relief and eventually put Islamic State on the defensive (BBC 2019b). The operations against Islamic State can therefore be seen as a significant example of internalisation of the military component of the responsibility to react, where military action halted a genocide.

Concerning the responsibility to react, the EU collectively issued sanctions against the Syrian regime, including an arms and oil embargo, asset freezes, and travel bans (Cavatorta and Turcotte 2019, 269). As the crisis dragged on and intensified, the EU correspondingly expanded its sanctions regime, consistent with the sanctions component of the responsibility to react. The only means truly left in terms of reaction to atrocities in Syria and therefore the last means to uphold the responsibility to protect in this case was military action.

Here, the EU member states that were at some points willing to consider these measures, such as France and the UK, were confronted with a Russian veto at the UN Security Council (RTÉ 2018). The only way around this would have been a Kosovo-type of intervention, lacking *ex-ante* authorisation by the Security Council, but, unlike in the Kosovo case, without any prospect of a *post hoc* authorisation. This was hardly an attractive option. Other factors that had to be considered were that the Libyan operation already drew a lot of resources from the UK and France and that the state's descent into chaos after the intervention did not make a great case for intervention in Syria. Any operations against the Assad regime would have also been militarily significantly more complicated and challenging than against the Gaddafi regime in Libya (Bumiller 2012).

Based on the above, two concluding remarks are in place. On the one hand, 12 years of civil war and atrocities seem to indicate that the EU and its member states have failed in their responsibility to protect in the Syrian case. On the other hand, when taking a close look at the different aspects of norm internalisation of R2P, the EU and its member states have made use of many tools in the R2P toolbox at different stages in the crisis. This includes the expression of formal support for R2P in statements on the crisis, the use of diplomatic steps as consistent with the responsibility to prevent, and the issuance of sanctions in line with the responsibility to react. The last tool available in the R2P toolbox, military action, has been considered by EU member states France and the UK, but, apart from limited strikes in response to chemical attacks in April 2018, this has not been a feasible option given the Russian and Chinese vetoes in the Security Council.

The 2015 European refugee crisis

While the number of refugees fleeing to Europe had already increased year after year, primarily due to the Arab uprisings, numbers dramatically increased in 2015. By the end of 2015, close to a million refugees and migrants had arrived on European shores since the start of the year, making it Europe's biggest refugee crisis since the Second World War (UNHCR 2015; BBC 2016a). At the same time, around 3770 people lost their lives or were reported missing during the perilous journey over sea. The vast majority of people fled conflict and persecution in Syria, Afghanistan, and Iraq (Spindler 2015). The large influx of refugees quickly propelled the EU into crisis mode.

It is noteworthy to identify the marked contrast in response to the arrival of refugees from different member states. While German Chancellor Merkel famously announced her government's *Willkommenspolitik* ('welcome policy') with which she opened Germany's borders to refugees in September 2015, Hungary's Prime Minister Orbán adopted a hard-line stance against migrants, at one point saying they were "looking like an army" (Agence France-Presse 2015). In response to the crisis, Hungary built a fence along its border with Croatia and Serbia to keep asylum seekers out (Feher 2015).

It is useful to more closely assess the discourse that Chancellor Merkel used during the refugee crisis. In her famous 'Wir schaffen das' speech of 31 August 2015, she highlighted a number of things. First, she spoke of 'atrocities' when describing the death of 70 refugees in a truck in Austria, left there by unscrupulous smugglers (Die Bundesregierung 2015). Another interesting aspect of her speech is when she discusses the European dimension of the refugee crisis. This is relevant to the self-image factor as identified in the analytical framework (factor 2), as here one of the regional powers describes the identity of the EU as a regional actor. "Until now, universal civil rights have been closely linked to Europe and its history. That is one of the founding impulses of the European Union. If Europe fails on the refugee question, this close connection with universal civil rights breaks down. It will be destroyed, and it will not be the Europe that we imagine and not the Europe that we, as the founding myth, must continue to develop today" (Die Bundesregierung 2015). With these words, Merkel discursively links Europe and its history to universal civil rights, which would also be constitutive of the EU itself. She then securitises the issue by saying that the existence of Europe as we now know it, as an actor that has civil rights ingrained in its identity, is at stake as it is being confronted by the refugee crisis. Failing on the refugee question means destroying the link between Europe and civil rights, which bring the whole European project in peril (Die Bundesregierung 2015). Merkel's speech shows that she sees Europe and the EU as normative actors that need to adequately address the refugee crisis to live up to their own standards. Her speech projects an EU identity that is based on underlying norms, rights, and values; that is supportive of R2P as a norm and that should put this into practice to protect refugees.

Hungary's Prime Minister Orbán had a very different take on the matter. He represented the arrival of refugees as an invasion and 'a flood of people'. He also portrayed refugees as a threat, arguing they are "able to destabilize governments, countries and the whole European continent", that they could include foreign fighters, that they exponentially increased the risks of terrorism and crime, and that they represented a threat to Hungary's "culture, way of life, customs and traditions" (Hungarian Government 2015a, 2015b). A key element in Orbán's discourse is sovereignty. In his view, it is ultimately up to Hungary itself whom it allows to live within its borders and whom not. Hungary's sovereignty is affirmed through the questioning of the supranational power of the EU (Mendelski 2019). The country's non-compliance with the EU's refugee quota system is an example of its challenge to the EU.

In many ways, the discourses and policies of Merkel and Orbán symbolise the deep divide between Western and Central-Eastern Europe over how to handle the refugee crisis. While Germany and other, mostly Western European, states believed Europe had a moral obligation to help refugees, Hungary and other, mostly Central-Eastern European (CEE), states believed Europe's focus should be on protecting its borders (Karnitschnig 2015). These clashing views on refugees and how states should deal with their arrival are also reflected in the figures of accepted asylum applications in EU member states in

2015. Germany topped the list with 148,000 accepted asylum applications, followed by Sweden, Italy, France, and the UK. Poland, Hungary, and the Czech Republic, the Visegrad states that were opposed to the reception of refugees, all granted positive decisions to less than a thousand people in the year 2015 (Eurostat 2016). When one takes the number of refugees per head of population, Sweden topped the list, followed by Malta, Cyprus, Austria, and Denmark. The CEE states were again on the lower end of the list (Full Fact 2016). The CEE states' resistance to letting in refugees also played out during EU negotiations around a refugees' redistribution key. When such a key was finally agreed upon, Poland, Hungary, and the Czech Republic refused to comply with it. European Court of Justice's advocate general, Eleanor Sharpston, indicated in October 2019 that the move by the three member states likely broke EU law (EURACTIV with AFP 2019).

In March 2016, the EU brokered a 'deal' (officially it is a statement, which means the European Court of Justice has no jurisdiction over it) with Turkey in which it was agreed that all 'irregular migrants' crossing from Turkey into Greece will be sent back. The idea was to have a 'one-for-one system' in which for each Syrian returned to Turkey, a Syrian migrant would be resettled in the EU. In return for taking back refugees, Turkey was offered financial aid, the removal of visa restrictions, and the resumption of Turkey's EU membership negotiations (BBC 2016b). In 2019, the European Commission called the EU-Turkey deal 'a game changer' as it reduced arrivals to Greece by 97% (European Commission 2019b). The deal has been heavily criticised by human rights organisations, however. Amnesty International called the grounds on which the deal was constructed – that Turkey is a safe place for refugees – flawed (Gogou 2017). This notion was backed by the rulings of Greece's asylum appeals committees, which ruled in many instances that Turkey does not provide effective protection for refugees. To Amnesty, all European leaders cared about was for the number of irregular arrivals to Europe to fall significantly. The humanitarian costs of the deal, such as the migrants who are in a legal limbo awaiting their status outcome in dire conditions on the Greek islands, seem to be a price Europe is willing to pay. The adverse conditions on the Greek islands have already resulted in deaths. One man living on one of the islands described the place as "a grave for humans. It is hell" (Gogou 2017). Amnesty has also documented "how some Syrian asylum-seekers have been forcibly returned to Turkey without having access to asylum and without being able to appeal against their return, in breach of international law" (Gogou 2017).

In an interview, Co-executive Director Kate Ferguson of the UK organisation Protection Approaches also mentioned the topic of migration as an area where the EU has failed to match its R2P rhetoric with R2P action. The Khartoum process, an interregional forum on migration covering the Horn of African and Europe, led by the AU and the EU, saw a clear prioritisation of the security agenda over the humanitarian agenda. Its aim was de facto – although of course not stated that way – to keep people out of Europe (Ferguson 2020). From an atrocity prevention perspective, it is indefensible to sign deals with countries like Sudan, which are major sources of refugees and whose leaders commit ongoing atrocities. So, it is in the area of migration where one witnesses the most flagrant failure by the EU to connect the security and protection agendas (Ferguson 2020). What one misses here is a moment in the decision-making process where someone raises how these migration measures will impact on atrocity prevention and how they will match the commitments the EU has under the three pillars of R2P. Despite the existence of the Atrocity Prevention Toolkit, at moments like these, when major interests are at stake, it is difficult for the protection agenda to compete with a very well-established security agenda (Ferguson 2020). This finding seems to suggest that R2P has not been internalised all the way through, since it has not become a concern that is habitually raised in relevant decision-making processes at the EU level, nor one that is habitually carried out in terms of policy action.

A discussion of the refugee crisis is appropriate in the context of this book as some authors have forged the link between asylum and the responsibility to protect, even though this link is absent in the relevant paragraphs of the 2005 World Summit Outcome Document. Newman (2018) critically raises the question if "a commitment to the international R2P principle entails a commitment to protect individuals fleeing persecution, including atrocities" (Newman 2018, 1). He observes that some scholars have suggested that a commitment to R2P implies a general responsibility to protect those fleeing atrocities (Newman 2018, 3). These scholars see the protection of refugees fleeing from atrocities as "one of the most direct ways of serving the R2P principle by countries which are capable of doing so" (Newman 2018, 3). Newman (2018, 3) argues there is arguably a special liberal commitment to offer protection to refugees for European countries as they "have tended to be champions of the R2P principle and thus explicitly commit themselves to a higher standard of humanitarianism."

However, as noted, the 2014–15 refugee crisis was strongly securitised by politicians and opinion makers. Defining the arrival of refugees as a security challenge opened the doors to exceptional measures, such as strengthening borders and enhancing exclusionary policies (Newman 2018, 13). The securitisation of the refugee debate led to a discourse in which the interests of citizens and those seeking protection were framed as incompatible or in conflict (Newman 2018, 15). In practice, it led to a situation in which European countries acted in ways that do not conform to what may be expected from supposed R2P champions (Newman 2018). The opposition of the Visegrad states to the EU's refugees' relocation scheme and the creation of the EU-Turkey deal are exemplary of this. More recent examples include the EU's decision to stop Mediterranean migrant rescue boat patrols in early 2019, under pressure from Italy's populist government at the time, and Italy's decision to criminalise NGO rescue missions on sea, a move which was strongly criticised by the UN (Rankin 2019; Tondo 2019). The dilemma that Panebianco and Fontana (2017) highlight in the EU management of the refugee crisis between 'border control' and 'duty of protection' seems to have been resolved in most cases in favour of the former, with as most notable exception Germany's *Willkommens-politik*.[1] An EP resolution adopted in April 2017 also concluded that "security and border protection were the predominant element in European migration spending" and it underlined that a European response "should not focus only on a security-based approach" (European Parliament 2017b). It can thus be concluded that most EU member states, with Germany as most notable exception, have inadequately internalised the norm of R2P when it 'hits home'. This is all the more significant given the assertion that Panebianco and Fontana (2017) have made that when the Security Council is blocked, such as in the case of Syria, it is important to explore other ways to implement R2P, such as through offering international asylum. Refugee protection seems to be in these cases indeed a critical and potentially only true alternative to action through the Security Council to uphold R2P (effectively making refugee protection a means of 'last resort' to uphold R2P when all other means have failed), which makes Europe's shortcomings in this respect all the more painful.

In terms of the different components of R2P, refugee protection would logically fall under the responsibility to react, as it entails measures that can be taken when atrocities are already taking place or have taken place. One can think of a case where sanctions have failed to dissuade a government from committing crimes against its own people and where a military intervention is not a feasible option due to vetoes in the Security Council. Syria would be a good example. In such case, the only option left to implement R2P, apart from rebuilding activities after the end of the conflict (falling under the responsibility to rebuild), is to provide protection to those fleeing violence and atrocities. The above analysis shows that apart from a few positive exceptions, such as Germany, the issue of refugee protection became extremely securitised within the EU and a not insignificant number of member states refused to take in hardly any refugees at all. This can only mean that the EU, as a whole, has not (yet) adequately internalised the refugee protection component of the responsibility to react. If it had, one would have expected a more unified effort at the European level to share the burden of refugee hosting and, at the very least, no resistance from member states against the European Commission's redistribution key.

The 2017 Rohingya crisis

In August 2017, Myanmar's security forces started a military campaign against the Rohingya, a Muslim minority predominantly living in Rakhine state. The campaign was a response to an attack of insurgents of the Arakan Rohingya Salvation Army (ARSA) on Myanmar police posts and an army base in the north of Rakhine state (Reuters 2019). The attack by the ARSA and Myanmar's response took place in a context of decades of discrimination and repression of the Rohingya under successive Burmese governments (Human Rights Watch 2019). Myanmar's 1982 Citizenship Law had effectively denied the Rohingya citizenship in the country, making them one of the largest stateless populations in the world (Human Rights Watch 2019). Amnesty International has asserted the situation of the Rohingya in Myanmar amounts to a 'system of apartheid', in which hundreds of thousands of Rohingya live in overcrowded camps and 'prison' villages where they are denied freedom of movement and have severely limited access to schools and health care (Amnesty International 2019).

The 2017 campaign by Myanmar's security forces forced an estimated 745,000 Rohingya out of their houses, who mostly sought refuge in neighbouring Bangladesh. During the campaign, according to the UN Office for the Coordination of Humanitarian Affairs (2019), "entire villages were burned to the ground, families were separated and killed, and women and girls were gang raped. Most of the people who escaped were severely traumatized after witnessing unspeakable atrocities." An estimated 25,000 Rohingya people were killed (Ellis-Petersen 2018). A damning UN report published in August 2018 accused Myanmar's military of genocide against the Rohingya. The UN report stated it found conclusive evidence that the actions of the country's armed forces "undoubtedly amounted to the gravest crimes under international law," amongst which war crimes and crimes against humanity (Ellis-Petersen 2018). In November 2019, The Gambia filed a case against Myanmar at the International Court of Justice (ICJ), including a charge of genocide (Bowcott 2019). The case was supported by the Organisation of Islamic Cooperation (OIC) of which The Gambia is a member. The prosecutor of the International Criminal Court (ICC) had previously opened a preliminary investigation against Myanmar (Bowcott 2019).

The EU's response to the Rohingya crisis was at first hesitant. High Representative Mogherini's first statement on the situation, on 6 September 2017, condemned the attacks on Myanmar security forces, but made no mention of the over-reaction by the country's security forces (European External Action Service 2017a; Smith 2018, 15). This changed rather soon, as EU messaging became much more focused on Myanmar's military forces later that month. In a speech to an urgent session of the EP on 14 September 2017, Mogherini stated: "We are very much aware and concerned about the excesses during the security operations conducted by Myanmar's security forces. This has led to a massive flow of refugees into Bangladesh – one of the most terrible refugee crises of our time" (European External Action Service 2017b; Smith 2018, 15). On the same day, the European Parliament issued its first resolution on the situation in which it condemned all attacks in Rakhine state and recalled the Myanmar authorities of its duty to protect all civilians from abuse (European Parliament 2017c). The Council of the EU addressed the situation in Myanmar in October 2017, noting there were reports of "serious human rights violations". It called for an "end to all violence", and for Myanmar's military to cease its operations and observe human rights law. It called on the government to cooperate with the UN Human Rights Council's fact-finding missions and it also declared it was suspending invitations to high-ranking military officers and reviewing defence cooperation. It signalled that additional measures, either positive or negative, would be considered depending on how the situation would evolve (Council of the European Union 2017). Some European leaders had already gone further by then. French President Macron used his address to the UN General Assembly in September 2017 to alert the world to what in his view amounted to the ethnic cleansing and genocide of the Rohingya. A few months later, in February 2018, UK Foreign Secretary Johnson told the House of Commons that "this has been ethnic cleansing on an industrial scale, and it may also have been genocide" (Smith 2018, 15).

European leaders, both from the member states and at the institutional level, thus condemned the persecution of the Rohingya, which constituted a textbook R2P case in which atrocities were being committed. To assess R2P internalisation in this specific case, it is needed to see if the behaviour of European actors was in line with what R2P as a norm would demand of external actors in the face of mass atrocities. Condemnation is a first step to signal disapproval to a target state that is committing atrocities, and, as was just shown, this step was taken by multiple European leaders. A next step, as was seen in the Syrian case, is further diplomatic measures, such as the calling back of one's own diplomats from the target state, the ousting of the target state's diplomats from one's own capital, and the suspension of membership of the target state in international and regional organisations. Generally, EU member states did not call back their ambassadors or expel Myanmar's ambassadors from their capitals. Other symbolic steps were taken, however. A number of British cities, for instance, withdrew the Freedom of City Awards from Myanmar's State Councillor Aung San Suu Kyi (Ratcliffe 2018).

In February 2018, the EU's Foreign Affairs Council condemned "ongoing widespread, systematic grave human rights violations" committed by Myanmar's military and security forces, it called upon Myanmar to address the issue of accountability and to create "conditions for voluntary, safe and dignified return of displaced persons." In its conclusions, the Council invited the High Representative to make proposals for sanctions (Council of the European Union 2018a). Those sanctions – the next logical step in the R2P toolkit when responding to atrocities – were eventually adopted in April 2018. The Council extended the existing arms embargo and it now also prohibited the export of dual-use goods and the equipment for monitoring communications that might be used for internal repression. Next to that, it prohibited the provision of military training to and military cooperation with the Myanmar army. The Council also adopted a legal framework for targeted restrictive measures against certain individuals from the Myanmar Armed Forces and the border guard police, allowing it to impose travel bans and asset freezes on individuals responsible for serious human rights violations, for obstructing the conduct of independent investigations and for obstructing the rapid and unimpeded passage of humanitarian assistance (Council of the European Union 2018b). In June 2018, the Council made use of this framework for the first time when it put sanctions on seven members of the Myanmar army, border guard, and police for their association with "atrocities and serious human rights violations committed against the Rohingya population" (Council of the European

Union 2018c). In the time that followed, the Council added individuals to the sanctions list on a regular basis. This use of the sanctions instrument is evidence of the internalisation of the sanctions component of the responsibility to react, where one should see the application of sanctions in response to atrocity crimes. The adoption of sanctions against Myanmar did not make the EU immune to criticism, which mostly came from civil society. As Smith (2018, 15) noted, the Burma Campaign UK called the measures "too little, too late", and added that they "are not an adequate or proportionate response given the scale and seriousness of violations of international law taking place" (Burma Campaign UK, 2018). Human Rights Watch had criticised the EU after earlier waves of violence against the Rohingya for not taking a stand against "Burmese army's rampant atrocities in Rakhine State" (Bolopion 2017).

The criticism from civil society begs the question of what the EU could have done differently in response to the atrocities committed against the Rohingya. When looking at the R2P toolbox, after condemnation, further diplomatic steps, and the adoption of sanctions, what remains is authorised military intervention. As in the case of Syria, the EU was confronted here with a veto in the Security Council, from both Russia and China. Even if these vetoes would not have been used, it would have been highly unlikely that any of the EU member states would have even considered getting militarily involved in Myanmar. The logistics of any such operation would have been very challenging given the long distance from the European continent and, more importantly, different from the Libyan and Syrian cases, European security interests were not directly involved in the case of Myanmar.

Staunton and Ralph (2019) provide an interesting account that aims to explain why the EU experienced such difficulty in engaging in effective atrocity prevention in Myanmar. They argue that Myanmar's human rights situation was on the radar of committed NGOs, states, and international organisations. This makes it all the more puzzling that the international community failed to prevent the Rohingya crisis. An important part of the explanation lies in the fact that external actors, such as the EU, were focused too much on democracy promotion in Myanmar in the post-2011 reforms period. In a way this was understandable, as Myanmar was making hopeful progress under reform-minded President U Thein Sein who came to power in 2011 (Staunton and Ralph 2019). Under his leadership, Myanmar witnessed improvements in press freedom and the release of political prisoners, including Suu Kyi. The EU, along with other external actors, aimed to encourage these reforms by first suspending and then lifting sanctions on Myanmar, with the exception of the arms embargo (Hodal 2012; Staunton and Ralph 2019). The first openly contested general election that took place in 2015 and that led to a victory for the opposition party NLD seemed to confirm that Myanmar was on 'the right path'. The EU's focus on Myanmar's progress and democratisation created a blind spot, however. Actors that looked at the country purely through an atrocity prevention lens, such as the US Holocaust Memorial Museum and the UN Advisers on the Prevention of Genocide and R2P, warned of the high risk of atrocity crimes and the vulnerability of the Rohingya population (Staunton and Ralph 2019, 11). As a matter of fact, as Bellamy (2015) argued, the democratic transition process and the opening up of free speech increased the risk of atrocities as it "sharply exacerbated inter-communal tensions and prejudice."

Contributing to this problem was that the EU had made linkages between norms as atrocity prevention, conflict prevention, and democracy promotion in its comprehensive approach to Myanmar. Although these linkages make sense from a conceptual point of view, they complicate a response when a situation actually demands trade-offs between these norms. In the case of Myanmar, the EU's focus on democracy promotion made it underestimate the risk of atrocities, and it complicated the response to the latter as it feared any negative measures would endanger the country's democratic transition (Staunton and Ralph 2019).

An EEAS official acknowledged in an interview that the EU response to the Rohingya crisis was suboptimal, as it was perceived by some as 'too little, too late'. One of the main challenges the EU faced in responding to the crisis was the quick mobilisation of resources. These challenges formed one of the main motivations for creating the Atrocity Prevention Toolkit, which was released in early 2019 (EEAS Policy Officer 2019). This toolkit has the potential to help the EU in meeting its responsibility to prevent duties. Concerning R2P internalisation in the Myanmar case, it can be said that the EU has shown signs of internalising the sanctions aspect. Preventive action fell short of what was needed, because of the EU's bias towards promoting Myanmar's transition to democracy, which came at the expense of attention for the situation of the Rohingya. This is arguably more problematic than the lack of internalisation of the military component of the responsibility to react in this case, since this option was blocked by *inter alia* China in the Security Council and the logistics of such an operation would have been extremely challenging given the long distance from the European continent.

Concerning the responsibility to rebuild, the EU led efforts of the donor community to assist the Rohingya community after the August 2017 ethnic cleansing campaigns. The EU co-hosted a donors' conference in October 2017, at which it pledged almost half of the overall funding. The EU also took the initiative to lead the resolution at the UN Human Rights Council to establish an independent, international Fact-Finding Mission for the situation in Northern Rakhine state (European Commission 2018). This is crucial as a first step in creating accountability, as the mission detailed the violence perpetrated against the Rohingya based on 875 detailed interviews. It documented atrocities and attributed responsibility, mostly to the Tatmadaw (Myanmar's armed forces) and its top military leaders (UN Human Rights Council 2018). EU member states later called for accountability for the persecution of the Rohingya, after the International Court of Justice (ICJ) imposed emergency "provisional measures" on Myanmar in January 2020 and instructed the state's government to respect the requirements and prevent genocidal violence against Rohingya Muslims and preserve evidence of past crimes (Marks 2018). EU member states urged Myanmar officials to "address the root causes of its conflicts in Rakhine state," as well as in Kachin and Shan states (Reinl 2020).

In 2019, the EU provided over €35 million to help refugees and host communities by providing critical health care, food assistance, and education in emergencies (European Commission 2020). Protection is also a key goal of this support, with a specific focus on registration and documentation. This is a significant step as most Rohingya have spent a lifetime without official documentation, which left them stateless and deprived of basic rights (UNHCR 2019). The documentation establishes the refugees' protection in host communities, and it establishes their right to return. The EU's post-atrocity activities aimed at the Rohingya community include R2P measures, such as support for the fact-finding mission and international accountability (acts that are signs of internalisation of the accountability aspect of the responsibility to react). The call from member states on Myanmar to address the root causes of the conflicts is an important element of the responsibility to rebuild and key in the prevention of future atrocities.

In short, the case of the Rohingya crisis demonstrates internalisation of the sanctions-aspect of R2P, consistent with the responsibility to react, whereas the EU fell short on prevention in this case. This was mainly because the EU's democracy promotion aims hampered the organisation to adequately assess the threat of atrocities in an early stage, in which preventive action could have made a difference. The use of force (in line with the military component of the responsibility to react) was a non-starter given vetoes in the Security Council, the difficult logistics in the absence of Council vetoes, and a lack of vital EU interests in Myanmar. Interestingly, the case actually demonstrated that the EU took some important measures under the responsibility to rebuild, such as the support for a fact-finding mission and the adoption of protection-oriented measures towards the Rohingya community, such as helping the Rohingya with official registration. Some organisational learning, therefore, seems to have taken place since the Libyan case, as the rebuilding efforts in Myanmar have a clearer protection aim than those taken in the aftermath of the Libya campaign. At the same time, the deficiencies of the EU response to the Rohingya crisis, especially in its early days, have again provided input to organisational learning in the EEAS, which among others resulted in the development of the EU's Atrocity Prevention Toolkit.

Case reflections and comparisons

The different cases have provided important insights into the extent the EU and its member states have internalised R2P and through which means they have done so. Generally, it can be observed that the EU is strong on formal support for R2P and it is willing to issue condemnations, to take diplomatic steps (in line with the responsibility to prevent), and to adopt sanctions in R2P situations (consistent with the sanctions component of the responsibility to react). The following sections will systematically discuss the internalisation of the different components of R2P, both at the general level and based on the case studies.

Formal support

Looking at the normative positions adopted, it is clear to see that most European actors are located in the proponents camp of R2P. A majority of EU member states has been very supportive of R2P at the declaratory level. This is evidenced by *inter alia* the large number of EU member states being member of the Group of Friends of R2P and the formal support many EU member states have voiced for the norm in international fora. The same counts for the EU as a whole and the EU institutions. The EU has a long history of issuing statements in support of R2P in international fora through its representatives, such as at the UN, while the European Parliament has consistently supported the norm in its resolutions and has kept the norm on the political agenda in Brussels, even in the face of backlashes against the norm, such as after the intervention in Libya (European Parliament 2013a). As Bloomfield (2016) demonstrated, though, there are various role conceptions even among supporters of normative change. Germany, for instance, seemed to have played the role of 'rival entrepreneur' in the case of Libya. Although it agreed with the UK and France that the Libyan civilian population needed to be protected, it disagreed that military means would be the best means to do so. This would be an example of applicatory contestation, where there is no disagreement on the norm itself, but about whether or how the norm applies in a particular case, in this case if the robust aspects of the R2P norm applied to the Libyan case.

Although the EP as a whole has been Europe's most important norm entrepreneur on R2P, this masks a minority position within it that rejects R2P. For instance, in a motion for a resolution on Yemen, the Confederal Group of the European United Left/Nordic Green Left (GUE/NGL) group specifically rejected the use of the notion of the 'responsibility to protect', as it would violate international law and it would not offer an adequate legal basis for justifying the unilateral use of force (GUE/NGL Group 2018). Such a hard rejection indicates that the GUE/NGL Group operates as a norm antipreneur in the European debate on R2P. It seems that the group has a narrow interpretation of R2P, equating it with military intervention. Given the group's anti-militarism, the resistance against R2P should thus not come as a surprise. As the GUE/NGL Group constitutes a small minority in the EP, it has not been able to steer the debate on the topic, nor has it been able to influence the EP's position as the EU's leading institutional proponent of R2P.

The strongest challenge to R2P probably came during the refugee crisis, in which predominantly the Visegrad states adopted rhetoric and policies that are directly at odds with any notion of protection. The strong emphasis that was put on national sovereignty (against 'EU interference'), by for instance Hungary, is also clearly at odds with R2P's qualified understanding of sovereignty and its notion of sovereignty as responsibility, whereby the state is accountable to domestic *and* international constituencies (Deng et al. 1996). The positioning of the Visegrad states in the refugee crisis thus qualifies them as R2P norm antipreneurs (at least in the context of this crisis), in which they use different frames to discredit R2P and to support rival norms, such as more absolute notions of sovereignty. This is fully in line with the expected behaviour of R2P norm antipreneurs, as formulated in the analytical framework: it seems that R2P antipreneurs do indeed engage in 'counter-campaigns', attempting to discredit R2P through the support of rival norms, when they come to see 'R2P expectations' (in this case the protection of refugees) in direct opposition to their own interests and values. This observation of R2P antipreneurship within the EU was confirmed in an interview with an EEAS official who alluded to the states' uncooperative stance in early consultations about developing an internal protection agenda in the EU (EEAS policy officer 2019). The policies of the EU in response to the crisis, such as the EU-Turkey deal, have, as noted, also been widely criticised by human rights organisations, such as Amnesty International and Human Rights Watch. At the EU level, there thus seems to have been a gap between protection-rhetoric and policy action. The latter has been dominated by the security concerns of member states.

This notwithstanding, overall, one can observe a strong, qualitative shift in terms of discourse at the EU-level since the norm of R2P was adopted at the UN level: member states and the EU-institutions have familiarised themselves with the 'R2P lexicon' and have increasingly come to frame atrocity (risk-) situations in R2P terms, which then subsequently informs policy action. For this reason, it can be reasonably concluded that the EU and its member states have internalised the formal aspect of the norm to a significant extent.

Responsibility to prevent

The different cases have provided important insights into the extent the EU and its member states have internalised the responsibility to prevent and through which means they have done so.

In terms of authoritative support, the European Parliament unequivocally expressed its support for atrocity prevention in its July 2017 resolution on 'addressing human rights violations in the context of war crimes, and crimes against humanity, including genocide.' It noted the duty of the international community to prevent atrocity crimes from taking place and it called upon the EU to "integrate into its comprehensive approach to external conflicts and crises the necessary tools for identifying and preventing any atrocity crime at an early stage" (European Parliament 2017a). The latter call stimulated the creation of the EU's Atrocity Prevention Toolkit, which can in and by itself be seen as authoritative support for the responsibility to prevent. The EP also stressed the need to address the root causes of violence and conflict as crucial to preventing genocide and crimes against humanity, a central element of the responsibility to prevent (European Parliament 2017a).

In terms of practice, the case of Libya showed that the EU and its member states take diplomatic steps early on, through condemnations of the actions by the Gaddafi regime and the early recognition of the Libyan opposition as the country's legitimate representative (Cowell and Erlanger 2011), which is in line with the responsibility to prevent. A similar scenario played out in the case of

Syria. Again, the EU and its member states condemned the violence against civilians early on and the EU declared through its High Representative that the Syrian regime had lost its political legitimacy in August 2011. If all opportunities in terms of structural or 'deep' prevention were seized remains an open question. The policy of constructive engagement with Syria prior to the Arab uprisings predominantly had an economic focus, and it failed to realise meaningful economic and political reforms in Syria (Cavatorta and Turcotte 2019). The EU did attempt to bring about political reforms through an emphasis on human rights and democratisation in the Association Agreement (AA) it negotiated with Syria at the time, which resonates to some extent with structural prevention under R2P. While the lack of effectiveness of the EU in realising reform may have had to do something with its own approach, it also was to a large extent the result of a changing international situation.

Syria had started to come out of its international isolation due to various factors, including the election of President Obama in the United States, which simply meant it now had the luxury to turn down an agreement with the EU which it did not see as in its own interest (Cavatorta and Turcotte 2019). This also shows the limits to deep prevention when target states have 'outside options': long-standing efforts to partner with countries can be quickly undermined if there is no intrinsic interest in these countries to reform and outside options become available that do not require domestic change. Hence, it is difficult to argue that opportunities for structural prevention have been missed because of the EU's constructive engagement towards Syria and the broader region. One caveat that is in order here is that the EU did not yet have a clear atrocity prevention framework in place during the 'constructive engagement period', which would have been appropriate given the Assad's regime's questionable human rights records at the time.

The case of Myanmar is more problematic in terms of prevention. The EU's focus on democracy promotion here barred it from seriously engaging with atrocity prevention in the years leading up to 2017, while all the warning signs for potential atrocities in Myanmar were flashing red according to organisations such as the US Holocaust Memorial Museum (Staunton and Ralph 2019). The way the EU interlinked different norms, such as democracy promotion and atrocity prevention, created blind spots when the situation on the ground demanded trade-offs between these norms. The emphasis on democracy promotion thus came at the expense of atrocity prevention, and this barred engagement with the responsibility to prevent in the case of Myanmar. The EU's focus on democracy promotion left it ill-positioned to address concerns about the treatment of the Rohingya minority, as the organisation did not want to alienate Myanmar's government on its path towards democracy (Staunton and Ralph 2019). Hence, in practice, protection aims under the responsibility to prevent received inadequate attention in Myanmar, raising doubts about the extent to which the EU had internalised the preventive component of R2P at the time. The development of the Atrocity Prevention Toolkit came partly in response to the problematic early response to the crisis in Myanmar and this could aid future engagement with the responsibility to prevent.

Overall, it can be concluded that the responsibility to prevent has been partially internalised by the EU and its member states. In the cases of Libya and Syria, the EU and its member states took several steps that are in line with the responsibility to prevent, such as the early public condemnation of human rights abuses. In the case of Myanmar, however, the focus on democracy promotion created blind spots in the EU's approach to the country and barred sufficient attention for atrocity prevention. While the Myanmar case would lead one to draw sober conclusions with regard to the EU's internalisation of the responsibility to prevent, the fact that the EU has been willing to reflect critically on its shortcomings in Myanmar is positive. This process of institutional learning was one of the major factors leading to the development and the adoption of the Atrocity Prevention Toolkit in early 2019. The fact that the EU has been willing to learn from the Myanmar case and given its more adequate responses in Libya and Syria, it seems reasonable to conclude that the EU and its member states have partially internalised the responsibility to prevent. Much depends on the actual practical implementation of the Atrocity Prevention Toolkit on the ground whether one will witness a more consistent and comprehensive internalisation of the responsibility to prevent in the future (R2P Advisor 2020). At least, the EU has institutionally equipped itself to strive towards this goal.

Responsibility to react

With regard to the responsibility to react, we have witnessed consistent EU-authoritative support for actions that fall under this component of R2P. This can be evidenced through EP resolutions in the various crises. The EP stressed the need for accountability for all parties responsible for atrocity crimes in Syria as recent as in a March 2021 resolution. In the same resolution, it called on the European Commission to present an EU action plan on impunity (European Parliament 2021). Similar calls for accountability were included in EP resolutions on Libya and Myanmar (European Parliament 2011a; European Parliament 2017c). Apart from supporting legal accountability for those responsible for human rights violations and atrocities, the EP also generally endorsed or called for the adoption of sanctions in atrocity cases. It fully endorsed the UN-imposed arms embargo, travel bans, and asset freezes in the case of Libya (European Parliament 2011a). It welcomed the restrictive measures adopted by the European Council against Syria, which included visa bans, asset freezes, and an arms embargo (European Parliament 2011b). Finally, in the case of Myanmar, it called upon the UN Security Council to impose a global comprehensive arms embargo on the state, as well as travel bans and asset freezes against individuals who appeared responsible for serious crimes under international law (European Parliament 2018a).

As was noted in the Libyan case study, the EP also showed a willingness to support the military component of the responsibility to react through a March 2011 resolution, in which it noted that no option under the UN Charter should be ruled out and it called upon EU member states to stand ready for a UNSC-authorised no-fly zone (European Parliament 2011a). A similar call was not made in the cases of Syria and Myanmar. In the case of Syria, this was possibly due to the fact that it was much harder to secure UN Security Council involvement in Syria given the ongoing situation in Libya (European Parliament 2011b). In Myanmar, the opposition of China in the Security Council and the remote likelihood that any EU member state would want to become militarily involved given limited interests and significant logistical challenges even with UNSC authorisation seem plausible reasons why the EP did not call for military measures in its resolutions on the Rohingya crisis. Regardless of this, the EP resolutions demonstrate strong authoritative support for the various measures under the responsibility to react, consistent across crises, which is indicative of discursive internalisation of the responsibility to react.

With regard to the practice-side of the internalisation of the responsibility to react, the EU and its member states adopted sanctions, including arms embargoes, visa bans, and asset freezes, in all three external crises. These sanctions often came in direct response to the commission of atrocities, demonstrating an important commitment to the sanctions component of the responsibility to react. The case of Libya has shown that some EU member states are even willing to use military means to protect civilians (relevant to the military component of the responsibility to react), although one should acknowledge that it is always difficult to pinpoint which factors are leading in intervention decision-making processes. It is therefore difficult to say that R2P was driving the UK and France to intervene in Libya, although it was definitely part of their calculus.

The cases of Syria and to some extent Myanmar have demonstrated that the EU is constrained in which steps it can take in atrocity situations when sanctions do not bring about desired change and one or more of the permanent members of the Security Council are actively using their veto rights. In the case of Syria, Russia and China blocked draft resolutions that did not even come close to calling for military measures against the Assad regime, as they feared 'a replay of Libya' in Syria. In practice, this meant that the Syrian people were left to the whims of the Assad regime, which resulted in appalling atrocities. The paralysis in the Security Council made that the international community flagrantly failed its responsibility to protect the Syrian people, when this international responsibility was activated by a regime that actively targeted its own people and therefore manifestly failed its primary responsibility to protect. It is difficult to conceive, however, what the EU and its member states can do in the case of a deadlocked Security Council. Intervening without a UN mandate seems to be a nonstarter since the Iraq intervention of 2003. Against this backdrop, France has taken initiative together with Mexico in 2015, when they co-launched a "Political Declaration on suspension of veto powers in cases of mass atrocities," open to all member states to support (Global Centre for the Responsibility to Protect 2022). The declaration, which in theory could make a significant contribution to the implementation of the responsibility to react, is as of April 2022 supported by 103 member states, and a similar initiative, the "Code of Conduct regarding Security Council action on genocide, war crimes, and crimes against humanity", has 119 signatories (as per 1 January 2019) (Global Centre for the Responsibility to Protect 2022; Global Centre for the Responsibility to Protect 2019). As three of the UN Security Council Permanent Members (P5) – the US, Russia, and China – have so far not supported either initiative, the initiatives have so far not been able to provide real protection to populations at risk of atrocity crimes.

In the cases of Syria and Myanmar, where Russia and China continue to make active use of their veto right, it means that the EU and its member states are denied the use of R2P's most robust tool, military intervention. It needs to be acknowledged though, that since Russia's direct involvement in Syria, any military action by EU member states has become unthinkable there. The same counts for Myanmar, in which China has major stakes. Concerning the internalisation of the military component of the responsibility to react, one can thus say that the EU has not (yet) been able to fully internalise this aspect of R2P. As was discussed, this is partly due to an inability to act when vetoes in the Security Council exclude forceful action and partly due to an unwillingness to become involved in conflicts in which one of the major powers has major stakes and/or already has a military presence on the ground. Some member states, and particularly Germany, are more generally wary about becoming militarily involved in atrocity cases and sceptical about the ability of military interventions to bring about positive change in these kinds of cases. Another reason for the limited internalisation of the military component of the responsibility to react is that the CSDP is institutionally the least developed policy area in terms of autonomous EU capability, which makes it difficult for the EU to act in this area.

The case of the refugee crisis demonstrated that the EU is in greater difficulty of living up to its 'R2P responsibilities' when R2P 'hits home', which supports the notion that the EU prefers to internalise R2P through its external policies (De Franco et al. 2016). The framing used by some European leaders, such as Hungarian Prime Minister Orbán, who likened refugees to 'an army', shows how deeply securitised the crisis became (Agence France-Presse 2015). It is important to note though that not only the leaders of the CEE-states engaged in securitisation and pictured migrants as a threat. At the height of the refugee crisis, border controls were reinstated throughout Europe and the EU-Turkey deal also demonstrates that the 'border protection'-argument eventually carried the day at the cost of the 'duty of protection'-discourse in Europe (Panebianco and Fontana 2017). A major clash over migration during a June 2018 EU Summit, in which the topic of migration dominated the agenda, shows that the EU will continue to struggle to implement R2P through refugee protection – logically part of the responsibility to react – as long as true European solidarity in this area is lacking (Gotev 2018).

To conclude, the EU and its member states have demonstrated strong signs of internalisation of the sanctions component of the responsibility to react, both through authoritative support and through the consistent use of sanctions in response to atrocities where less forceful means turned out to be inadequate. The picture related to the military component of the responsibility to react is much more complex and for a multiplicity of reasons, ranging from a lack of capabilities and political to geopolitical constraints, this aspect has been internalised to a much lesser extent. The only analysed internal crisis, the refugee crisis, shows furthermore that many EU member states are reluctant to embrace the responsibility to react when 'R2P hits home'. With some notable exceptions, such as Germany and Sweden, most member states prioritised security concerns over protection aims and limited the number of refugees they were willing to let in. Overall, weighing the evidence above, it seems reasonable to conclude that the EU has partially internalised the responsibility to react.

Responsibility to rebuild

The EP expressed authoritative support for the responsibility to rebuild on various occasions, including in a May 2018 resolution on the situation in Libya. In the resolution, the EP called upon the Council to support the stabilisation of Libya, through a political and inclusive national reconciliation process, reconstruction, reconciliation, and state building. It also highlighted the need to foster institution building, including the development of civil society and the private sector, while supporting Libyan efforts to work on a new constitutional order (European Parliament 2018b). With regard to Syria, various EU political actors have expressed the position that any EU rebuilding efforts are conditional on a meaningful, political transition in the state (European Parliament 2019a; Dacrema 2019). In the case of the Rohingya in Myanmar, on the other hand, the EP has on multiple occasions expressed support for reconstruction measures, including food, medical and psychological assistance, protection from gender-based violence, and registration and documentation efforts (European Parliament 2018a; European Parliament 2018c; European Parliament 2019b).

In terms of practice, the aftermath of the Libya intervention witnessed limited rebuilding efforts by the EU. While these measures, such as the rebuilding of infrastructure, schools, and hospitals, made a positive contribution to the situation in Libya, the question is to what extent they are tailored to R2P ends, i.e. preventing future atrocity crimes. Concerning member states, the UK spent less than half of its spending on the intervention in Libya on reconstruction, which gives away that rebuilding may not have been an immediate priority. Much more problematic, though, are the actions of France, which has provided support for General Haftar, who started an armed campaign in 2019 in Libya and who has been accused of committing war crimes. These observations raise important questions about the commitment of some of the larger EU member states to the responsibility to rebuild after an intervention that was supposedly at least partially informed by the R2P framework.

Syria has not witnessed rebuilding efforts similar to those in Libya, partly because the conflict is not over there at the time of writing, but mostly because Western actors, including the EU and its member states, are unwilling to pay for reconstruction as long as there is no meaningful political transition in the country (Calamur 2019).

In contrast with the Libyan case, EU activities aimed at the Rohingya community since the 2017 crisis seem to have been more tailored towards protection ends. The EU's international advocacy for the creation of an international fact-finding mission and its calls more generally for accountability for the atrocities against the Rohingya are important to ensure future protection of the minority group. The provision of documentation to the Rohingya has also been an important protection step, as their statelessness has deprived them of basic rights for decades. These various steps are therefore more in line with the responsibility to rebuild as outlined in the analytical framework of this book ("to provide, particularly after a military intervention, full assistance with recovery, reconstruction, and reconciliation, addressing the causes of the harm the intervention was designed to halt or avert") (Crossley 2016, 82). Even though there was no military intervention in Myanmar, the serious atrocities warranted rebuilding efforts, particularly in societal terms, where the position of the Rohingya within Myanmar's society urgently needed to be addressed. The steps taken by the EU have directly addressed these concerns, by recognising Rohingya's position in Myanmar and the years of neglect and oppression they have faced. Providing documentation to the Rohingya minority has been a first step to give them legal recognition and to strengthen their position in Myanmar. Whether these steps will pay off and will actually give the Rohingya a firmer position in Myanmar is still an open question and the current signs, especially with increased oppression after the military coup in 2021, are not hopeful (BBC 2022). Nevertheless, the actions of the EU in the aftermath of the 2017 atrocities against the Rohingya have demonstrated its ability to learn from the lack of rebuilding in Libya and the limited extent to which rebuilding efforts there were tailored towards protection ends. This shows then that since Libya, the EU and its member states have made concrete steps towards internalising the responsibility to rebuild.

All in all, efforts of the EU and its member states regarding the responsibility to rebuild seem to suggest a partial internalisation of the responsibility to rebuild. The targeted rebuilding measures after the Rohingya crisis demonstrate institutional learning since the Libyan crisis, where rebuilding efforts were more limited and less tailored towards R2P ends. If this progress can be sustained, this offers hope for even deeper and more comprehensive internalisation of the responsibility to rebuild in future cases.

General assessment of norm internalisation of R2P by the EU: a case of norm accommodation

Overall, one can conclude that the EU's internalisation of R2P reflects norm accommodation. The appointment of an EU R2P Focal Point, the setting up of a division in the EEAS focusing on R2P and related areas, the creation of the Atrocity Prevention Toolkit, and the integration of atrocity prevention in existing policies and programmes largely represent the adaptation of existing processes, policies, and institutions, while their essential features have remained largely unchanged. The steps taken are too substantial to be called cosmetic, therefore going beyond norm absorption, but they are arguably not groundbreaking enough to fundamentally change or replace existing policies, therefore stopping short of transformation (Börzel and Risse 2003).

A similar observation can be made in the analysis of the different cases. The response of both EU member states and EU institutions to R2P cases seems to have been generally informed and framed by R2P, but it is difficult to argue that atrocity responses have fundamentally shifted since the adoption of R2P in 2005. Prior to 2005, one could expect the EU and its member states to condemn atrocities, to take diplomatic steps, to adopt sanctions (as against the Former Republic of Yugoslavia (FRY) in 1996–2000), and, in rare cases, to use military force (Giumelli 2013, 43–44). The 1999 NATO Allied Force campaign against the FRY, which was conducted in response to the ethnic cleansing of Albanians by Serbian forces, and to which EU member states France, the UK, Italy, Belgium, Denmark, the Netherlands, Norway, Spain, and Germany contributed is an example of the latter (Roberts 1999; US Department of Defense 1999). Rebuilding was also practiced, for instance through the deployment of the police mission EUFOR and the rule-of-law-mission EULEX in Kosovo (Korski and Gowan 2009).

Post-2005, the norm of R2P has offered the EU and its member states a framework for conceptualising and responding to atrocities, which was visible in the case analyses, but it seems difficult to argue that the norm has fundamentally changed patterns of atrocity response at the EU level. Accommodation and adaptation through institutional learning, which happened in response to the Libyan and Rohingya crises, seems to be a more appropriate label for the way the EU has responded to the norm of R2P.

One level at which the norm has made a significant difference is at the discursive level, most clearly demonstrated by the EP. The EP has consistently referred to R2P in various crisis situations, and it has used it as leverage to spur the EU and its member states into action. This is a significant discursive change compared to the pre-2005 situation. It has kept the pressure on the EU and its member states to act in R2P cases and to continue to develop EU understandings of the norm, while signalling internationally the commitment of the EU to the norm.

Having analysed how and to what extent the EU has internalised the norm of R2P, and having discussed how various European norm entrepreneurs have contributed to the construction of the global norm, it is now time to assess how the various regional factors hold up when assessed against the empirical evidence.

Assessment of the regional factors and the likelihood of internalisation of R2P

As was discussed in the analytical framework, the EU resembles a regional security community (Adler and Greve 2009). References to the EU in official circles and the academic community, such as the 'EU as a peace project'-discourse and the 'civilian/normative/cosmopolitan/Europe'-debate, suggest that EU elites and observers also perceive the EU as such (Von der Leyen 2019; Tusk 2019; Duchene 1972; Habermas 2003; Manners 2002). As was argued in the analytical framework of this book, a security community subscribes to shared norms and values and facilitates peace among its members (Deutsch 1957; Adler and Barnett 1998; Adler and Greve 2009). This allows member states to focus on matters beyond state security, such as the defence of human rights through for instance R2P. The norm-based nature of security communities further increases the attention for human rights issues. The EU, as a security community, can therefore be expected to have a positive disposition to R2P. This has indeed been the case. The EU issued strong rhetorical support for R2P in international fora in the early years of R2P, and has more recently, starting in 2016 with the appointment of the EU R2P Focal Point, followed up on this at the policy level. An interview with a senior EU policy official in Brussels revealed there is an implicit assumption, at least among some EU elites, that R2P is of limited concern to the EU internally, as the organisation is founded upon respect for human rights, which it has codified through a long series of treaties and it has applied externally through conditionality (European Commission official 2018). Other interviewees, particularly civil society representatives and academics, acknowledged there are potential protection issues internally, for instance, when it comes to the refugee crisis (Ferguson 2020; Ralph 2019; UN Official in Brussels 2018; Ralph and Souter 2017). Some interviewees alluded to the start of an internal-protection conversation within the EU as of 2018, potentially through DG JUST, but this was still in the very early stages and it was seen as a sensitive issue area (UN Official in Brussels 2018).

It is insightful at this point to contrast the EU with regional hegemonic systems. Contrary to regional hegemonic systems, the EU has a few big member states rather than one. The lack of a single hegemon may have had some important repercussions for the internalisation of R2P in the EU. Whereas in ECOWAS, Nigeria as the hegemon was one of the states pushing the R2P agenda, the absence of such a hegemon in the EU may have prevented a similar push in the EU. Importantly, the EU's most influential member states have often not seen eye to eye on R2P. This was most visible during the Libyan crisis, in which France and the UK pushed for a robust application of R2P, whereas Germany attempted to constrain this. The conflicting agendas of the EU's leading member states prevented the emergence of collective leadership on R2P that could somehow mirror hegemonic leadership at the EU level. An ALDE-MEP at the time (2018) alluded that the need for consensus in CFSP decision-making has proved an important obstacle to achieving EU-wide consensus on R2P. Arguably, collective leadership from the EU's leading states on R2P would have gone a long way in forging this consensus. The absence of a hegemon, or in the EU's case, collective leadership, could thus be seen as a factor that hampered the internalisation of R2P at the European level.

Concerning the security environment of the EU there is significant fear of the use of hard power, mostly experienced by member states that fear Russia's behaviour since the Crimean annexation of 2014 and even more so since the invasion of Ukraine in 2022. While some eastern member states fear intervention directly, in many member states in Western Europe, debates are being held about Russian elections interference, funding for populist parties etc. (Flanagan et al. 2019; Brattberg and Maurer 2018). The first factor hypothesised that fear of the use of hard power would likely create resistance against R2P in regional fora, as R2P could serve as legitimation for an interventionist agenda. However, generally, it seems that Russian interference and R2P are, apart from an unsuccessful Russian attempt to invoke R2P during the 2008 Georgia intervention (Global Centre for the Responsibility to Protect 2008), viewed as two distinct issue areas that are not often connected in the EU. So, this factor only applies to the EU to a limited extent. Concerning the role of hard power inside the region, it was argued that the more prevalent the role of power in regional systems, the more likely one will witness concerns about the norm of R2P. This is, again, because states with significant hard power could use R2P as an excuse for an interventionist agenda. In the EU, where there is a limited supply of hard power compared to other regions in the world, for the states that do possess significant hard power, it is unconceivable they would project this power *within* the region. The empirical evidence thus indicates that fear of the use of hard power was not a factor that created resistance against R2P within the EU.

The third regional factor related to available capacities and preferences for the use of certain means and resources over others. It was expected that the closer a particular provision of R2P matches the available and preferred regional resources, the more likely the regional organisations will internalise that particular provision. For the EU, this would mean that one should see internalisation of R2P most pronounced in areas where the regional organisation has an edge and it prefers to engage, such as in diplomacy, conflict prevention, and development. Concerning R2P internalisation, one would thus expect a strong internalisation of formal support (as it relates to diplomacy), prevention (as it relates to conflict prevention and diplomacy, and, when assessing long-term prevention, also on development cooperation). As hard power is less readily available, one would expect a less ready internalisation of the military component of the responsibility to react. In the different cases, one saw these expectations confirmed: the EU institutions, particularly the EP, have voiced strong support for R2P at international fora, the EU engages in preventive diplomacy and in long-term prevention and it is more comfortable applying sanctions than using military means. A concrete example of how existing EU capacities and strengths may have informed its specific engagement with R2P is the development of the *Atrocity Prevention Toolkit*, which builds on the area of conflict prevention, one of the EU's traditional strengths and preferred policy approaches.

The fourth and final factor deals with the degree of regional institutionalisation. When there is a high degree of regional institutionalisation, this is likely to increase the chance of an institutional response to new global norms as opposed to an ad hoc response. As the EU is highly institutionalised, one would expect an institutional response (Sweet et al. 2001; Smith 2004). As discussed in this chapter, this has indeed been the case. R2P has been institutionalised in the EU through the appointment of the EU R2P Focal Point and the division within the EEAS that works on R2P. Other examples are the creation of the Atrocity Prevention Toolkit and the integration of R2P and mass atrocity prevention in existing policies and programmes. These institutionalisation practices can aid with the internalisation of R2P, as it provides the EU with the tools to translate the norm into policy action.

Conclusion

This chapter has analysed how and to what extent the EU and its member states have internalised the norm of R2P. Concerning the 'how', it has been shown that the EU has a clear preference to implement R2P externally, i.e. through foreign policy. The fact that the EU focal point on R2P and the policy divisions that work on R2P are located in the EEAS is telling in this respect. Discussions are taking place on the development of an internal protection agenda, but this is at the time of writing still in the early stages (UN official in Brussels 2018; European External Action Service 2019). Initially, the EU tended to subsume R2P and mass atrocity prevention under a general conflict prevention approach, in which it had already built significant experience (De Franco et al. 2016). Recently, this has been addressed by the development of the Atrocity Prevention Toolkit by the EEAS and the integration of the prevention of atrocities into the EU's CSDP missions and operations and into the EU's capacity-building programmes (Schmidt 2019). This specific attention for atrocity prevention is important for the implementation of R2P, as it enables the EU to detect early warning signals of atrocities in a way that was much more challenging under its more general conflict prevention approach.

With regard to local norm construction, it was shown that European norm entrepreneurs such as Blair, Kouchner, and Fischer advocated for important precursors of the R2P norm, such as liberal interventionism and *le droit d'ingérence*. It was also noted that while Blair delivered some important contributions to the R2P norm, the humanitarian discourse he used to defend the unmandated Iraq intervention did most likely more damage than good to the norm.

The four cases have shown that the EU is generally united when it comes to expressing formal support for R2P, condemning the use of force against civilians, taking diplomatic steps in line with the responsibility to prevent, and adopting sanctions in atrocity cases – all important indicators of internalisation of the norm of R2P as identified in the analytical framework of this book. When these measures are insufficient and threats to civilians continue, the picture becomes more complicated. In the cases of Syria and Myanmar, vetoes by Russia and China on the Security Council excluded any possibility of intervention to protect civilians, denying the EU and its member states this measure of last resort under R2P (although the question has been raised if member states would have even considered using these measures in the absence of the vetoes). In the case where the veto was not in the way of forceful measures to protect civilians, i.e. in Libya, this robust application of R2P strongly divided European member states. France and the UK led the case for intervention, while Germany abstained on the crucial UN Security Council vote (UN Security Council 2011b). The case showed that the EU as a whole has not internalised the military component of the responsibility to react. This notion has been dominant in the existing literature on the case, and it has for instance led to the conclusion that the Libyan crisis demonstrated "the extent of disagreement between major European governments about R2P, and the resulting paralysis of the European Union as a whole to support or implement R2P in practice" (Brockmeier et al. 2014, 445). What my framework adds to this analysis is that this EU paralysis does not apply to R2P as a whole, but only to the military component of the responsibility to react. The EU and its member states actually showed unity on other aspects of R2P during the Libyan crisis, such as jointly taking diplomatic steps and adopting sanctions. Adding this nuance is important as R2P is about more than military intervention in atrocity cases alone.

The limited rebuilding efforts in Libya and the fact that they were generally not tailored to preventing future atrocity crimes show that this aspect of the norm has also not been fully internalised by the EU. The actions by some member states in the post-intervention period, and in particular France's support for General Haftar who has been accused of war crimes, is even more damning in this respect. The EU-reconstruction measures taken in the aftermath of the Rohingya crisis are more promising, however, as some of them are directly tailored to protection and atrocity prevention. This demonstrates a willingness of the EU to critically reflect on past experiences and to use these lessons to improve future engagement with the responsibility to rebuild.

The case of the refugee crisis has demonstrated that Europe struggles the most when R2P 'hits home'. While Germany and a few others proved a positive exception, offering generous protection to refugees in 2015, the refugee crisis was generally characterised by a strong degree of securitisation, unilateral steps by member states at the expense of a joint approach and the dominance of security and border protection concerns. The Visegrad states, among which Hungary, went furthest in their 'refugees-as-a-threat' framing and their border protection measures, but the EU as a whole also received widespread criticism from human rights organisations for its approach to the crisis, such as the creation of the EU-Turkey deal. The notion that refugee protection may be the only viable last resort to implement R2P in case of deadlocks in the UN Security Council, an idea advanced by some scholars, means that the EU still has important homework to do it if it truly wants to present itself as "staunch supporter of R2P" (Panebianco and Fontana 2017; European External Action Service 2019).

At the end of the chapter, it was noted that the EU response to R2P largely represents norm accommodation, in which it accommodated the R2P norm by adapting existing processes, policies, and institutions, without changing their essential features and the underlying collective understandings attached to them (Börzel and Risse 2003, 70). This was also visible in the cases, where actions were often informed or framed by R2P, but where adaptation, such as in response to the Rohingya crisis, rather than transformation occurred.

Note

1 Sweden has also been very receptive of refugees during the 2015–16 refugee crisis. The country received a total of 156,000 asylum applications in 2015, and granted 34,470 applicants asylum in the same year (Pew Research Center 2016; Eurostat 2016).

Bibliography

Abboud, Samer. 2016. *Syria*. Cambridge: Polity Press.

Adams, Simon. GCR2P Executive Director. 2018. Interviewed by Jochem Rietveld, Skype, 21 June 2018.

Adler, Emanuel and Michael Barnett, eds. 1998. *Security Communities*. Cambridge: Cambridge University Press. DOI:10.1017/CBO9780511598661.

Adler, Emanuel and Patricia Greve. 2009. "When Security Community Meets Balance of Power: Overlapping Regional Mechanisms of Security Governance." *Review of International Studies* 35 (1): 59–84. DOI:10.1017/S0260210509008432.

Adler-Nissen, Rebecca and Vincent Pouliot. 2014. "Power in Practice: Negotiating the International Intervention in Libya." *European Journal of International Relations* 20 (4): 889–911. DOI:10.1177%2F1354066113512702.

Advisory Council on International Affairs. 2010. "The Netherlands and the Responsibility to Protect: The Responsibility to Protect People from Mass Atrocities." June 4. www.advisorycouncilinternationalaffairs.nl/documents/publications/2010/06/04/the-netherlands-and-the-responsibility-to-protect (May 28, 2020).

Agence France-Presse. 2015. "Refugees 'Look Like an Army', Says Hungarian PM Viktor Orban." *The Guardian*. October 23. www.theguardian.com/world/2015/oct/23/refugees-look-like-an-army-says-hungarian-pm-viktor-orban (December 9, 2019).

ALDE MEP. 2018. Interviewed by Jochem Rietveld, email correspondence, July 2018.

Amnesty International. 2019. "Myanmar: Two Years since Rohingya Exodus, Impunity Reigns Supreme for Military." *Amnesty International*. August 21. www.amnesty.org/en/latest/news/2019/08/myanmar-two-years-since-rohingya-crisis/ (December 9, 2019).

Assad, Abdulkader. 2019. "Mediapart: French Warplanes Sold to Egypt Used to Back up Haftar in Libya." *Libya Observer*. September 21. www.libyaobserver.ly/news/mediapart-french-warplanes-sold-egypt-used-back-haftar-libya (April 17, 2020).

BBC. 2013. "Syria Crisis: Cameron Loses Commons Vote on Syria Action." *BBC*. August 30. www.bbc.com/news/uk-politics-23892783 (December 9, 2019).

BBC. 2016a. "Migrant Crisis: Migration to Europe Explained in Seven Charts." *BBC*. March 4. www.bbc.co.uk/news/world-europe-34131911 (December 9, 2019).

BBC. 2016b. "Migrant Crisis: EU-Turkey Deal Comes into Effect." *BBC*. March 20. www.bbc.co.uk/news/world-europe-35854413 (December 9, 2019).

BBC. 2019a. "Libya Conflict: French Missiles Found on Pro-Haftar Base." *BBC*. July 10. www.bbc.com/news/world-africa-48935242 (April 17, 2020).

BBC. 2019b. "Syria Profile." *BBC*. January 14. www.bbc.com/news/world-middle-east-14703995 (December 9, 2019).

BBC. 2022. "Myanmar: What has been Happening since the 2021 Coup?" *BBC*. February 1. www.bbc.com/news/world-asia-55902070.

Bellamy, Alex. 2009. *Responsibility to Protect: The Global Effort to End Mass Atrocities*. Cambridge: Polity.

Bellamy, Alex. 2015. "Protecting the Rohingya: Delivering on a Shared Responsibility." *Global Observatory*. June 12. https://theglobalobservatory.org/2015/06/rohingya-myanmar-asean-r2p/ (December 9, 2019).

Black, Ian and Chris McGreal. 2012 "Syrian Diplomats Expelled from Countries around the World." *The Guardian*. May 29. www.theguardian.com/world/2012/may/29/syrian-ambassadors-expelled-britain-france (December 9, 2019).

Bloomfield, Alan. 2016. "Norm Antipreneurs and Theorising Resistance to Normative Change." *Review of International Studies* 42 (2): 310–333. DOI:10.1017/S026021051500025X.

Bolopion, Philippe. 2017. "EU Risks Complicity in Crimes against Rohingya." *Human Rights Watch*. March 15. www.hrw.org/news/2017/03/15/eu-risks-complicity-crimes-against-Rohingya (December 9, 2019).

Börzel, Tanja and Thomas Risse. 2003. "Conceptualising the Domestic Impact of Europe." In *The Politics of Europeanisation*, eds. Kevin Featherstone and Claudio Radaelli. Oxford: Oxford University Press, 55–78. DOI:10.1093/0199252092.003.0003.

Bowcott, Owen. 2019. "Gambia Files Rohingya Genocide Case against Myanmar at UN Court." *The Guardian*. November 11. www.theguardian.com/world/2019/nov/11/gambia-rohingya-genocide-myanmar-un-court (December 9, 2019).

Brattberg, Erik and Tim Maurer. 2018. "Russian Election Interference: Europe's Counter to Fake News and Cyber Attacks." May 23. *Carnegie Endowment for International Peace, paper*. https://carnegieendowment.org/2018/05/23/russian-election-interference-europe-s-counter-to-fake-news-and-cyber-attacks-pub-76435 (May 28, 2020).

Brockmeier, Sarah. 2013. "Germany and the Intervention in Libya." *Survival* 55 (6): 63–90. DOI:10.1080/00396338.2013.862937.

Brockmeier, Sarah, Gerrit Kurtz and Julian Junk. 2014. "Emerging norm and rhetorical tool: Europe and a responsibility to protect. *Conflict, Security & Development* 14 (4): 429–460. DOI:10.1080/14678802.2014.930587.

Bucher, Jessica, Lena Engel, Stephanie Harfensteller and Hylke Dijkstra. 2013. "Domestic Politics, News Media and Humanitarian Intervention: Why France and Germany Diverged over Libya et al." *European Security* 22 (4): 524–539. DOI:10.1080/09662839.2013.766597.

Bumiller, Elisabeth. 2012. "Military Points to Risks of a Syrian Intervention." *The New York Times*. March 11. www.nytimes.com/2012/03/12/world/middleeast/us-syria-intervention-would-be-riskypentagon-officials-say.html?pagewanted=all&_r=2& (December 9, 2019).

Burma Campaign UK. 2018. "EU Burma Response: Too Little, Too Late." *Burma Campaign UK*. February 26. http://burmacampaign.org.uk/eu-burma-response-too-little-too-late/ (December 9, 2019).

Calamur, Krishnadev. 2019. "No One Wants to Help Bashar al-Assad Rebuild Syria." *The Atlantic*. March 15. www.theatlantic.com/international/archive/2019/03/where-will-money-rebuild-syria-come/584935/ (February 20, 2022).

Cameron, David and Sarkozy, Nicolas. 2011. "Letter from David Cameron and Nicolas Sarkozy to Herman Van Rompuy." March 10. www.theguardian.com/world/2011/mar/10/libya-middleeast (April 17, 2020).

Cavatorta, Fransesco and Pierre-Michel Turcotte. 2019. "The European Union and Syria." In *The War for Syria. Regional and International Dimensions of the Syrian Uprising*, eds. Raymond Hinnebusch and Adham Saouli. London: Routledge, 261–276.

Cohen, Zachary and Joshua Berlinger. 2019. "Libyan General Praised by Trump Accused of Possible War Crimes." *CNN*. May 16. https://edition.cnn.com/2019/05/15/politics/libya-war-crimes-allegations-intl/index.html (April 17, 2020).

Council of the European Union. 2011. "Libya: EU Imposes Arms Embargo and Targeted Sanctions." 7081/11. www.consilium.europa.eu/uedocs/cms_data/docs/pressdata/EN/foraff/119524.pdf (October 4, 2019).

Council of the European Union. 2017. "Council Conclusions on Myanmar/Burma." 13099/17. https://data.consilium.europa.eu/doc/document/ST-13099-2017-INIT/en/pdf (December 9, 2019).

Council of the European Union. 2018a. "Council Conclusions on Myanmar/Burma." 6418/18. http://data.consilium.europa.eu/doc/document/ST-6418-2018-INIT/en/pdf (December 9, 2019).

Council of the European Union. 2018b. "Myanmar/Burma: EU Extends and Strengthens its Arms Embargo, and Adopts a Framework for Targeted Measures against Officials Responsible for Serious Human Rights Violations." www.consilium.europa.eu/en/press/press-releases/2018/04/26/myanmar-burma-eu-extends-and-strengthens-its-arms-embargo-and-adopts-a-framework-for-targeted-measures-against-officials-responsible-for-serious-human-rights-violations/ (December 9, 2019).

Council of the European Union. 2018c. "Myanmar/Burma: EU Sanctions 7 Senior Military, Border Guard and Police Officials Responsible for or Associated with Serious Human Rights Violations against Rohingya Population." www.consilium.europa.eu/en/press/press-releases/2018/06/25/myanmar-burma-eu-sanctions-7-senior-military-border-guard-and-police-officials-responsible-for-or-associated-with-serious-human-rights-violations-against-rohingya-population/ (December 9, 2019).

Cowell, Alan and Steven Erlanger. 2011. "France becomes First Country to Recognize Libyan Rebels." *The New York Times*. March 10. www.nytimes.com/2011/03/11/world/europe/11france.html (May 13, 2022).

Crossley, Noële. 2016. *Evaluating the Responsibility to Protect: Mass Atrocity Prevention as a Consolidating Norm in International Society*. New York: Routledge.

Dacrema, Eugenio. 2019. "Why Europe won't rebuild Syria." *Atlantic Council*. May 8. www.atlanticcouncil.org/blogs/syriasource/why-europe-won-t-rebuild-syria/ (February 20, 2022).

Daily Express. 2012. "Cameron: Give Assad a Safe Passage." *Daily Express*. November 6. www.express.co.uk/news/world/356472/Cameron-Give-Assad-a-safe-passage (December 8, 2019).

Davidson, Jason. 2013. "France, Britain and the Intervention in Libya: An Integrated Analysis." *Cambridge Review of International Affairs* 26 (2): 310–329. DOI:10.1080/09557571.2013.784573.

De Franco, Chiara, Christoph Meyer and Karen Smith. 2016. "Europe and the European Union." In *The Oxford Handbook of the Responsibility to Protect*, eds. Alex Bellamy and Tim Dunne. Oxford: Oxford University Press, 391–408. DOI:10.1093/oxfordhb/9780198753841.013.21.

Deng, Francis M., Sadikiel Kimaro, Terrence Lyons, Donald Rothchild and William Zartman. 1996. *Sovereignty as Responsibility: Conflict Management in Africa*. Washington, DC: Brookings Institution Press.

Deutsch, Karl. 1957. *Political Community and the North Atlantic Area: International Organization in the Light of Historical Experience*. Princeton: Princeton University Press.

Die Bundesregierung. 2015. "Sommerpressekonferenz von Bundeskanzlerin Merkel." August 31. www.bundesregierung.de/breg-de/aktuelles/pressekonferenzen/sommerpressekonferenz-von-bundeskanzlerin-merkel-848300 (April 20, 2020).

Duchene, Francois. 1972. "Europe's Role in World Peace." In *Europe Tomorrow: Sixteen Europeans Look Ahead*, ed. Richard Mayne. London: Fontana/Collins, 32–47.

EEAS Policy Officer. 2018. Interviewed by Jochem Rietveld, Telephone Interview, 11 July 2018.

EEAS Policy Officer. 2019. Interviewed by Jochem Rietveld, Brussels, February 2019.

Ellis-Petersen, Hannah. 2018. "Myanmar's Military Accused of Genocide in Damning UN Report." *The Guardian*. August27. www.theguardian.com/world/2018/aug/27/myanmars-military-accused-of-genocide-by-damning-un-report (December 9, 2019).

EU Sanctions. 2020. "Sanctions Profile: Syria." www.europeansanctions.com/region/syria/ (April 20, 2020).

EURACTIV with AFP. 2019. "Czech Republic, Hungary and Poland 'Breached EU Law' by Refusing Refugees." *EURACTIV*. November 1. www.euractiv.com/section/politics/news/czech-republic-hungary-and-poland-breached-eu-law-by-refusing-refugees/ (December 9, 2019).

European Commission. 2018. "EU Steps up Support to Address the Rohingya Crisis in Bangladesh." https://ec.europa.eu/commission/presscorner/detail/en/IP_18_201 (April 20, 2020).

European Commission. 2019a. "EU Emergency Trust Fund for Africa." *Libya*. https://ec.europa.eu/trustfundforafrica/region/north-africa/libya_en (October 11, 2019).

European Commission. 2019b. "A Step-Change in Migration Management and Border Security." https://ec.europa.eu/home-affairs/sites/homeaffairs/files/what-we-do/policies/european-agenda-migration/20190306_managing-migration-factsheet-step-change-migration-management-border-security-timeline_en.pdf (December 9, 2019).

European Commission. 2020. "Rohingya Crisis: EU Allocates €31 million for Bangladesh and Myanmar." March 3. https://ec.europa.eu/commission/presscorner/detail/en/IP_20_371 (June 16, 2022).

European Commission Official. 2018. Interviewed by Jochem Rietveld, Brussels, June 2018.

European External Action Service. 2017a. "Statement by the High Representative/Vice-President Federica Mogherini on the Situation in Rakhine State, Myanmar." https://eeas.europa.eu/delegations/myanmar-burma/31738/statement-high-representativevice-president-federica-mogherinisituation-rakhine-state-myanmar_en (December 9, 2019).

European External Action Service. 2017b. "Speech by Federica Mogherini at the European Parliament Urgent Debate on Myanmar, in Particular the Situation of Rohingyas." https://eeas.europa.eu/delegations/myanmar-burma/32123/speech-federica-mogherini-european-parliament-urgentdebate-myanmar-particular-situation_en (December 9, 2019).

European External Action Service. 2018. "Libya: Hope for a Normal Life." https://eeas.europa.eu/headquarters/headquarters-homepage_en/51028/Libya:%20hope%20for%20a%20normal%20life (October 10, 2019).

European External Action Service. 2019. "EU Statement – United Nations General Assembly: Debate on the Responsibility to Protect and the Prevention of Genocide." https://eeas.europa.eu/delegations/un-new-york/64721/eu-statement-%E2%80%93-united-nations-general-assembly-debate-responsibility-protect-and-prevention_en (December 10, 2019).

European Parliament. 2005. "European Parliament Resolution on the Outcome of the United Nations World Summit of 14–16 September 2005. P6_TA(2005)0362." www.europarl.europa.eu/sides/getDoc.do?pubRef=-//EP//TEXT+TA+P6-TA-2005–0362+0+DOC+XML+V0//EN (October 4, 2019).

European Parliament. 2011a. "European Parliament Resolution of 10 March 2011 on the Southern Neighbourhood, and Libya in Particular." www.europarl.europa.eu/doceo/document/TA-7-2011-0095_EN.html (February 18, 2022).

European Parliament. 2011b. "European Parliament Resolution of 7 July 2011 on the Situation in Syria, Yemen and Bahrain in the Context of the Situation in the Arab World and North Africa." www.europarl.europa.eu/doceo/document/TA-7-2011-0333_HR.html (February 18, 2022).

European Parliament. 2012. "European Parliament resolution of 13 September 2012 on Syria." www.europarl.europa.eu/sides/getDoc.do?pubRef=-//EP//TEXT+TA+P7-TA-2012-0351 + 0+DOC+XML+V0//EN&language=EN (December 8, 2019).

European Parliament. 2013a. "European Parliament Recommendation to the Council of 18 April 2013 on the UN Principle of the 'Responsibility to Protect' ('R2P')." P7_TA(2013)0180. www.europarl.europa.eu/sides/getDoc.do?type=TA&reference=P7-TA-2013-0180&language=EN (October 5, 2019).

European Parliament. 2013b. *European Neighbourhood Policy, Working towards a Stronger Partnership: EP's Position on the 2012 Progress Reports.* www.europarl.europa.eu/sides/getDoc.do?pubRef=-//EP//TEXT+TA+P7-TA-2013-0446 + 0+DOC+XML+V0//EN&language=EN (December 8, 2019).

European Parliament. 2016. *European Parliament resolution of 24 November 2016 on the Situation in Syria.* www.europarl.europa.eu/doceo/document/TA-8-2016-0449_EN.html?redirect (October 5, 2019).

European Parliament. 2017a. *European Parliament Resolution of 4 July 2017 on Addressing Human Rights Violations in the Context of War Crimes, and Crimes against Humanity, Including Genocide (P8_TA(2017)0288).* www.europarl.europa.eu/doceo/document/TA-8-2017-0288_EN.html (October 7, 2019).

European Parliament. 2017b. *European Parliament Resolution of 5 April 2017 on Addressing Refugee and Migrant Movements: The Role of EU External Action.* www.europarl.europa.eu/doceo/document/TA-8-2017-0124_EN.html?redirect (December 10, 2019).

European Parliament. 2017c. *European Parliament Resolution of 14 September 2017 on Myanmar, in Particular the Situation of Rohingyas.* www.europarl.europa.eu/doceo/document/TA-8-2017-0351_EN.html (December 9, 2019).

European Parliament. 2018a. *European Parliament Resolution of 13 September 2018 on Myanmar, Notably the Case of Journalists Wa Lone and Kyaw Soe Oo.* www.europarl.europa.eu/doceo/document/TA-8-2018-0345_EN.html (February 18, 2022).

European Parliament. 2018b. *European Parliament Recommendation of 30 May 2018 to the Council, the Commission and the Vice-President of the Commission/High Representative of the Union for Foreign Affairs and Security Policy on Libya.* www.europarl.europa.eu/doceo/document/TA-8-2018-0227_EN.html (February 20, 2022).

European Parliament. 2018c. *European Parliament Resolution of 14 June 2018 on the Situation of Rohingya Refugees, in Particular the Plight of Children.* https://eur-lex.europa.eu/legal-content/EN/TXT/PDF/?uri=CELEX:52018IP0261&from=EN (June 16, 2022).

European Parliament. 2019a. "EU Strategy for Syria." *European Parliament.* November 20. www.europarl.europa.eu/legislative-train/theme-europe-as-a-stronger-global-actor/file-eu-strategy-for-syria (February 18, 2022).

European Parliament. 2019b. *European Parliament Resolution of 19 September 2019 on Myanmar, Notably the Situation of the Rohingya.* www.europarl.europa.eu/doceo/document/TA-9-2019-0018_EN.html (June 16, 2022).

European Parliament. 2021. *European Parliament Resolution of 11 March 2021 on the Syrian conflict – 10 Years after the Uprising.* www.europarl.europa.eu/doceo/document/TA-9-2021-0088_EN.html (February 18, 2022).

European Parliament, Council, Commission. 2006. "The European Consensus on Development. 2006/C 46/01)." *Official Journal of the European Union.* https://eur-lex.europa.

eu/LexUriServ/LexUriServ.do?uri=OJ%3AC%3A2006%3A046%3A0001%3A0019%3AEN%3APDF (October 4, 2019).

European Union. 2008. *Report on the Implementation of the European Security Strategy-Providing Security in a Changing World, Brussels. S407/08.* www.consilium.europa.eu/ueDocs/cms_Data/docs/pressdata/EN/reports/104630.pdf (October 4, 2019).

European Union. 2011. *Declaration by the High Representative Catherine Ashton on behalf of the European Union on Libya. 6966/1/11 REV 1.* https://europa.eu/rapid/press-release_PESC-11-36_en.htm (October 4, 2019).

European Union. 2012. *Statement by the High Representative Catherine Ashton Condemning the Continued Repression and Violence in Syria and Marking the Anniversary of the Uprising. A 123/12.* www.consilium.europa.eu/uedocs/cms_data/docs/pressdata/EN/foraff/129013.pdf (December 9, 2019).

European Union. 2016. *Shared Vision, Common Action: A Stronger Europe. A Global Strategy for the European Union's Foreign and Security Policy*. Belgium: European Union.

Eurostat. 2016. "Asylum Decisions in the EU. EU Member States Granted Protection to More than 330 000 Asylum Seekers in 2015." *Eurostat.* April 20. https://ec.europa.eu/eurostat/documents/2995521/7233417/3-20042016-AP-EN.pdf/34c4f5af-eb93-4ecd-984c-577a5271c8c5#page=3 (December 9, 2019).

Fabbrini, Sergio. 2014. "The European Union and the Libyan Crisis." *International Politics* 51 (2): 177–195. https://dx.doi.org/10.2139/ssrn.2423286.

Feher, Margit. 2015. "Hungary Completes Croatia Border Fence to Keep Migrants Out." *The Wall Street Journal.* October 15. www.wsj.com/articles/hungary-completes-croatia-border-fence-to-keep-migrants-out-1444927774 (December 10, 2019).

Ferguson, Kate. Co-executive Director Protection Approaches. 2020. Interviewed by Jochem Rietveld, Skype, January 31.

Finnemore, Martha and Kathryn Sikkink. 1998. "International Norm Dynamics and Political Change." *International Organization* 52 (4): 887–917. DOI:10.1162/002081898550789.

Fiott, Daniel and Marie Vincent. 2013. "The European Union." In *An Institutional Approach to the Responsibility to Protect*, ed. Gentian Zyberi. Cambridge: Cambridge University Press, 199–219.

Flanagan, Stephen, Jan Osburg, Anika Binnendijk, Marta Kepe and Andrew Radin. 2019. "Deterring Russian Aggression in the Baltic States Through Resilience and Resistance." *RAND Corporation Research Report.* www.rand.org/content/dam/rand/pubs/research_reports/RR2700/RR2779/RAND_RR2779.pdf (May 28, 2020).

Full Fact. 2016. "Asylum seekers, the UK and Europe." *Full Fact.* October 25. https://fullfact.org/immigration/asylum-seekers-uk-and-europe/ (December 9, 2019).

Gifkins, Jess. 2012. "The UN Security Council Divided: Syria in Crisis." *Global Responsibility to Protect* 4 (3): 377–393. DOI:10.1163/1875984X-00403009.

Giumelli, Francesco. 2013. "How EU sanctions work: A new narrative." *Chaillot Papers, EU Institute for Security Studies.* May. https://www.iss.europa.eu/content/how-eu-sanctions-work-new-narrative (November 17, 2022).

Global Centre for the Responsibility to Protect. 2008. "The Georgia-Russia Crisis and the Responsibility to Protect: Background Note." *GCR2P.* www.globalr2p.org/wp-content/uploads/2021/07/the-georgia-russia-crisis-and-the-r2p-background-note.pdf. (July 7, 2022).

Global Centre for the Responsibility to Protect. 2019. "List of Signatories to the ACT Code of Conduct." www.globalr2p.org/resources/list-of-signatories-to-the-act-code-of-conduct/ (May 5, 2022).

Global Centre for the Responsibility to Protect. 2022. "Political Declaration on Suspension of Veto Powers in Cases of Mass Atrocities." www.globalr2p.org/resources/

political-declaration-on-suspension-of-veto-powers-in-cases-of-mass-atrocities/ (May 5, 2022).

Gogou, Kondylia. 2017. "The EU-Turkey Deal: Europe's Year of Shame." *Amnesty International.* March 20. www.amnesty.org/en/latest/news/2017/03/the-eu-turkey-deal-europes-year-of-shame/ (December 9, 2019).

Goldman, Russell. 2019. "Kurds, Turkey and the U.S.: 5 Years of Tension, Alliances and Conflict." *The New York Times.* October 10. www.nytimes.com/2019/10/10/world/middleeast/turkey-syria-kurds-history-facts.html (April 17, 2020).

Gotev, Georgi. 2018. "EU Summit Approves Tortured Conclusions on Migration after Sleepless Night." *EURACTIV.* June 29. www.euractiv.com/section/global-europe/news/eu-summit-approves-tortured-conclusions-on-migration-after-sleepless-night/ (December 10, 2019).

Government Europa. 2019. "Humanitarian Assistance to Libya Boosted." April 4. www.governmenteuropa.eu/humanitarian-assistance-to-libya/92816/ (October 10, 2019).

GUE/NGL Group. 2018. *Motion for a Resolution. European Parliament Resolution on the situation in Yemen (B8-0450/2018).* www.europarl.europa.eu/doceo/document/B-8-2018-0450_EN.html (October 5, 2019).

Habermas, Jurgen. 2003 "Making Sense of the EU: Towards a Cosmopolitan Europe." *Journal of Democracy* 14 (4): 86–100. http://doi.org/10.1353/jod.2003.0077.

Hinnebusch, Raymond and Omar Imady. 2018. *The Syrian Uprising: Domestic Origins and Early Trajectory.* London: Routledge. DOI:10.4324/9781315143798.

Hodal, Kate. 2012. "EU lifts Burma Sanctions for One Year." *The Guardian.* April 23. www.theguardian.com/world/2012/apr/23/eu-lifts-burma-sanctions (December 9, 2019).

Human Rights Watch. 2019. "Rohingya Crisis." *Human Rights Watch.* www.hrw.org/tag/rohingya-crisis (December 9, 2019).

Hungarian Government. 2015a. "Viktor Orban's Speech Address in the European People's Party Congress in Madrid." October 22. www.kormany.hu/en/the-prime-minister/the-prime-minister-s-speeches/speech-of-viktor-orban-at-the-epp-congress20151024 (April 17, 2020).

Hungarian Government. 2015b. "Viktor Orban's Speech Address in the Hungarian Parliament, Budapest." November 16. www.kormany.hu/en/the-prime-minister/the-prime-ministers-speeches/prime-minister-viktor-orban-s-address-in-parliament-before-the-start-of-daily-business (April 17, 2020).

International Court of Justice. 2007. "Application of the Convention on the Prevention and Punishment of the Crime of Genocide (Bosnia and Herzegovina v. Serbia and Montenegro), Judgment." February 26. p. 166 § 297. General List No. 91.

Karnitschnig, Matthew. 2015. "Orbán Says Migrants Threaten 'Christian' Europe." *Politico.* September 3. www.politico.eu/article/orban-migrants-threaten-christian-europe-identity-refugees-asylum-crisis/ (December 9, 2019).

Keranen, Outi. 2016. "Libyan Lessons: Bring Back the Responsibility to Rebuild." *Oxford Research Group.* November 11. www.oxfordresearchgroup.org.uk/blog/libyan-lessons-bring-back-the-responsibility-to-rebuild (October 7, 2019).

Kirkpatrick, David and Kareem Fahim. 2011. "Qaddafi Warns of Assault on Benghazi as U.N. Vote Nears." *The New York Times.* March 17. https://nyti.ms/2zLFDiP (October 4, 2019).

Kirkup, James. 2013. "David Cameron: World Setting a 'Dangerous' Precedent not Intervening in Syria. *The Telegraph.* September 6. www.telegraph.co.uk/news/worldnews/middleeast/syria/10291207/David-Cameron-world-setting-a-dangerous-precedent-not-intervening-in-Syria.html (December 9, 2019).

Korski, Daniel and Richard Gowan. 2009. "Can the EU Rebuild Failing States? A Review of Europe's Civilian Capacities." *European Council of Foreign Relations* 1–99.

Kurtz, Gerrit, Dr. 2019. Interviewed by Jochem Rietveld, Skype, November, 12.

Louw-Vaudran, Liesl. 2015. "Libya the Key to Stopping Terror in the Sahel." *Institute for Security Studies*. https://issafrica.org/amp/iss-today/libya-the-key-to-stopping-terror-in-the-sahel (May 29, 2020).

Manners, Ian. 2002. "Normative Power Europe: A Contradiction in Terms?" *Journal of Common Market Studies* 40 (2): 235–258. DOI:10.1111/1468-5965.00353.

Marks, Simon. 2018. "EU Urges Prosecutions for Myanmar Crimes against Rohingya." *Politico*. September 14. www.politico.eu/article/myanmar-rohingya-un-eu-urges-prosecutions-for-myanmar-crimes-against-rohingya/ (April 17, 2020).

McGreal, Chris and Martin Chulov. 2011. "Syria: Assad Must Resign, Says Obama." *The Guardian*. August 19. www.theguardian.com/world/2011/aug/18/syria-assad-must-resign-obama (December 9, 2019).

Mendelski, Bruno. 2019. "The Rhetoric of Hungarian Premier Victor Orban: Inside X Outside in the Context of Immigration Crisis." In *The Palgrave Handbook of Ethnicity*, ed. S. Ratuva. Singapore: Palgrave Macmillan, 1829–1852. DOI:10.1007/978-981-13-0242-8_155-1.

Newman, Edward. 2018. "The Limits of Liberal Humanitarianism in Europe: The 'Responsibility to Protect' and Forced Migration." *European Review of International Studies* 4 (2 + 3): 59–77. DOI:10.3224/eris.v4i2-3.04.

Newman, Edward and Christina Stefan. 2020. "Normative Power Europe? The EU's Embrace of the 'Responsibility to Protect' in a Transitional International Order." *Journal of Common Market Studies* 58 (2): 472–490.

Panebianco, Stefania and Iole Fontana. 2017. "When Responsibility to Protect 'Hits Home': The Refugee Crisis and the EU Response." *Third World Quarterly* 39 (1): 1–17. DOI:10.1080/01436597.2017.1369035.

Pew Research Center. 2016. "Number of Refugees to Europe Surges to Record 1.3 Million in 2015." *Pew Research Center*. August 2. www.pewresearch.org/global/2016/08/02/number-of-refugees-to-europe-surges-to-record-1-3-million-in-2015/ (February 20, 2022).

R2P advisor. 2020. Interviewed by Jochem Rietveld, Skype, January 2020.

Ralph, Jason. 2019. Interviewed by Jochem Rietveld, Skype, December 2019.

Ralph, Jason and Souter, James. 2017. "Introduction: The Responsibility to Protect and the Refugee Protection Regime." *Ethics and International Affairs* 31 (1): 47–50.

Rankin, Jennifer. 2019. "EU to Stop Mediterranean Migrant Rescue Boat Patrols." *The Guardian*. March 27. www.theguardian.com/world/2019/mar/27/eu-to-stop-mediterranean-migrant-rescue-boat-patrols (December 9, 2019).

Ratcliffe, Rebecca. 2018. "Aung San Suu Kyi Stripped of Amnesty's Highest Honour over 'Shameful Betrayal'" *The Guardian*. November 12. www.theguardian.com/global-development/2018/nov/12/aung-san-suu-kyi-amnesty-highest-honour-shameful-betrayal (December 9, 2019).

Reinl, James. 2020. "Europeans Demand Rohingya Justice at UN." *Anadolu Agency*. February 4. www.aa.com.tr/en/europe/europeans-demand-rohingya-justice-at-un/1724370 (April 17, 2020).

Republic of Slovenia. 2013. "UNGA Fifth Informal Interactive Dialogue on the Responsibility to Protect: State Responsibility and Prevention. Statement by Ambassador Andrej Logar." September 11. http://responsibilitytoprotect.org/Slovenia%2013.pdf (May 28, 2020).

Republic of Slovenia, Ministry of Foreign Affairs. 2019. "Responsibility to Protect." http://mzz.arhiv-spletisc.gov.si/en/foreign_policy_and_international_law/responsibility_to_protect/ (October 9, 2019).

Rettman, Andrew. 2014. "EU Countries Give France Green Light to Arm Iraqi Kurds." *EU Observer*. August 13. https://euobserver.com/foreign/125245 (April 17, 2020).

Reuters. 2019. "Two Years on, a Look at the Rohingya Crisis." *Reuters*. August 23. www.reuters.com/article/us-myanmar-rohingya-timeline/two-years-on-a-look-at-the-rohingya-crisis-idUSKCN1VD044 (December 9, 2019).

Roberts, Adam. 1999. "NATO's 'Humanitarian War' in Kosovo." *Survival* 41 (3): 102–123.

RTÉ. 2018. "Russia's 12 UN Vetoes on Syria." *RTÉ*. April 11. www.rte.ie/news/world/2018/0411/953637-russia-syria-un-veto/ (December 9, 2019).

Schmidt, Julia. 2019. "The European Union and the Responsibility to Protect." *European Foreign Affairs Review* 24 (3): 309–326.

Smith, Karen. 2018. "The EU and the Responsibility to Protect in an Illiberal Era." *Dahrendorf Forum IV Working Paper No. 03*. http://eprints.lse.ac.uk/90083/ (November 17, 2022).

Smith, Michael. 2004. "Institutionalization, Policy Adaptation and European Foreign Policy Cooperation." *European Journal of International Relations* 10 (1): 95–136. DOI:10.1177%2F1354066104040570.

Spindler, William. "2015: The Year of Europe's Refugee Crisis." *UNHCR UK*. December 8. www.unhcr.org/news/stories/2015/12/56ec1ebde/2015-year-europes-refugee-crisis.html (December 9, 2019).

Staunton, Eglantine and Jason Ralph. 2019. "The Responsibility to Protect Norm Cluster and the Challenge of Atrocity Prevention: An Analysis of the European Union's Strategy in Myanmar." *European Journal of International Relations* 26 (3): 660–686.

Stavridis, Stelios. 2016. "The European Parliament's Contribution to the R2P Debate: Lessons from the Libyan and Syrian Conflicts." *Global Affairs* 2 (2): 187–201. DOI:10.1080/23340460.2016.1178872.

Stefan, Christina and Edward Newman. 2020. "Europe's Progress and the Road ahead at R2P's 15th Anniversary." *Global Responsibility to Protect* 12 (4): 369–371. DOI:10.1163/1875-984X-01204004.

Sweet, Alec Stone, Wayne Sandholtz and Neil Fligstein, eds. 2001. *The Institutionalization of Europe*. Oxford: Oxford University Press. DOI:10.1093/019924796X.001.0001.

Theron, Julien. 2019. "French Foreign Policy in Libya and Syria (2003–2017): Strategic Adaptability in Quickly Changing Environments." In *The World Community and the Arab Spring*, eds. Cenap Çakmak and Ali Onur Özçelik. London: Palgrave Macmillan, 205–231. DOI:10.1007/978-3-319-60985-0_10.

Tondo, Lorenzo. 2019. "Italy Adopts Decree that Could Fine Migrant Rescuers up to €50,000." *The Guardian*. June 15. www.theguardian.com/world/2019/jun/15/italy-adopts-decree-that-could-fine-migrant-rescue-ngo-aid-up-to-50000 (December 9, 2019).

Trombetta, Lorenzo. 2014. "The EU and the Syrian Crisis as Viewed from the Middle East." *The International Spectator* 49 (3): 27–39. DOI:10.1080/03932729.2014.937134.

Tusk, Donald. 2019. "Remarks by President Donald Tusk after his Meeting with Taoiseach Leo Varadkar." February 6. www.consilium.europa.eu/en/press/press-releases/2019/02/06/remarks-by-president-donald-tusk-after-his-meeting-with-taoiseach-leo-varadkar/ (October 2, 2020).

UN General Assembly 2005. *Resolution Adopted by the General Assembly on 16 September 2005. 60/1.2005 World Summit Outcome*. ttps://www.un.org/en/development/desa/population/migration/generalassembly/docs/globalcompact/A_RES_60_1.pdf (October 11, 2019).

UN Official in Brussels. 2018. Interviewed by Jochem Rietveld, Brussels, June 2018.

UN Security Council. 2011a. Resolution 1970. S/RES/1970. www.undocs.org/S/RES/1970%20(2011) (October 7, 2019).

UN Security Council. 2011b. *Resolution 1973. S/RES/1973.* www.undocs.org/S/RES/1973%20(2011) (October 7, 2019).

UNHCR. 2015. "Global Trends. Forced Displacement in 2015." www.unhcr.org/576408cd7.pdf (April 20, 2020).

UNHCR. 2019. "Registration Gives Many Rohingya Refugees Identification for the First Time." *The UN Refugee Agency*. May 17. www.unhcr.org/news/latest/2019/5/5cde66b84/registration-gives-rohingya-refugees-identification-first-time.html (June 16, 2022).

United Nations. 2011. *The Role of Regional and Subregional Arrangements in Implementing the Responsibility to Protect. A/65/877 – S/2011/393.* https://undocs.org/A/65/877 (December 9, 2019).

United Nations Human Rights Council. 2018. "Myanmar: UN Fact-Finding Mission releases its Full Account of Massive Violations by Military in Rakhine, Kachin and Shan States." www.ohchr.org/EN/HRBodies/HRC/Pages/NewsDetail.aspx?NewsID=23575 (April 20, 2020).

United Nations Office for the Coordination of Humanitarian Affairs. 2019. "Rohingya Refugee Crisis." www.unocha.org/rohingya-refugee-crisis (December 9, 2019).

US Department of Defense. 1999. "Operation Allied Force." 21 June. https://archive.defense.gov/specials/kosovo/ (29 September 2020).

Von der Leyen, Ursula. 2019. "A Union that Strives for More. My Agenda for Europe." https://ec.europa.eu/commission/sites/beta-political/files/political-guidelines-next-commission_en.pdf (October 2, 2020).

Vorster, Nico. 2015. "Just War and Virtue: Revisiting Augustine and Thomas Aquinas." *South African Journal of Philosophy* 34 (1): 55–68.

WANEP. 2016. "Institutional Capacities for the Implementation of R2P in West Africa: A Case Study of Ghana." *West Africa Network for Peacebuilding* 1–52.

Weller, Marc. 2018. "Syria Air Strikes: Were they Legal?" *BBC*. April 14. www.bbc.co.uk/news/world-middle-east-43766556 (December 10, 2019).

5 ECOWAS and R2P

West African inspirations of a global norm

Introduction

This empirical chapter assesses how and to what extent ECOWAS has internalised the norm of the Responsibility to Protect (R2P), since the norm's adoption at the UN in 2005. This chapter thus aims to provide answers to the research question for the West African case, with the previous chapter having analysed the EU.

The first part of this chapter looks at the normative status quo in the region at the time that R2P emerged and its implications for norm entrepreneurs and antipreneurs of R2P. This analysis will pave the way for a discussion of how the norm of R2P has generally been received in ECOWAS since 2005. Before this can be discussed, it is needed to go back in time though, as some of R2P's roots were laid in the West African region in the 1990s. West African norm entrepreneurs such as Kofi Annan subsequently elevated the West African institutional approaches and policy practices to tackle mass atrocities to the global level, where they served as important inspiration for the R2P norm. Providing this context is important as it will set the stage for the cases that will be analysed in the third part of the chapter. The selected cases, the crises in respectively Guinea, Ivory Coast, and Mali, are relevant for assessing the internalisation of R2P in ECOWAS, as they all involved the commission of atrocity crimes at some point. There is also variance in terms of R2P response, as Guinea and Ivory Coast saw the applications of sanctions, whereas in Mali, ECOWAS troops eventually became involved.

The subsequent part offers some case reflections and case comparisons. The cases and reflections together will demonstrate how and to what extent ECOWAS and its member states have internalised the different aspects the norm of R2P in practice and how different West African actors have operated during crises. Towards the end of the chapter, the regional factors as identified in the theory chapter of this book will be systematically assessed. References to these factors are made throughout the chapter, but it is in this section that they are comprehensively assessed based on the presented empirical evidence. The final part offers some concluding remarks.

DOI: 10.4324/9781003230731-5

The normative status quo in ECOWAS pre-2005: fertile ground for R2P

As was discussed in the contextual chapter, traditional notions of sovereignty were far from entrenched in ECOWAS in the early 2000s, when the norm of R2P first emerged and negotiations around it started. ECOWAS had already accumulated extensive experience with sovereignty-pooling in the field of peace and security, usually one of the areas where doing so is most sensitive. One can thus assert that rather than enjoying an entrenched status, sovereignty's normative status quo in ECOWAS was already unstable in the period when R2P as a global norm emerged. Analysing the normative context was the first necessary step identified in the analytical framework. The 'unstable normative status quo' comes with a number of expectations. First, in a context of an unstable status quo, entrepreneurs are expected to be advantaged over antipreneurs. In the case at hand, one should expect R2P norm entrepreneurs to be well positioned to seize the opportunity produced by the unstable normative status quo to problematise the status quo and advocate for a new norm to address the problem. In the case of ECOWAS, the normative status quo around 2005 was, however, already one in which intervention norms had taken root in regional protocols. R2P norm entrepreneurs, such as Ghana, thus had little problematising to do, as R2P strongly resonated with the existing security norms in ECOWAS.

If there is an unstable status quo, antipreneurs are expected to be less successful in exploiting blocking opportunities. Given sovereignty's contested status in ECOWAS, it will be difficult for norm antipreneurs to defend traditional notions of sovereignty in the advent of the norm of R2P. The first blocking opportunity they have, to maintain there are no problems with the current status quo, will thus be difficult to seize. In the case of ECOWAS, norm antipreneurship against R2P around the 2005 World Summit has not been documented. This is not to say that this automatically means there were no sceptics. Rather, as Hartmann and Striebinger (2015, 81) would argue, in case there would have been sceptics, they would have likely believed they could agree to R2P while avoiding a radical implementation of the norm-mirroring their expectations about the ECOWAS protocols that were adopted in the 1990s and 2000s.

The norm of R2P and ECOWAS

To assess how ECOWAS has dealt with the norm of R2P, it is needed to go back in time, as some of the roots of R2P can be traced back to regional practices and institutional developments in ECOWAS in the 1990s. In the interviews that were conducted with ECOWAS officials in the context of this research, it was striking to see how they all consistently emphasised the West African roots of the norm of R2P. This is significant as the wider R2P literature generally does cite the African Union's 'non-indifference principle' as a regional precursor to R2P, but generally fails to mention the multiple West African precursors that both predated and inspired the AU's non-indifference principle (Acharya 2013; Welsh 2013; Williams 2017). These West African roots are particularly visible in the 1999 Protocol relating to the Mechanism and the 2001 Protocol on Democracy and Good Governance, two documents that institutionalised ECOWAS' role in peace and security (the 1999 Mechanism) and political affairs (the 2001 Protocol), which were discussed in the contextual chapter of this book. Article 25 of the 1999 Mechanism specifies under which conditions intervention is allowed, which includes cases of "humanitarian disaster" and "massive violations of human rights and the rule of law" (ECOWAS 1999). Article 45 (1) of the 2001 Protocol states that "where there is massive violation of Human Rights in a Member State, ECOWAS may impose sanctions on the State concerned" (ECOWAS 2001).

The 1999 Mechanism was established because of a variety of factors, of which two were dominant. First, ECOWAS member states felt the necessity to increase ECOWAS' security utility because they perceived the Security Council had failed to act quickly enough in the cases of Liberia and Sierra Leone. Second, the 1993 Revised Treaty had given an impetus to institutional change as it included a new security mechanism whose details needed to be worked out (Koga 2016, 117). Togo took the initiative in the process of creating the 1999 Mechanism as it convened the Fourth Extraordinary Summit in Lomé in December 1997. The aim of this summit was to reach an agreement on the conditions of intervention that were suitable for the new regional security environment, which would in practice mean reformulating or replacing the existing conditions established by the PNA (1978) and the PMAD (1981) (see the contextual chapter of this book). During the summit, ECOWAS leaders created a committee to this end, "the ECOWAS Ministers of Foreign, Defense, Internal Affairs and Security" (the Ministers Committee). The committee would become a norm entrepreneur of the 1999 Mechanism. Hartmann and Striebinger (2015) argue "there is generally a lack of empirical data on the decision-making processes leading to the 1999 Protocol" (here referred to as 'the Mechanism'). On the basis of their research, it seems certain, though, that at least Nigeria, Benin, Niger, and Mali lobbied for the Mechanism (Hartmann and Striebinger 2015, 76).

The authors hypothesise that the democratic lock-in hypothesis is behind this. Throughout the 1990s, the number of democracies slowly increased in the West African region and the democracies were for the first time in the majority just before the signing of the protocol (Hartmann and Striebinger 2015, 76). A few military coups against democratically elected governments in the late 1990s showed the newly elected presidents how fragile their democratic institutions remained. A regional protection mechanism such as the 1999 Mechanism and later the 2001 Protocol was thus certainly welcome. Concerning the specific role of Nigeria, the authors assert that the Mechanism and Protocol would have been unimaginable without Nigeria's involvement and consent (Hartmann and Striebinger 2015). In 1999, democracy was reinstated in Nigeria with the election of President Obasanjo. President Obasanjo used his election not only to democratise Nigeria but to push for this in the region as well. This reflects the regional self-image factor as captured in the theory chapter, in which actors within the region shape normative responses in the region based on their own experiences and identity. Some experts have wondered why Nigeria, as the region's hegemon, would ever agree to the creation of a body, the Mediation and Security Council (MSC), in which it could be outvoted. Some have argued it would reduce transaction costs when dealing with crises and to share legal and political responsibility in avoiding further regional instability with other ECOWAS member states in a time when it was expected accountability would increase inside Nigeria (Hartmann and Striebinger 2015). Coleman (2007) comes up with a different hypothesis, namely that the specific features of the 1999 Protocol create the procedural legitimacy for military interventions pursued at the regional level with very few institutional restrictions in place (the 1999 Mechanism allows decisions to intervene to be taken with a majority instead of unanimity). This, in effect, maintains Nigeria's capacity of military intervention in neighbouring states. In many ways, Nigeria's leadership in realising the 1999 Mechanism and the 2001 Protocol is reflective of the hegemonic stability thesis outlined in the theory chapter. It was under these conditions of hegemonic stability that a leadership role of the hegemon in driving the institutionalisation of R2P was expected, provided there was an interest in the norm in the region. Nigeria's behaviour as regional hegemon has been in line with these expectations, as it delivered an important contribution to institutionalising some of the most significant West African precursors to the R2P norm.

The 2008 ECOWAS Conflict Prevention Framework (ECPF), which aims "to provide a framework for identifying, designing and implementing programs and activities for operation and structural conflict prevention in ECOWAS member states," directly refers to R2P (ECOWAS 2019). In Article 41, it states that ECOWAS has the power and the legitimacy "to intervene to protect human security in three distinct ways," namely the responsibility to prevent, the responsibility to react, and the responsibility to rebuild (ECOWAS 2008). The inclusion of provisions that are this directly related to R2P in constitutive regional documents is something that was not seen in the EU case and it represents a very strong indicator of formal internalisation of the norm of R2P.

As was addressed in the contextual chapter of this book, there are strong similarities between the language in different provisions of ECOWAS' 1999 Mechanism, 2001 Protocol, and 2008 Framework and that of R2P as it was adopted at the UN in 2005. The language contained in the 1999 Protocol of "humanitarian disaster" and "massive violations of human rights and the rule of law" (ECOWAS 1999) and in the 2001 Protocol – Article 45 (1) speaking of "massive violation of Human Rights in a Member State." (ECOWAS 2001) – are roughly synonyms for mass atrocities. It is these mass atrocity crimes (genocide, war crimes, crimes against humanity, and ethnic cleansing) against which R2P, as it was adopted at the UN World Summit in 2005, aims to offer protection. The contextual chapter noted that the essential difference here is the level of specification, with ECOWAS' instruments, adopted around the turn of the century, broadly phrasing these massive human rights violations, while the R2P norm specified them a few years later. What is important to note is that ECOWAS' protocols are activated in occasions where R2P does not apply, such as the "unconstitutional maintenance or seizure of power" (Article 1c, ECOWAS 2001). So, in this sense, ECOWAS' protocols are more far-reaching and inclusive than R2P ever could be, as the scope of the latter had to be narrowed to ensure consensus at the global level.

Two officers of the West Africa Network for Peacebuilding (WANEP), a leading regional peacebuilding organisation that has over 500 members across West Africa and has a partnership with ECOWAS, argued that ECOWAS' impact on the norm-building of R2P has consequences for how the norm in the region can be analysed. According to them, ECOWAS would rarely use the R2P discourse or invoke R2P as a reason to become involved in a particular crisis. Instead, it would refer to its own human rights provisions in its protocols and frameworks (WANEP Policy Officers 2019). It would therefore be unproductive to look for the use of specific 'R2P discourse' in the region as a benchmark to assess the regional internalisation of the R2P norm. Taking this discourse aspect into consideration, it would be particularly important to assess how the locally applied language converges with or diverges from the global R2P discourse and if ECOWAS' actions are in line with R2P's prescriptions.

One of the interviewees, an ECOWAS Commission policy officer, similarly argued that my original research question of how ECOWAS has internalised R2P should be turned upside down: rather than asking how and to what extent ECOWAS has internalised R2P, one should look at how ECOWAS has inspired and contributed to the norm-building of R2P (ECOWAS Commission Policy Officer 2019). Another ECOWAS official added to that that ECOWAS had been leading normative developments on the African continent, as its protocols and practices influenced the adoption of African Union (AU) documents and principles, such as its well-known non-indifference principle enshrined in its Constitutive Act (ECOWAS Commission Official 2020). ECOWAS' norm entrepreneurship in this regard has also been acknowledged by the UN. In the 2011 report on "The role of regional and subregional arrangements in implementing the responsibility to protect", the Secretary General noted that "Regional and subregional bodies, such as the Economic Community of West African States (ECOWAS), the African Union and the Organization for Security and Cooperation in Europe (OSCE), were in the vanguard of international efforts to develop both the principles of protection and the practical tools for implementing them. The United Nations has followed their lead" (UN 2011, 2). ECOWAS' interventions in Liberia and Sierra Leone were also mentioned in the 2001 report of the International Commission on Intervention and State Sovereignty (ICISS), arguably R2P's 'founding document' (International Commission on Intervention and State Sovereignty et al. 2001).

Unfortunately, there is a lack of empirical information on how West African norm entrepreneurs influenced the R2P norm at the global level. It is evident that UN Secretary General Annan, coming from Ghana, was a crucial norm entrepreneur from the region. He was shaped by the experiences in his own region in the 1980s and 1990s, where civil wars and continuous political instability unsettled the lives of many. Another event that had a big impact on Annan was the Rwandan genocide. He was chief of UN peacekeeping at the time and he would later call the genocide "a very painful and traumatic experience" both for himself and the UN (PBS Frontline 2004). The sense of failure that Annan experienced first over Rwanda and later over Srebrenica made him determined to make the UN equipped to prevent future genocides. That determination powerfully inspired his norm entrepreneurship for R2P (Thakur and Weiss 2009). Besides Annan, accounts of the World Summit 2005 negotiations mention that Africa as a whole was supportive of R2P, evidenced by the Ezulwini Consensus adopted by the African Union (AU) in March 2005, which included a cautious endorsement of R2P (Bellamy 2009, 80). Specific states are mentioned as well as supporters of R2P in the 2005 negotiations, such as Rwanda, South Africa, Tanzania, and Ghana, although specifics about their lobbying activities are lacking for most of these (Bellamy 2009). In any case, according to Bellamy (2009), Ghana was thus already a West African R2P norm entrepreneur before the norm was adopted in 2005. The state has continued its advocacy of the norm ever since, both nationally, through the adoption of a Peace Council and various other institutions, and regionally and globally, through its advocacy for the institution of the R2P national focal point (WANEP Policy Officers 2019).

Besides the provisions in its protocols and frameworks that are directly relevant to R2P, ECOWAS also has a number of institutions that operate in this area. The ECOWAS Warning and Response Network (ECOWARN) is one of them. ECOWARN is ECOWAS' sub-regional peace and security observation system that was established by the 1999 Mechanism and is operated by the ECOWAS Early Warning Department. ECOWARN is unique in the sense that it is bottom-up and driven by grassroots participation of civil society organisations (CSOs), led by WANEP. The system is mostly focused on state instability, civil unrest, and criminality. None of the indicators is specifically related to mass atrocity prevention, although some of them do speak to identity-based violence (Traore 2016). The inclusion of specific mass atrocity prevention indicators could make ECOWARN more relevant for R2P purposes. Given the fact that the institutional infrastructure is already in place, adding these indicators would be a cost-effective way to contribute to R2P internalisation in the region. This would mostly contribute to the internalisation of the responsibility to prevent. The ability to take preventive measures in R2P cases depends after all on accurate and timely information. It is exactly that kind of information that ECOWARN, when equipped with specific mass atrocity prevention indicators, could supply.

Given West Africa's early experience with protocols and instruments similar to R2P, it should come as no surprise that all ECOWAS member states agreed to the norm of R2P at the 2005 World Summit (UN General Assembly 2005). Member states have since then reaffirmed their support during the annual dialogues on R2P in the UN General Assembly (UNGA). Nigeria, the most powerful state in the region and probably the most important driving force behind ECOWAS, expressed its support for R2P during the UNGA debate on R2P in 2009: "Today's debate should not have the effect of rolling back, weakening or undermining the 2005 consensus, but should rather aim at strengthening that commitment to ensuring the more effective implementation of the R2P" (Nigeria 2009). It also reminded the audience of the African roots of R2P, such as article 4(h) of the AU Constitutive Act, the ECOMOG interventions that helped to rescue trapped populations and ECOWAS' early warning zones. A few years later, Nigeria appointed an R2P focal point and opened a Human Rights desk in its military (Nigeria 2018). Finally, the state has called on the international community to help it in its efforts to protect its people against Boko Haram, the jihadist terrorist organisation based in north-eastern Nigeria, an act which is consistent with pillar II of R2P, namely invoking the assistance of the international community to help a state meet its primary responsibility to protect (International Coalition for the Responsibility to Protect 2015).

Ghana has been a strong supporter of R2P in the region and it has led efforts together with Australia to make R2P a formal agenda item of the UNGA, in which it has succeeded. In 2018, the first formal debate on R2P in many years (the last dated 2009, after which there were yearly informal dialogues on R2P in the UNGA) was held in the UNGA (UN General Assembly 2018). In 2010, Ghana and Denmark established the national R2P Focal Points initiative, in collaboration with the GCR2P. The latter sees Ghana as an R2P norm entrepreneur as it

> "facilitated the spread of mass atrocity prevention values internationally, and particularly among its West African neighbours, by launching the Global Network of R2P Focal Points and hosting the third meeting of the network in Accra in 2013. In the two years following that meeting, four additional West African states-Ivory Coast, Guinea, Liberia, and Sierra Leone, have signalled their deepening commitment to mass atrocity prevention through the appointment of R2P Focal Points"
>
> (Streitfeld-Hall 2015, 8)

This norm dynamic is reminiscent of Finnemore and Sikkink's (1998) notion of a norms cascade, in which more and more states in the international community start to adopt (aspects of) a norm after initial advocacy efforts by a norm entrepreneur, in this case Ghana. Ghana's role as regional norm entrepreneur on R2P has also been recognised by WANEP (GhanaWeb 2015).

Smaller states in the region have expressed their support for R2P as well. In 2013, in its contribution to that year's UNGA informal interactive dialogue on

R2P, Togo stated that even in the absence of judicial obligations, it was convinced "here exists a moral obligation to provide societies with the means of protecting populations against criminal atrocities" (Togo 2013). The country has contributed troops to regional efforts to manage crises in the sub-region, such as those in Liberia, Ivory Coast, and Guinea-Bissau (Togo 2013). Guinea-Bissau expressed its support for R2P during the 2009 UNGA debate on R2P: it stated the concept of R2P was not open for renegotiation, and that the focus should now be on implementation. It also subscribed to the notion of sovereignty as responsibility with reference to Dr. Deng, who pioneered in the 1990s with the notion that sovereignty comes with responsibility, both domestically and internationally (Deng et al. 1996). In line with his work, Guinea-Bissau expressed that sovereignty should not be simply understood as the ability of a sovereign state to do what it wants within its territorial limits, but rather as going hand in hand with a responsibility towards its citizens (Guinea-Bissau 2009). Interestingly, the state later became itself a country of concern, due to a coup in 2012 and an election crisis in 2016/2017 (Hirsch 2012). Sierra Leone backed R2P during the 2009 UNGA debate on R2P. Its representative explained this support was based on the country's own history, where the Revolutionary United Front (RUF)-led rebellion had resulted in atrocities for over a decade. Sierra Leone referred to the African roots of the norm as well and it emphasised the importance of prevention (Sierra Leone 2009). The R2P frame it used was state-centred, in the sense that it attributed atrocities to the actions of non-state actors, with the country as a victim.

ECOWAS member states, both big and small, have thus supported the norm of R2P in the post-World Summit period, both rhetorically, in the UN General Assembly debates, and through policy action, such as through the appointment of R2P focal points, and, as will be seen in the case studies, through participation in regional diplomatic initiatives and military interventions.

When reflecting on the above discussion through the lens of local norm construction, a few observations can be made. First, West African norm entrepreneurs such as Annan and Obasanjo built their advocacy for R2P (Annan) and some of its ECOWAS precursors (Obasanjo) on their experiences with a region frequently disrupted by civil war and the commission of atrocities. This means that the approaches they were suggesting should be able to speak to other localities where there is a threat of or actual commission of atrocities as well. Importantly, the ECOWAS' regional precursors to R2P showed a degree of success, providing a firm legal and institutional basis for ECOWAS to intervene in intrastate conflicts with a high risk of atrocities. This success has been recognised by the UN, among other actors (UN 2011). Thirdly, it was recognised that local norm construction would be facilitated if some local actors emerged as global norm entrepreneurs. In the case of ECOWAS and West Africa, this role was clearly embodied by former UN Secretary General Kofi Annan. As a Ghanaian diplomat, he was profoundly shaped by the experiences in his region, which together with other experiences, such as overseeing UN peacekeeping efforts at the time of the genocide in Rwanda, powerfully informed his global advocacy to tackle mass atrocities. It was *inter alia* through Annan's norm entrepreneurship that some of the West African protocols and practices came to constitute the building blocks of the global R2P norm.

Against this background, it is time to further investigate ECOWAS' actions in various crisis situations, and how and to what extent these conform with R2P expectations. Given the way that ECOWAS and its member states responded to R2P and the experience the organisation built with its own protocols and mechanisms prior to 2005, one can come up with some expectations of how ECOWAS will likely respond to cases. The adoption of the 2008 ECOWAS Conflict Prevention Framework, which includes explicit references to R2P, and ECOWAS' tradition of shuttle-diplomacy in (pre-)crisis situations create the expectation of a strong engagement through the responsibility to prevent. Concerning the responsibility to react, one can expect the application of sanctions, as ECOWAS has done so for many years in crisis situations. Regarding the use of force, the other application of the responsibility to react, there is a history of interventions in the region through ECOMOG. While occasionally there has been some criticism of these interventions from smaller member states, the use of force seems to be generally less hotly contested in ECOWAS than in the EU. Concerning the responsibility to rebuild, as was noted in the previous chapter, many of the relevant measures have a prevention-logic underpinning them, so this could position ECOWAS well to engage with this component of R2P.

The 2009/2010 Guinean crisis

On 28 September 2009, opposition supporters organised a demonstration in a stadium in Conakry, the capital of Guinea, to protest against junta leader Captain Dadis Camara's reported intention to break his promise to hand over power to civilian rule in the January 2010 elections (Streitfeld-Hall 2015). Although the protests were peaceful, security forces opened fire on the crowd, and they committed widespread rape and sexual violence. Their actions resulted in over 150 deaths and 1200 injuries. An international commission of inquiry that investigated the massacre reported that members of Camara's junta had prior knowledge of the planned demonstration and had incited the security forces to commit violence against civilians (Global Centre for the Responsibility to Protect 2019). Deputy prosecutor of the ICC, Fatou Bensouda, stated after a preliminary investigation into the incident that the killing of opposition supporters amounted to a crime against humanity (ICC 2010).

Guinea had already triggered increased regional and international attention in December 2008, when, following President Conte's death, Captain Moussa Dadis Camara seized control of the government through a coup. The AU and ECOWAS quickly suspended the country's membership as both organisations have provisions against the unconstitutional change of government in their respective constitution and protocols (Hartmann 2013, 37). ECOWAS appointed a Special Representative to monitor the situation and, even though

Guinea was suspended, engage with junta leaders (Kikoler 2015). ECOWAS and the AU established the International Contact Group on Guinea (ICG-G) to coordinate regional and international diplomatic efforts. The ICG-G also included the UN, the EU, African Security Council members, La Francophonie, and the Mano River Union. The ICG members were able to persuade Captain Camera to transition to civilian rule and he publicly affirmed he would not stand in the 2010 elections (Kikoler 2015). In the months after the coup, Camara's rule started to be increasingly repressive, with serious restrictions on opposition activity, a ban on political gatherings and demonstrations and arbitrary detentions (Kikoler 2015). This repression found its climax in the September 2009 massacre in the stadium in Conakry.

Kikoler (2015) correctly notes that Guinea committed to uphold R2P at the 2005 World Summit and therewith accepted the primary responsibility to protect Guinea's populations against mass atrocity crimes. This responsibility shifted to the country's junta after it came to power through the December 2008 coup. In practice, upholding R2P should have meant ensuring that Guinea's security forces exercised restraint, abided by international law and standards on the use of force, and protected all Guineans irrespective of their ethnic identity (Witt 2013; Kikoler 2015). By committing crimes against humanity, the security forces manifestly failed to uphold their responsibility to protect. The ruling junta was demonstrably complicit in the crimes and appeared both unable and unwilling to tackle the risk of ethnic violence and prevent further instances of atrocity crimes after the massacre. The massacre in Conakry heightened the need for preventive diplomacy efforts that had been initiated by domestic, regional, and international actors after the coup. Now that Guinea failed to uphold its primary responsibility to protect, it was up to the international community to step in to protect the Guinean people. For external actors, it meant that their goal was no longer only to restore the constitutional order in Guinea. The prevention of a recurrence of atrocity crimes became a priority too.

ECOWAS took the lead in responding to the September 2009 massacre. In October 2009, Nigeria organised an extraordinary session of the Authority of Heads and Government of ECOWAS to discuss the latest developments in Guinea (ECOWAS 2009). The communique it released after the summit adopted a frame with a clear focus on the committed atrocities, which is visible in the following excerpt: "The Summit expressed deep concern over *the mass violation of human rights and humanitarian law* in Guinea and roundly *condemned the brutal acts of massacre, rape and other atrocities* perpetrated by the security forces under the authority of the CNDD against unarmed women and civilians on 28 September 2009. It characterised the acts of impunity and the rapidly deteriorating political, security and human rights situation in Guinea as seriously damaging to the democratic process in the country and a real threat to the peace, security and stability of the region" (ECOWAS 2009, 3, emphasis added). The organisation thus condemned the violence of the security forces and advocated for the establishment of an international commission of inquiry. After the September 2009 massacre, which took the international community by surprise, it became crucial to prevent further instances of atrocities. Condemning the atrocities showed that, from now on, the international community would be watching, while ECOWAS' advocacy for the establishment of an international commission of inquiry raised the spectre of accountability, which is relevant to the accountability aspect of the responsibility to react. These constitute crucial measures to prevent further instances of atrocities, consistent with the responsibility to prevent. ECOWAS also appointed a mediator "to re-establish dialogue among the Guinean political actors" (ECOWAS 2009, 4; Kikoler 2015, 310). Furthermore, it imposed an arms embargo on Guinea and, as co-chair of the ICG-G, it coordinated the approach of group members, much more so than the other co-chair, the AU (Streitfeld-Hall 2015). Other international actors followed ECOWAS' lead. The United States, for instance, implemented targeted travel bans and suspended aid to Guinea while endorsing the ECOWAS arms embargo. The arms embargo was a direct response to the September 2009 massacre and aimed to reduce the capacity of the regime to commit similar atrocities in the future. The embargo can therefore be seen as an important indicator of internalisation of the sanctions component of the responsibility to react.

In December 2009, Captain Camara was shot by a lieutenant who feared Camara would assign all blame for the September 2009 massacre to him while he was being investigated by the ICC. Camara then had to leave the country to receive medical treatment. This led to the appointment of Konate, a popular former defence minister, as interim leader. Konate's appointment created an unexpected opening for preventive diplomacy, as contrary to Camara, this was a leader the international community could work with (Kikoler 2015). ECOWAS mediator Blaise Compaore engaged in shuttle diplomacy together with his UN and AU counterparts to ensure that Camara stayed outside the country, to get Konate to agree to a transitional government and to secure his commitment that none of the junta members would stand in elections to be held in six months (Kikoler 2015, 313). The diplomatic efforts were successful as it led to the signing of the Ouagadougou Accord in January 2010, in which the junta pledged to restore the country to civilian rule, establish a national unity government, hold elections within six months, ensure that the army maintained discipline and kept the peace, and that Camara would take time to recover outside of Guinea.

The next focus was on creating an environment conducive to peaceful elections. Tailored to atrocity prevention, priorities were to deter future crimes by stressing accountability and to ensure the security forces would exercise restraint. The preventive efforts of ECOWAS and the other international actors together with Konate's responsible leadership led to a peaceful first round of elections in June 2010. Tensions built up again, however, in the lead up to the second round, as supporters of the two remaining candidates already started to doubt the integrity of the upcoming elections (Kikoler 2015, 315). ECOWAS, the AU, and the UN continued their shuttle diplomacy to reduce tensions between the two political camps, which resulted in the signing of a pact on

3 September 2010 by the two presidential candidates outlining their intention to hold a peaceful election. The vote was postponed several times for multiple reasons, with each delay escalating tensions. The UN expressed its concerns about the security forces' heavy-handedness in maintaining public order, which included indiscriminate shooting at unarmed civilians. Interim leader Konate performed a crucial role at this time by visiting military barracks to urge the soldiers to remain neutral (Kikoler 2015, 316). Other religious, ethnic, and political leaders also urged calm, such as the interim prime minister who emphasised the importance of public order in the period before the election and made an appeal to the presidential candidates to control their language and their supporters. The AU, ECOWAS, and the UN had moved the presidential candidates themselves to stress at key moments the need for calm and to deplore deadly clashes that broke out in Conakry. To Kikoler (2015, 317), the fact that the situation did not deteriorate was the result of a strong desire on the part of Guineans for a peaceful transition, demonstrated by Guinean civil society campaigning for peaceful and fair elections, and consistent international pressure on the presidential candidates and the military to uphold R2P. This shuttle diplomacy of ECOWAS, together with other international actors, is a strong sign of the implementation of R2P preventive efforts in practice, and therefore of internalisation of the preventive aspect of R2P.

Generally, ECOWAS has shown signs of internalisation of R2P in the case of Guinea. After the coup of December 2008, it engaged with the country to make sure it would transition back to constitutional rule. In this period, ECOWAS did not take specific atrocity prevention measures as the junta regime did not yet seem to pose a threat in this regard. When the September 2009 stadium massacre proved that the junta was capable of committing atrocities, ECOWAS adjusted its approach. Restoring Guinea to constitutional rule remained a priority, but this was now accompanied by measures to ensure accountability for crimes and to prevent future atrocities. ECOWAS publicly condemned the atrocities against civilians and imposed an arms embargo on Guinea corresponding to the 'sanctions component' of the responsibility to react. ECOWAS' shuttle diplomacy was crucial in signalling to Guinea that it was being scrutinised and in helping prepare the country for peaceful elections. These are important measures to prevent future atrocity crimes, and they are thus indicative of internalisation of the responsibility to prevent. ECOWAS' active engagement and the pressure it put on the transitional authorities in Guinea to ensure a peaceful climate in the lead up to the elections have definitely contributed to further atrocity prevention after the 2009 stadium massacre and are therefore indicative of R2P internalisation by the regional organisation (Kikoler 2015).

The 2010/2011 Ivory Coast election crisis

When Ivory Coast prepared for its 2010 presidential elections, this came against the backdrop of a turbulent recent past. Ivory Coast's economy struggled in the 1990s, while politically, ethno-nationalism carried the day. Ivorian President

Bedie coined the term *ivorité* (the quality of being "a true Ivorian") and codified this into law, meaning that political candidates and voters must be born of two native Ivorian parents (Ipinyomi 2012, 157). This move fostered xenophobia and in effect disenfranchised most of the north of Ivory Coast, where ethno-linguistic groups like the Malinke and Dioula, despite having lived in the country for centuries, did not qualify as 'true Ivorians'. These ethno-political tensions and a failed coup led to an outbreak of civil war in Ivory Coast in 2002 (Ipinyomi 2012). UN and ECOWAS peacekeepers, together with French troops, eventually managed to separate the warring parties. The civil war had heavily divided the country though, with a rebel-held north and a government-controlled south (Bassett and Strauss 2011). A series of peace accords eventually culminated in the Ouagadougou Peace Accord of March 2007, in which, among other things, the parties agreed on the planning of elections. These elections were postponed multiple times, until 2010.

The 2010 Ivorian presidential elections started off peacefully. The first round, held on October 31, proceeded orderly with a high turnout of 84 percent and it was certified by the UN operation in the country (Bassett and Straus 2011, 132). Incumbent President Gbagbo came in first place with 38 percent, while former Prime Minister Ouattara came second with 32 percent. The second round, held on November 28, took place in a much more volatile context. Gbagbo's and Ouattara's supporters engaged in violent clashes. All the same, over 80 percent of the electorate turned out and EU and the UN observers found the election, on balance, to be fair and transparent. The Independent Electoral Commission (IEC) announced the provisional results on December 2, declaring that Ouattara had won with 54 percent of the vote. The Constitutional Council, however, which was headed by a Gbagbo loyalist, invalidated the vote in seven regions in the north (where Ouattara had clear majorities) "because of serious irregularities in the integrity of the poll" (Bassett and Straus 2011, 132). According to the Council, this resulted in an election victory by Gbagbo with 51.45 percent of the vote. The UN special representative, Choi, disagreed with the Council's proclamation and his office certified the IEC tally based on the office's independent count. The situation led both contestants to claim the presidency, to the concern of the international community (Bassett and Straus 2011).

ECOWAS quickly decided that Ouattara was the legitimate winner of the elections and that Gbagbo had to stand down. ECOWAS thereby recognised the decision of the IEC and it consequently suspended Ivory Coast's membership. These decisions were communicated in its Communique of 7 December 2010 (ECOWAS 2010a). Its decision to recognise Ouattara as President-elect gained international credibility as the UNSC issued a Press Statement backing the ECOWAS position (Hunt 2016). ECOWAS' Communique of 24 December 2010 marked a shift in discourse, which partly reflected changes on the ground in Ivory Coast. While the 7 December Communique focused exclusively on the electoral crisis in the country, the 24 December Communique widened its attention to the deteriorating security environment and the perpetration of atrocities. This is evidenced by quotes as

> "the Heads of State and Government expressed deep concern over the fast deteriorating political and security environment in Cote d'lvoire characterised by escalating violence, the use of mercenaries to perpetrate atrocities, loss of life, and the heightening of ethnic tensions, as well as the threat of civil war, with its negative consequences on regional peace and security," and "they expressed deep concern over the unacceptably high number of lives lost since 7 December 2010 and warned all those responsible that they will face international trial for human rights violations at the earliest opportunity" (ECOWAS 2010b)

The 24 December Communique thus started to frame the crisis in Ivory Coast more in terms of an 'atrocity crisis'. The statement is reminiscent of the one that was released after the 2009 stadium massacre in Guinea, in the sense that violence was condemned and accountability for those responsible was raised. These are important diplomatic steps under the accountability-aspect of the responsibility to react and the responsibility to prevent, as they make (would be-) perpetrators aware of international scrutiny and accountability, raising the costs of committing further atrocities. ECOWAS also communicated to Gbagbo that if he did not stand down, he could expect "legitimate force" (BBC 2010). Some regional states distanced themselves from that statement, however, such as Ghana, which expressed its desire to stay neutral (Cocks and Kpodo 2011). These divisions weakened the signalling function of ECOWAS' 'use of force threat', which falls under the military component of the responsibility to react.

The organisation proceeded by taking diplomatic steps, as it organised a joint AU-ECOWAS visit to Abidjan to negotiate a deal. This diplomatic mission did not succeed in ending the stalemate, however. In March 2011, ECOWAS called on the UNSC to adopt strict sanctions against Gbagbo and bolster the mandate of the UN peacekeeping mission in the country, "enabling the mission to use all necessary means to protect life and property and to facilitate the immediate transfer of power to Mr. Alassane Ouattara" (Reuters 2011). Stronger action was deemed necessary as diplomatic steps did not lead to desired results and violence from both sides resulted in over a thousand casualties (UN News 2011). One of the problems with the diplomatic effort was that there were some disagreements within the five-person High-Level Panel that was set up by the AU to resolve the crisis. Although the Panel had a clear mandate from the AU that it formulate its proposals on the basis of prevailing AU and ECOWAS declarations and the UN Secretary General's five principles that should guide the Panel's work, members showed a lack of common ground on the task at hand, especially on the question whether Gbagbo should directly resign (Babbitt 2014, 9–10). The panel frustrated the work of ECOWAS, in a crisis which fell within its remit. Tensions came particularly to the fore in February 2011, when the panel members visited Ivory Coast without the West African representative Blaise Compaoré and without the president of the ECOWAS Commission, Gbeho. ECOWAS expressed its disapproval in a very critical communiqué issued on 22 February 2011 (International Crisis Group 2011, 14; ECOWAS 2011).

By this time, the human rights and security situation at Ivory Coast had drastically deteriorated. As clear-cut as the picture looked electorally, with the overwhelming majority of the international community recognising Ouattara as the country's new president, making Gbagbo's position obstructionist, the picture on the ground looked differently. Here, there was no 'good side' to be discerned, as both pro-Gbagbo troops and pro-Ouattara fighters committed serious human rights abuses, clearly violating international humanitarian law in their armed campaigns. These abuses were generally strongly ethnically motivated. Human Rights Watch documented the human rights violations from both sides. Pro-Gbagbo troops and allied militias targeted real and perceived supporters of Ouattara and singled out immigrants from neighbouring West African countries as well. The violence against West African immigrants was instigated by Gbagbo's "youth minister", Goudé, who publicly called on 25 February 2011 for "real Ivorians" to denounce foreigners (Human Rights Watch. 2011a). In early March, the Burkina Faso ambassador received violent threats aimed at his nationals living in Ivory Coast from a militant pro-Gbagbo group. Gbagbo's forces also abducted members of Ouattara's party, fired at peaceful demonstrations, engaged in sexual violence against women and girls, committed extrajudicial executions and used excessive and indiscriminate force more generally (Human Rights Watch 2011a). Human Rights Watch concluded that the atrocities committed by Gbagbo's forces amounted to crimes against humanity (Human Rights Watch 2011a). Pro-Ouattara forces committed reprisal killings of civilians and extrajudicial executions against detained pro-Gbagbo forces. Prisoners were tortured as well. A later Human Rights Watch report documented rape and other sexual violence, the recruitment of child soldiers, and a mass killing in the place Duékoué, in which hundreds were massacred. The organisation concluded that the transgressions of pro-Ouattara fighters amounted to crimes against humanity and war crimes (Human Rights Watch 2011b). While atrocities were being committed by both sides, the military status quo started to shift at the end of March 2011.

Forces loyal to Ouattara started a country-wide offensive on 28 March 2011. While the offensive was successful in the sense that Ouattara's forces quickly gained terrain across the country, this came at a high cost: mass atrocities were again reported with hundreds killed and thousands displaced (Babbitt 2014; Bassett and Straus 2011). On 30 March 2011, the UN Security Council adopted Resolution 1975, recalling its authorisation, and stressing its full support given to the UNOCI (the UN force present in Ivory Coast since the country's civil war) "to use all necessary means to carry out its mandate to protect civilians under imminent threat of physical violence" (UN Security Council 2011). The battle for Abidjan, the capital of Ivory Coast, started on 1 April. Ten days later, operations ended, after French and UN attack helicopters destroyed the heavy weapons encircling the presidential residence and the Republican Forces arrested Gbagbo (Bassett and Straus 2011).

The question is to what extent ECOWAS acted in line with R2P's prescriptions in the Ivorian crisis, i.e. to what extent it showed signs of internalisation of R2P in this specific case. First, it is important to note that the crisis started as an electoral crisis and not directly as a crisis involving atrocity crimes. However, given the country's recent history, characterised by civil war, atrocities, and postponed elections, concerns over potential atrocities when Gbagbo refused to step down were not far-fetched. As was noted, ECOWAS was quick in taking diplomatic steps, backing Ouattara's election victory and suspending Ivory Coast's membership based on the 2001 Protocol. This represents the application of sanctions as consistent with the responsibility to react. When Gbagbo persevered, ECOWAS leaders warned it would consider the use of force as a last resort to resolve the crisis. The organisation eventually did not follow through on this threat, which has been linked to concerns over risk to West African nationals living in Ivory Coast, ECOWAS' financial constraints, and the fact that the head of ECOWAS at the time, Nigerian President Goodluck Jonathan, was preoccupied with his re-election campaign (Bassett and Straus 2011). This comes to show that ECOWAS has not fully internalised the military component of the responsibility to react. Had it done so, it would not have reneged from its threat to use force to address the Ivorian crisis. ECOWAS was instrumental, though, in laying the groundwork for UN Security Council Resolution 1975, which included a use of force-mandate, as it adopted its own resolution a few days earlier calling on the Security Council to strengthen the UN's mandate in Ivory Coast (ECOWAS 2011).

One problematic aspect of ECOWAS' response to the crisis from an atrocity prevention point of view is that the organisation did not explicitly condemn the violence perpetrated by pro-Ouattara fighters. In a March 2011 resolution, ECOWAS condemned the deliberate targeting of and the violence against civilians and personnel of the UN Operation in Ivory Coast (ECOWAS 2011). The resolution puts the blame for the crisis on Gbagbo, due to his resistance to accept the elections outcome, which seems, given the UN certified election results, sensible enough. In line with those findings, the resolution calls for "more stringent international targeted sanctions against Laurent Gbagbo and his associates" (ECOWAS 2011). Whenever Ouattara is mentioned in the resolution, it is in the context of the election results and the need for Gbagbo to transfer power to Ouattara. Since his name is only mentioned in this context, the text of the resolution seems to suggest that the earlier mentioned deliberate targeting of and violence against civilians and UN personnel are all attributable to Gbagbo's forces and militias, which is not the case. The atrocities committed by pro-Ouattara fighters had by the time of the drafting of the resolution (late March 2011) been well documented by Human Rights Watch and other organisations. From a perspective of atrocity prevention, an inclusion of a call on both Gbagbo *and* Ouattara to reign their forces, to publicly condemn committed atrocities, and to stress accountability for these crimes should have been warranted in the resolution. It seems that the constitutional element of the Ivorian crisis, namely the resistance of Gbagbo to transfer power to his rival, took precedence in the response of ECOWAS to the crisis, also in the later stages when atrocities had been committed by both sides and this had been widely reported on. In this light, a parallel can be made with the EU's response to the Rohingya crisis in Myanmar, where the need to promote democracy came at the expense of applying an atrocity prevention lens in the lead up to the crisis. It therefore seems safe to say that regional organisations struggle with applying R2P and atrocity prevention when these norms compete with other norms.

To relate this back to the research question of this book, this finding has something to say about the 'to what extent' part of the research question. The response to the Ivory Coast crisis seems to suggest that ECOWAS has not internalised R2P all the way through, given that when atrocity prevention considerations compete with other considerations, the former do not necessarily prevail. Given R2P's origins in ECOWAS, in which it is more broadly conceived, and the unconstitutional maintenance of power is also a cause for concern and a justification for intervention (think of the 2001 Protocol), it is understandable that ECOWAS paid attention to this (ECOWAS 2001). However, the commission of atrocities is equally a trigger for regional involvement, so even given ECOWAS' protocols broader scope, it is problematic from an R2P point of view that the constitutional element of the crisis clearly prevailed over the need to address atrocities, whichever side they came from.

The 2012 Mali crisis

The Mali crisis started in 2012. A coup d'état was conducted in March 2012 which was soon followed by an Islamic insurgency in the north of the country. The coup makers were dissatisfied with the weak leadership of the country and the inability of the government to deal with an armed rebellion in the north, spearheaded by the Movement for National Liberation of Azawad (MNLA) (Karlsrud 2016, 786). The confusion that the coup d'état created was exploited by the MNLA, which, together with some armed Islamist groups, quickly won terrain in their advance south in the direct aftermath of the coup. In April 2012, the rebels declared the independence of the 'Republic of Azawad', and they imposed sharia law in northern Mali. The rebel insurgence forced over 400,000 people to flee their homes, becoming either internally displaced or finding refuge in neighbouring countries.

ECOWAS responded by denouncing the March coup and by urging the junta to relinquish power to the rightful government. It also appealed to the MNLA to lay down its arms (Haysom 2014, 4). On 30 March 2012, it imposed economic and diplomatic sanctions on Mali, while ECOWAS member states bordering Mali closed their borders, blocking the country's access to neighbouring seaports. Subsequently, ECOWAS focused on political negotiations to remove the military junta by sending a mediation team to Mali. Although the mediation process faced its setbacks, with the junta reasserting control at some point, it did result in the formation of a government of national unity in August 2012 (Haysom 2014, 4). The situation in Mali quickly deteriorated though, as fighting broke out between the MNLA and various other rebel groups and the former was side-lined by its Islamist allies. In a short period of time, all areas in the north were held by various Islamist groups. Soon after, international NGOs started reporting that war crimes were being committed by the Islamist groups, making the situation in northern Mali of R2P concern (Karlsrud 2016). Both ECOWAS and the AU have provisions in their respective protocols and constitution that allow the organisations to intervene in cases of 'mass human rights violations'. The threat that the Islamist groups posed to the territorial integrity of Mali and to regional security also formed an important motivation for ECOWAS and the AU to act. They prepared to intervene in northern Mali and they asked for a Security Council mandate for an African military force (Karlsrud 2016, 786). Progress on this front was, however, slow. One reason was that there was reluctance to help the coup-makers, while there were also disagreements on the political strategy between ECOWAS and the AU (Lacher and Tull 2013).

The difficulty external actors faced was that human rights violations were both committed by the different groups in the north and by government forces serving the coup-makers in Bamako. Amnesty International reported that the latter included the repression of opponents to the military coup, through illegal detention of several politicians and the absence of condemning or responding to physical assaults on political leaders of civil society demonstrating against the coup (Amnesty International 2012, 12). In its fight against the MNLA, the Malian army also indiscriminately attacked populations and civilian targets in violation of international humanitarian law. These actions included indiscriminate bombings, extra-judicial killings, and ill-treatments of prisoners (Amnesty International 2012, 13). The human rights violations committed by the MNLA and Islamist groups in the north of Mali included sexual violence against women and female minors, deliberate and arbitrary killings, the recruitment of child soldiers, and the imposition of Sharia law (Amnesty International 2012). The fact that human rights violations occurred at both sides meant that any outside intervention would be marred by dilemmas.

Despite these dilemmas, ECOWAS developed a concept of operations together with the UN Secretary General, which received endorsement from the AU in November 2012. The UN Security Council subsequently endorsed the operation on 20 December 2012. The resolution authorised the deployment of an African-led International Support Mission in Mali (AFISMA) and it captured the stated desire of ECOWAS and the AU to be given a strong mandate to deal with atrocities unfolding on the ground and "to defend the unity and territorial integrity of Mali" (UN Security Council 2012a). AFISMA received the mandate, among others,

(a) To support the Malian authorities in recovering the areas in the north of its territory under the control of terrorist, extremist, and armed groups and in reducing the threat posed by terrorist organisations, including AQIM, MUJWA, and associated extremist groups, while taking appropriate measures to reduce the impact of military action upon the civilian population;
(b) To support the Malian authorities in their primary responsibility to protect the Population.

(UN Security Council 2012b)

The deployment of AFISMA was eventually delayed as it was overtaken by events on the ground. In early January 2013, the Islamist groups that had conquered the north moved south at alarming speed, which prompted the Malian government, fearing the loss of its capital Bamako, to ask France to intervene (Karlsrud 2016, 787).

France launched Operation Serval, in which Chadian troops also participated, which was successful in liberating the north of Mali from Islamist groups. A few weeks later, AFISMA was deployed, month ahead of its anticipated deployment in September 2013. According to the African Institute for Peacebuilding and Conflict Transformation (AIPECT), the French military intervention and AFISMA "was most significant in bringing about a rapid and decisive military end to the conflict in northern Mali" (AIPECT 2018). The crisis management mechanisms adopted in Mali by AFISMA – which in July 2013 was incorporated in the UN mission MINUSMA – were, however, not adequate "in broadly dealing with the issues in contention; governance failure, political exclusionism and uneven distribution of national wealth, manipulation of ethnic and religious differences for political ends, abuse and violation of citizens' rights, among others." So, while the French and AFISMA managed to put out the fire (dislodging the terrorist groups, recapturing northern Mali, and re-establishing democratic governance in the country), they failed to address what had caused the fire in the first place (AIPECT 2018). This would then also explain the resurgence of hostilities in northern Mali that again threaten the stability of the country and the West African sub-region at large.

When assessing signs of R2P internalisation by ECOWAS in the case of Mali, a few things stand out. It both condemned the military campaign of the MNLA with its Islamist allies in the north and the subsequent coup in Bamako. It also specifically condemned atrocities committed by both sides. These are relevant measures in the light of the responsibility to prevent. By condemning and exposing perpetrators of atrocities, the hope is they will be deterred from committing these crimes in the future. Sanctions were put in place to signal disapproval about the coup and they were relieved when the junta expressed its willingness to take steps to restore Mali's constitutional order. ECOWAS also prepared for a military intervention, but this faced delays. The critique that AFISMA, to which ECOWAS strongly contributed, failed to effectively deal with the root causes of the Mali crisis, such as governance failure and political exclusionism, does have implications for the assessment of ECOWAS' internalisation of the responsibility to rebuild component of R2P. Although ECOWAS' long-term commitment to the stabilisation efforts in Mali is important for the future of the country, these efforts have so far insufficiently addressed the root causes of the conflict that led to atrocities. At least based on the Mali case, it can be concluded that ECOWAS has only internalised the responsibility to rebuild component of R2P to a limited extent.

Case reflections and comparisons

Formal support

The different cases have provided important insights into how and to what extent ECOWAS and its member states have internalised R2P. Generally, it can be observed that ECOWAS actively engages with atrocity crises in the West African region. It already started this involvement in the late 1980s, with the Liberian civil war. This activism was recognised by the UN when Secretary General Ban Ki Moon acknowledged that ECOWAS was one of the leading regional players inspiring the development of R2P (UN 2011). It should therefore come as no surprise that all ECOWAS member states signed up to R2P at the 2005 World Summit and that different member states have reaffirmed their support during annual UNGA dialogues on R2P. ECOWAS also made direct reference to R2P in its 2008 ECPF (ECOWAS 2008), although it needs to be acknowledged that this document is generally not referred to during crisis situations in the ECOWAS region. Of all the ECOWAS member states, Ghana has most likely been the most significant R2P norm entrepreneur. Its pioneering efforts in setting up a Global Network of R2P Focal Points with Denmark in 2010 resulted in multiple ECOWAS member states appointing focal points of their own.

In the cases analysed above, it has become apparent that ECOWAS and its member states do not ordinarily use the 'R2P lexicon' when responding to atrocity situations. Instead, the organisation tends to refer to its own protocols and mechanisms, that predate the R2P norm. While this is understandable, it means that formal support for the R2P norm is less visible during crisis situations when compared to the EU.

Responsibility to prevent

The ECOWAS heads of state expressed their strong support for mediation and other diplomatic efforts to resolve the analysed crises, which reflects authoritative support for the responsibility to prevent (ECOWAS 2009; ECOWAS 2010a). This support for preventive measures was also previously institutionally expressed in the 2008 ECPF (ECOWAS 2008).

With regard to practice, in almost all of the cases, we have witnessed the conduct of shuttle-diplomacy in the early stages of tensions or a crisis, led by pre-eminent (ex-)leaders in the region or representatives of ECOWAS itself. This shuttle diplomacy is a key preventive measure, aiming to prevent volatile situations from spilling further out of control and in some cases to ensure the prevention of future violence and/or atrocities after initial violence. Once ECOWAS becomes engaged, it generally sustains this engagement for a prolonged period of time which is important to signal to the state in question there is regional commitment to domestic crises. At the same time, it signals to potential spoilers that they are being watched, which carries the potential to deter them from committing future atrocities and violent acts.

In the meantime, ECOWAS has made steps towards prioritising prevention more generally in its institutions. The adoption of the 2008 ECPF represented an important step in this direction. This should allow the organisation to step in much earlier in the conflict cycle and to engage in structural prevention as well, addressing the root causes that may lead to future violence. Equally, ECOWAS' early warning and response network ECOWARN has the potential of making an important contribution to the internalisation of the responsibility to prevent. The fact that ECOWARN receives significant bottom-up input from CSOs in the region led by WANEP is an important aiding factor in this respect. One factor that hampers ECOWARN from contributing significantly to the regional internalisation of the responsibility to prevent in practice is the absence of indicators that are specifically related to mass atrocity prevention (Traore 2016).

A critical note that was highlighted in the case studies section related to the crisis in Ivory Coast. Although ECOWAS in many ways followed the R2P playbook in this case, it did not explicitly condemn violence committed by Ouattara's followers. As ECOWAS recognised the election victory of the opposition leader and supported this position throughout the crisis, the constitutional element made it difficult to take a stance against Ouattara's followers when they too committed atrocities. This is a prime example of how two regional norms, zero tolerance for unconstitutional maintenance of power (which Gbagbo engaged in) and atrocity prevention clashed, in this case leading to the prioritisation of the former over the latter in ECOWAS' dealing with Ouattara and his followers. This does raise some important questions about the extent to which ECOWAS has internalised the responsibility to prevent.

Overall, one can conclude that ECOWAS has partially internalised the responsibility to prevent. The adoption of the ECPF and early mediation and shuttle-diplomacy are indicators of internalisation of the responsibility to prevent. One cannot conclude the organisation has fully internalised this component of R2P though, as there is still a need to integrate specific atrocity prevention indicators in ECOWARN. Besides, there is a need to improve case responses at times, as demonstrated during the Ivory Coast election crisis, in which ECOWAS failed to condemn atrocities committed by Ouattara fighters.

Responsibility to react

With regard to the responsibility to react, ECOWAS has showed important signs of internalising this aspect of R2P. In terms of authoritative support, it stresses legal accountability for atrocity crimes in most cases, such as seen in the cases of Guinea (support for the International Commission of Inquiry) and Ivory Coast (support for international trial for human rights violations), which constitutes important discursive support for the legal side of the responsibility to react (ECOWAS 2009; ECOWAS 2010a). In the case of Mali, while the heads of state did condemn atrocities committed in the north, there was no direct mentioning of legal accountability, potentially because ECOWAS was distracted by the coup taking place in the country at the same time and by the consequences of the armed rebellion in the north for Mali's territorial integrity (ECOWAS 2012). In its statements during crises, the ECOWAS Heads of State also express authoritative support for sanctions, and, on certain occasions, military action.

With regard to practice, parallel to diplomatic efforts that were discussed under the responsibility to prevent, and depending on the severity of the situation, the organisation puts sanctions in place in all cases, such as the suspension of membership of the regional body (Guinea, Ivory Coast, and Mali) (Hartmann 2013; ECOWAS 2010a; BBC 2012), the implementation of an arms embargo (Guinea) (Streitfeld-Hall 2015), travel bans (Guinea, Mali) (BBC 2009; Reuters 2012), border closures (Mali) (Look 2012), and asset freezes (Mali) (Reuters 2012). This demonstrates a strong practice in line with the sanctions component of the responsibility to react. These policy responses are, though based on ECOWAS' protocols and frameworks that go beyond R2P in their scope (e.g. they are also activated in cases where power is obtained or maintained by unconstitutional means, which falls outside the remits of R2P), what one may expect on the basis of R2P. Public condemnations, diplomatic steps and the issuance of sanctions are all part of the R2P toolkit, as outlined in the aspects of internalisation in the analytical framework of this book. In the case of Mali, ECOWAS even prepared a military intervention and asked the UN multiple times for authorisation before ECOWAS troops were eventually deployed as part of an AU-mission in 2013. This observation shows the willingness of ECOWAS to engage with the robust aspects of R2P and thus to internalise the military component of the responsibility to react. The question needs to be asked in this case, however, if atrocity crimes were the primary concern for ECOWAS to consider a military response. Based on the communiques the organisation released, the decision to intervene was more based on the violation of the territorial integrity of Mali and the threats that the rebels and Islamist groups posed to regional peace and security than in response to atrocities committed by them.

This question is also relevant more broadly, beyond the decision to intervene militarily. What is apparent is that ECOWAS' primary reason to become involved in the analysed cases was not because of concerns about atrocities. In Guinea, ECOWAS became involved after the December 2008 coup; in Ivory Coast, it stepped up its efforts after Gbagbo refused to step down after losing the November 2010 presidential elections; and in Mali, ECOWAS stepped in after the rebellion in the north and the coup in Bamako in 2012. What all crisis situations have in common is that they are characterised by an unconstitutional transfer or maintenance of power. The coups in Guinea and Mali and the military campaign by armed groups in the north of Mali amounted to unconstitutional seizures of power, whereas Gbagbo's refusal to hand over the presidency in Ivory Coast constituted an unconstitutional maintenance of power. These actions therefore violated provisions of the 2001 Protocol on Democracy and Good Governance, which declares "zero tolerance for power obtained or maintained by unconstitutional means" (ECOWAS 2001, Art. 1c). ECOWAS also referred to the violated provisions of the 2001 Protocol as a legitimation to become involved.

The fact that ECOWAS initially engaged with the analysed crises because of the unconstitutional seizure or maintenance of power does not mean that it was unconcerned about atrocities that happened down the line in these cases. Importantly, some of the steps taken by the organisation came in direct response to the commission of atrocities and therefore show that ECOWAS responds in R2P cases. For instance, regional condemnations and sanctions in the case of Guinea came in direct response to the September 2009 stadium massacre in Conakry. The massacre was later classified as a crime against humanity by the ICC and therefore constituted one of the crimes covered by R2P (ICC 2010). Another example of a response to atrocities is the 24 December 2010 Communique in which ECOWAS expressed concern over the unacceptably high number of lives lost in Ivory Coast and stressed accountability measures (international trials) for human rights violations (ECOWAS 2010b). The involvement of ECOWAS in the analysed crises shows again its broad mandate, which ranges from the maintenance of regional peace and security to the defence of principles of democracy and good governance and the protection of human rights and the rules of international humanitarian law (ECOWAS 1993; ECOWAS 1999; ECOWAS 2001; ECOWAS 2008).

The fact that ECOWAS often works side by side with other international actors, such as the UN and the AU, sometimes leads to coordination problems and strains between the organisations. One example is the Ivory Coast crisis in which it took the AU a long time to recognise Ouattara as winner of the elections. This frustrated ECOWAS as it wanted to step up its response in the crisis with all actors on board. In the Mali case, the EU pledged funding directly to ECOWAS which upset the AU and increased ECOWAS-AU tensions (Vanheukelom 2017). These examples show there is a need to further clarify the relationship between these regional organisations and also to establish standard operating procedures in crisis situations, so that it is clear for all actors *ex ante* who takes the lead in the international response. This is also crucial to be able to adequately act in R2P cases. The example of Ivory Coast shows that a divided international community can send a diluted message to leaders who are responsible for atrocities, in this case President Gbagbo. Regarding internalisation, this implies that even though ECOWAS demonstrated internalisation of R2P in this case, when it works in conjunction with other regional organisations, this is not necessarily sufficient to bring about an effective and timely R2P response.

Overall, it can be argued that ECOWAS has demonstrated an important commitment to the responsibility to react, through consistently stressing judicial accountability for atrocity crimes and applying sanctions to those responsible for atrocities. The case of Mali shows that ECOWAS is prepared to escalate its response in cases where diplomacy and the application of sanctions have not delivered desired results. Albeit it was helped in its mission by the French mission Serval, ECOWAS was willing to put boots on the ground to bring an end to the conflict and ongoing atrocities in Mali. This demonstrates its preparedness to use costly measures to implement R2P, a clear indicator it has internalised the military component of the responsibility to react to a significant extent. It needs to be noted though that there are cases in which the use of force is more disputed and ECOWAS does not manage to find consensus on the use of force. This was the case in Ivory Coast, where the organisation threatened incumbent Gbagbo with the use of force because of his intransigent stance, but where Ghana publicly distanced itself from this statement as it believed forceful measures were not appropriate in this situation. In itself, this is not a problem when assessing the internalisation of the military component of the responsibility to react: the use of force will not always be appropriate in every 'R2P case' and Ghana may therefore have been right in contesting the robust application of R2P during the Ivorian election crisis. What is important for this component of R2P is that there is not a consistent rejection of R2P's means of last resort by particular member states in the region. The fact that ECOWAS did find consensus on forceful measures in Mali, as well as in many other crisis situations not analysed in this book, shows that ECOWAS is generally able to take this step when a situation requires it and hence shows that the organisation has internalised the military component of the responsibility to react to a significant extent.

Responsibility to rebuild

ECOWAS issued authoritative support for the responsibility to rebuild in the 2008 ECPF, which it defined as "actions taken to ensure recovery, reconstruction, rehabilitation and reconciliation in the aftermath of violent conflicts, humanitarian or natural disasters" (ECOWAS 1999, art. 41c). In the period pre-dating the R2P norm, the organisation expressed similar authoritative support in its 1999 Mechanism. ECOWAS stated to "endeavour to assist Member States emerging from conflicts to increase their capacity for national, social, economic and cultural reconstruction" (ECOWAS 1999, art. 42). Various member states, under which Nigeria and Ghana, have also expressed support for rebuilding activities such as in Mali (Voice of America 2013).

With regard to practice, the responsibility to rebuild mostly came to the fore in the case of Mali. Here, we saw that ECOWAS, together with its international partners in AFISMA (and later MINUSMA) and French troops, managed to bring an end to the conflict in the north of Mali. While this constitutes a successful application of the responsibility to react, responding effectively and decisively to the commission of atrocities, the jury on the implementation of the responsibility to rebuild in this case is more mixed. It was noted that the crisis management mechanisms adopted in Mali by AFISMA and its UN successor mission MINUSMA – to which ECOWAS member states actively contributed – did not adequately deal with some of the root causes of the conflict, which constitutes a crucial element of the responsibility to rebuild. Some of these root causes, such as political exclusionism and manipulation of ethnic and religious differences for political ends, are direct warning signs for atrocity crimes, so it is of vital importance that these are addressed to prevent the resurgence of atrocity crimes in Mali. The fact that ECOWAS has insufficiently engaged with these root causes gives rise to the notion that it has only internalised the responsibility to rebuild to a limited extent and work remains to be done to fully internalise this important aspect of R2P.

General assessment of norm internalisation of R2P by ECOWAS: a case of norm absorption

In the analysed cases, it has been demonstrated that ECOWAS is willing to issue condemnations, take diplomatic steps and adopt sanctions in R2P cases. Importantly, and here the organisation differs from the EU, whenever ECOWAS becomes involved in crises with an atrocity component, the R2P discourse is usually absent in its communiques and statements. Instead, it draws on a rich body of regional security protocols and frameworks that were developed from the early 1990s onwards to tackle the precarious security situation in the West African region. Another difference with the EU is that the analysed cases concern internal cases for ECOWAS, whereas most R2P cases the EU had to respond to were outside Europe. In this respect, ECOWAS takes up the role the UN originally had in mind for regional organisations in the implementation of R2P, namely as taking the lead in responding to crises occurring within their region (UN 2011).

The crises in Guinea, Ivory Coast, and Mali demonstrate a habitualised response from ECOWAS. Generally, the organisation is quick in condemning the situation and those responsible for atrocities and in setting up a mediation mission, consistent with preventive activities in R2P cases. ECOWAS often engages in these efforts next to other international actors, such as the UN and the AU.

In terms of the depths of change in response to R2P, it seems that ECOWAS has engaged in norm absorption vis-à-vis the UN-agreed R2P. It incorporated the norm in its programs, specifically the 2008 ECPF, but without substantially modifying existing processes, policies, and institutions. In effect, the degree of change directly in response to R2P has been low (Börzel and Risse 2003). This reaction of norm absorption, rather than a more transformative response, is of course understandable given the pre-existence of 'R2P clauses' in the 1999 Mechanism and 2001 Protocol. The adoption of these documents and the regional intervention practice that started to emerge in the late 1980s *is* indicative of transformational change.

If one bears in mind where ECOWAS was in the 1980s and where it is now, the change is quite astonishing. In the 1980s, ECOWAS was a very young subregional organisation, with predominantly an economic mandate and some early security protocols, which focused very much on traditional interstate security and collective defence. The security protocols also appeared to be 'paper tigers' as not much attention was paid to them (Alter et al. 2013, 771). It was the sharply deteriorating security situation in the West African region, with a multitude of civil unrest and civil conflicts, that brought regional security into sharp relief. Nigeria, as the regional hegemon, took up the task to step into the void and lead regional interventions through ECOMOG, while ECOWAS caught up by introducing new institutional mechanisms and protocols to codify this new regional security role. As was widely discussed both in this and in the contextual chapter, the mechanisms and protocols were multidimensional, not only covering security, but democracy, good governance, and human rights (abuses) as well. ECOWAS was thus a 'first mover' in this area, as it already tackled questions of what to do in cases of "humanitarian disasters" and "serious and massive violations of human rights", years before R2P was created in response to these issues (ECOWAS 1999). ECOWAS thus underwent transformative changes in the 1990s and the 2000s in the area or regional security broadly conceived. When R2P as a global norm emerged, partly inspired by the events and practices in West Africa, the region was already well equipped to deal with 'R2P challenges'. Hence, the direct change in response to R2P itself was rather minimal and would strictly count as norm absorption (Börzel and Risse 2003).

Having analysed how and to what extent ECOWAS has internalised the norm of R2P, and having discussed how ECOWAS and other West African actors have contributed to the construction of the global norm, it is now time to assess how the various regional factors fare when assessed against the empirical evidence.

Assessment of the regional factors and the likelihood of internalisation of R2P

ECOWAS, as a regional actor, has the characteristics of a regional hegemonic system, in which Nigeria is clearly the hegemon. The state contributes about 70 percent of regional GDP and accounts for about half of West Africa's population (African Development Bank Group 2018; World Bank 2020). In the analytical framework, different hegemonic systems were identified, which were the hegemonic stability system, hegemonic dominance system, and hegemonic isolationist system. Nigeria has played an active role in the region, ruling out a hegemonic isolationist system. Even though tensions still exist between Anglophone (to which Nigeria belongs) and Francophone states, and Nigeria is sometimes criticised of unilateralism, there is a general recognition of the need for Nigeria's leadership in the region (Adebajo 2000). Nigeria has exercised this leadership by committing significant resources to ECOWAS, thereby contributing to the regionalisation process in West Africa (Lopez 2014). ECOWAS thus resembles a hegemonic stability system, in which the hegemon largely plays a constructive role and promotes hegemonic stability (Adler and

Barnett 1998). The region is generally also perceived this way by Nigeria and other West African states (Adebajo 2000; Lopez 2014). Concerning hegemonic regional systems, it was stated that if states in a 'hegemonic region' have positive perceptions of the role the hegemon plays, this will increase the likelihood of internalisation of R2P. If there is an interest in R2P in the region, the hegemon may ensure a stable institutionalisation of the norm within the region in line with its own preferences, which corresponds with the 'hegemonic stability thesis' (Gilpin 1981). Something along these lines seems indeed to have happened in West Africa in the late 1980s and 1990s, when ECOMOG intervened under Nigeria's leadership in various civil wars. This practice of intervention was subsequently institutionalised with the 1999 Mechanism, one of the West African precursors to R2P. Based on the case of ECOWAS, there is thus some preliminary support for the proposition that regional hegemonic stability systems offer facilitating structural conditions for internalisation of R2P.

Regarding the security environment of ECOWAS, there could be concerns about the use of hard power in the region. It was hypothesised that fear of the use of hard power would likely create resistance against R2P in regional fora, as R2P could serve as legitimation for an interventionist agenda. When assessing the role of external powers, France has been militarily active in several ECOWAS member states, most prominently in Mali. Generally, ECOWAS member states have, however, approved of France's military involvement in the region as it delivers an important contribution to the fight against extremism in the region (Nussbaum 2020). Hence, fear of the use of hard power by external powers seems to be limited in the region and therefore it is unlikely this had a significant effect on the region's attitude towards R2P. Internally, there is a limited supply of hard power in ECOWAS compared to other regions in the world. However, the states that do possess significant hard power have demonstrated a willingness to project this power *within* the region, as illustrated by the ECOMOG interventions led by Nigeria. For states that are at the receiving end of these interventions, this could create scepticism towards R2P. While some states in the region have voiced their concern about Nigeria's role in the region from time to time (Adebajo 2000), no evidence was found that these 'hegemonic interventions' have created resistance against R2P in West Africa. This counters the proposition that the fear (of the use of) of hard power would act against the regional internalisation of R2P.

The third regional factor relates to available capacities and preferences for the use of certain policy measures and resources over others. Concerning capacities, the closer the available resources match a particular provision of R2P, the more likely the regional organisations will internalise that particular provision. For ECOWAS, this would mean that one should see internalisation of R2P most pronounced in areas where the regional organisation has an edge, such as in diplomacy, conflict prevention and conflict management. Concerning R2P internalisation, one would thus expect a strong internalisation of formal support (as it relates to diplomacy), prevention (as it relates to conflict prevention and diplomacy) and reaction (as it relates to conflict management). In the cases, we saw these expectations confirmed. ECOWAS engages in preventive diplomacy, often in the form of shuttle-diplomacy, it applies sanctions and it does not shy away from using force when needed. Based on the empirical evidence, the proposition that regional organisations will internalise those aspects of R2P they have prior experience with and that fits with their policy preferences thus receives support.

The final regional factor deals with the degree of regional institutionalisation. When there is a high degree of regional institutionalisation, this is likely to increase the chance of an institutional response to new global norms as opposed to an ad hoc response. One could argue that ECOWAS, with its many protocols and frameworks, has a high degree of institutionalisation in the area of security. The specifics of the case here are that ECOWAS already had an elaborate security architecture resonant with R2P in place when the norm of R2P came back to the region from the global level. Therefore, ECOWAS did not come up with a very institutionalised response to R2P post-2005, effectively reflecting norm absorption: since ECOWAS' protocols and frameworks already contained ample R2P provisions, there simply was no institutional need to do so, which was echoed in interviews with multiple ECOWAS officials (ECOWAS Commission Official 2020; ECOWAS Commission Policy Officer 2019).

Conclusion

This chapter has analysed how and to what extent ECOWAS and its member states have internalised the norm of R2P. Concerning the 'how', contrary to the EU, it has been shown that ECOWAS has implemented R2P internally, through regional policies. As ECOWAS has been dealing with R2P-related questions for a long time and has incorporated provisions in its protocols regarding it, one can say that processes of local norm construction and diffusion of 'R2P' have started in ECOWAS before the adoption of the norm at the UN in 2005. The 1999 Mechanisms and the 2001 Protocol specify that ECOWAS may impose sanctions or intervene in cases of "humanitarian disaster" or where there are "massive violations of human rights and the rule of law" (ECOWAS 1999; ECOWAS 2001). ECOWAS had by then already established a practice of intervening in conflicts in its member states where atrocities were taking place. The 2008 ECPF came after the 2005 World Summit and some of the R2P terminology found its way in this document, as it states that ECOWAS is tasked to protect human security, through the responsibility to prevent, the responsibility to react, and the responsibility to rebuild (ECOWAS 2008). It must be noted though that in the analysed crises, references were made to the 1999 Mechanism and 2001 Protocol, but not to the 2008 ECPF, let alone the specific R2P clauses in that framework. In the Mali and Ivory Coast crises, ECOWAS referred to violated provisions of the 2001 Protocol on Democracy and Good Governance, which declare "zero tolerance for power obtained or maintained by unconstitutional means," as a reason to become involved (ECOWAS 2001, Art. 1c).

As was argued in this chapter, this shows that ECOWAS was initially triggered by a constitutional element in the different crises. Down the line, when concerns over atrocities intensified, its actions started to widen in scope to target atrocities as well. In terms of R2P internalisation, this means that regional organisations do not necessarily have to be triggered by atrocities in the first instance to become involved in regional crises of R2P relevance. What matters is that they subsequently act when atrocities become a concern as well. ECOWAS has demonstrably done so, taking both preventive and reactive action during crises in accordance with the prescriptions of the R2P norm. It has thereby shown signs of internalisation of the different facets of R2P as outlined in the analytical framework of this book.

The fact that ECOWAS generally does not refer to the R2P clauses in its 2008 ECPF, but rather to its 1999 and 2001 Protocols, gives away clues about its type of internalisation of R2P. It seems that ECOWAS has engaged in norm absorption vis-à-vis the UN-agreed R2P, in the sense that it incorporated the norm in its programs, specifically the 2008 ECPF, but without substantially modifying existing processes, policies, and institutions. In effect, the degree of change directly in response to R2P has been low (Börzel and Risse 2003). This reaction of norm absorption, rather than a more transformative response, is of course understandable given the pre-existence of "R2P-clauses" in the 1999 Mechanism and 2001 Protocol. The adoption of these documents, however, and the regional intervention practice that started to emerge in the late 1980s, *is* indicative of transformational change.

The analysed cases have shown that ECOWAS generally condemns the use of force against civilians, takes diplomatic steps, and adopts sanctions (in line with the sanctions component of the responsibility to react) in atrocity cases. It has even resorted to the (threat of the) use of force in Ivory Coast and Mali (consistent with the military component of the responsibility to react). In this regard, ECOWAS seems relatively unhampered by Security Council vetoes, unlike the EU member states which faced vetoes in the cases of Syria and Myanmar. Apparently, the interests of the permanent five are not great enough in West Africa to warrant their vetoes of 'use-of-force-resolutions'. Another explanation for this observation might be that ECOWAS' active involvement in its own region means that outside global powers cannot and do not need to similarly weigh in this region as they do in other regions. Concerning the responsibility to rebuild, it is positive that ECOWAS committed to a long-term deployment in Mali, as part of MINUSMA. At the same time, the mission has been criticised for inadequately dealing with the root causes of the conflict, that led to atrocities in the first place. In the analytical framework of this book, the responsibility to rebuild was defined as "to provide, particularly after a military intervention, full assistance with recovery, reconstruction, and reconciliation, addressing the causes of the harm the intervention was designed to halt or avert" (Crossley 2016, 82). ECOWAS' post-conflict activities in Mali, as part of MINUSMA, seem to have particularly fallen short of the latter, i.e. "addressing the causes of the harm the intervention was designed to halt or avert." So, the case of Mali, where rebuilding activities have been most prominent out of the three cases analysed, seems to suggest that ECOWAS has not (yet) internalised the rebuilding component of the responsibility to protect to the extent that the norm prescribes. The presence of spoilers in the country may also be an explanation for the lack of implementation of measures focusing on atrocity prevention, however (Lederer 2018).

Given the fact that ECOWAS often has to respond to complex crises, it is sometimes hard to establish if the measures that it takes are in response to atrocities or other aspects of a crisis. In the analysed cases, the reason for ECOWAS to become involved initially was not the commission of atrocities but the unconstitutional maintenance of seizure of power. Once ECOWAS engaged with these crises and atrocities took place down the line, the organisation addressed those as well. This fits into the picture of a regional organisation that has a broad mandate to deal with questions ranging from regional peace and security to atrocity prevention and response. Despite its critics, who state that there is sometimes a gap between ECOWAS' progressive protocols and frameworks and its actual response on the ground, there are few other regional organisations that have so actively engaged, whether through diplomacy, the use of sanctions or the use of force, with situations of R2P concern. Even though R2P may not be strongly present in the regional discourse, the actions of ECOWAS are a testament to the norm. So, it seems that the regional organisation that formed one of the main sources of inspiration of the R2P norm ensures that it is being carried forward in the new decade.

Bibliography

Acharya, Amitav. 2013. "The R2P and Norm Diffusion: Towards a Framework of Norm Circulation." *Global Responsibility to Protect* 5 (4): 466–479.

Adebajo, Adeyeke. 2000. "Nigeria: Africa's New Gendarme?" *Security Dialogue* 31 (2): 185–199. DOI:10.1177%2F0967010600031002005.

Adler, Emanuel and Michael Barnett. 1998. *Security Communities*. Cambridge: Cambridge University Press. DOI:10.1017/CBO9780511598661.

African Development Bank Group. 2018. "West Africa Economic Outlook 2018." *African Development Bank*. www.afdb.org/fileadmin/uploads/afdb/Documents/Publications/2018AEO/African_Economic_Outlook_2018_West-Africa.pdf (April 15, 2020).

AIPECT. 2018. AFISMA and the Mali Crisis Rethinking Security Intervention and Democratic Consolidation in Africa" http://aipectinstitute.com/articles/afisma-and-the-mali-crisis-rethinking-security-intervention-and-democratic-consolidation-in-africa/ (February 17, 2020).

Alter, Karen J., Laurence R. Helfer, and Jacqueline R. McAllister. 2013. "A New International Human Rights Court for West Africa: The ECOWAS Community Court of Justice." *The American Journal of International Law* 107: 737–779. https://dx.doi.org/10.2139/ssrn.2107427.

Amnesty International. 2012. "Mali: Five Months of Crisis." *Amnesty International*. May 16. https://reliefweb.int/report/mali/five-months-crisis-armed-rebellion-and-military-coup%E3%80%80 (February 16, 2020).

Babbitt, Eileen. 2014. "Mediation and the Prevention of Mass Atrocities." In *The International Politics of Human Rights: Rallying to the R2P Cause?* eds. Monica Serrano and Thomas Weiss. London: Routledge, 29–47.

Bassett, Thomas and Scott Strauss. 2011. "Defending Democracy in Côte d'Ivoire: Africa Takes a Stand." *Foreign Affairs* 90 (July/August): 130–140.

BBC. 2009. "Sanctions Imposed on Guinea junta." *BBC*. October 29. http://news.bbc.co.uk/1/hi/world/africa/8333026.stm (May 12, 2022).

BBC. 2010. "Ecowas Bloc Threatens Ivory Coast's Gbagbo with Force." *BBC*. December 25. www.bbc.co.uk/news/world-africa-12077298 (February 14, 2020).

BBC. 2012. "Mali Suspended from Regional Bloc Ecowas over Coup." *BBC*. March 28. www.bbc.com/news/world-africa-17526575 (May 12, 2022).

Bellamy, Alex. 2009. *The Responsibility to Protect. The Global Effort to End Mass Atrocities.* Cambridge: Polity Press.

Börzel, Tanja and Thomas Risse. 2003. "Conceptualising the Domestic Impact of Europe." In *The Politics of Europeanisation*, eds. Kevin Featherstone and Claudio Radaelli. Oxford: Oxford University Press, 55–78. DOI:10.1093/0199252092.003.0003.

Cocks, Tim and Kwasi Kpodo. 2011. "Ghana Neutral on Ivory Coast, Opposes Force: President." January 7. www.reuters.com/article/us-ivorycoast/ghana-neutral-on-ivory-coast-opposes-force-president-idUSTRE6BU1ZX20110107 (February 17, 2020).

Coleman, K.P. 2007. *International Organisations and Peace Enforcement: The Politics of International Legitimacy*. Cambridge: Cambridge University Press. DOI:10.1017/CBO9780511491290.

Crossley, Noële. 2016. *Evaluating the Responsibility to Protect: Mass Atrocity Prevention as a Consolidating Norm in International Society*. New York: Routledge.

Deng, Francis M., Sadikiel Kimaro, Terrence Lyons, Donald Rothchild and William Zartman. 1996. *Sovereignty as Responsibility: Conflict Management in Africa*. Washington, DC: Brookings Institution Press.

ECOWAS. 1993. *Revised Treaty of ECOWAS*. Abuja: ECOWAS.

ECOWAS. 1999. *Mechanism for Conflict Prevention, Management, Resolution, Peace-Keeping and Security*. Abuja: ECOWAS.

ECOWAS. 2001. *Protocol on Democracy and Good Governance*. Abuja: ECOWAS.

ECOWAS. 2008. *The ECOWAS Conflict Prevention Framework*. Abuja: ECOWAS.

ECOWAS. 2009. "Extraordinary Summit of ECOWAS Heads of State and Government." October 17. https://emansion.gov.lr/doc/Final_communiqu__of_ECOWAS_HS_17%20October_2009.pdf (February 17, 2020).

ECOWAS. 2010a. "Extraordinary Session of the Authority of Heads of State and Government on Cote d'Ivoire." December 7. www.ecowas.int/wp-content/uploads/2015/02/2010-7-december-Extra.pdf (March 10, 2022).

ECOWAS. 2010b. "Extraordinary Session of the Authority of Heads of State and Government on Cote d'Ivoire." December 24. www.ecowas.int/wp-content/uploads/2015/02/2010-24-december-Extra.pdf (February 17, 2020).

ECOWAS. 2011. "Resolution A/RES.1/03/11 of the Authority of Heads of State and Government of the Economic Community of West African States on the situation in Côte d'Ivoire." www.securitycouncilreport.org/atf/cf/%7B65BFCF9B-6D27-4E9C-8CD3-CF6E4FF96FF9%7D/Cote%20d%27Ivoire%20s%202011%20182.pdf (February 17, 2020).

ECOWAS. 2012. "Final Communique from the Extraordinary Summit of ECOWAS Heads of State and Government." March 27. https://reliefweb.int/report/mali/final-communique-extraordinary-summit-ecowas-heads-state-and-government (March 10, 2022).

ECOWAS. 2019. "ECOWAS Launches Plans of Action for its Conflict Prevention Framework." January 25. www.ecowas.int/ecowas-launches-plans-of-action-for-its-conflict-prevention-framework/ (February 17, 2020).

ECOWAS Commission Official. 2020. Interviewed by Jochem Rietveld, Skype, January 2020.

ECOWAS Commission Policy Officer. 2019. Interviewed by Jochem Rietveld, Skype, April 2019.

Finnemore, Martha and Kathryn Sikkink. 1998. "International Norm Dynamics and Political Change." *International Organisation* 52 (4): 887–917. DOI:10.1162/002081898550789.

GhanaWeb. 2015. "Ghana is an Important Player in Responsibility to Protect – Bombande." *GhanaWeb*. January 11. www.ghanaweb.com/GhanaHomePage/NewsArchive/Ghana-is-an-important-player-in-Responsibility-to-Protect-Bombande-342102 (April 15, 2020).

Gilpin, Robert. 1981. *War and Change in World Politics*. Cambridge: Cambridge University Press. DOI:10.1017/CBO9780511664267.

Global Centre for the Responsibility to Protect. 2019. "Guinea." www.globalr2p.org/countries/guinea/ (February 16, 2020).

Guinea-Bissau. 2009. "Statement by Guinea-Bissau." www.responsibilitytoprotect.org/Guinea%20Bissau_ENG.pdf (February 16, 2020).

Hartmann, Christoff. 2013. "Governance Transfer by the Economic Community of West African States (ECOWAS)." *SFB-Governance Working Paper Series* 47 (December).

Hartmann, Christoff and Kai Striebinger. 2015. "Writing the Script? ECOWAS's Military Intervention Mechanism." In *Governance Transfer by Regional Organizations. Patching Together a Global Script*, eds. Tanja Börzel and Vera van Hüllen. Basingstoke: Palgrave Macmillan, 68–82. DOI:10.1057/9781137385642_4.

Haysom, Simone. 2014. "Security and Humanitarian Crisis in Mali. The Role of Regional Organisations." March. *Humanitarian Policy Group Working Paper*. www.odi.org/sites/odi.org.uk/files/odi-assets/publications-opinion-files/8829.pdf (February 17, 2020).

Hirsch, Afua. 2012. "Guinea-Bissau Coup Suspected as Military Seizes Parts of Capital." April 13. www.theguardian.com/world/2012/apr/13/guinea-bissau-coup-suspected (February 17, 2020).

Human Rights Watch. 2011a. "Côte d'Ivoire: Crimes Against Humanity by Gbagbo Forces. As Crisis Deepens, Grave Abuses Committed by Both Sides." *Human Rights Watch*. March 15. www.hrw.org/news/2011/03/15/cote-divoire-crimes-against-humanity-gbagbo-forces (February 16, 2020).

Human Rights Watch. 2011b. "Côte d'Ivoire: Ouattara Forces Kill, Rape Civilians During Offensive. New Government Should Investigate and Prosecute Atrocities by Both Sides." *Human Rights Watch*. April 9. www.hrw.org/news/2011/04/09/cote-divoire-ouattara-forces-kill-rape-civilians-during-offensive (February 16, 2020).

Hunt, Charles. 2016. "Côte d'Ivoire." In *The Oxford Handbook of the Responsibility to Protect*, eds. Allex J. Bellamy and Tim Dunne. Oxford: Oxford University Press, 693–716. DOI:10.1093/oxfordhb/9780198753841.013.37.

International Coalition for the Responsibility to Protect. 2015. "Q&A: The Responsibility to Protect (RtoP) and Nigeria."http://responsibilitytoprotect.org/Nigeria%20Q(2).pdf (February 16, 2020).

International Commission on Intervention and State Sovereignty, Gareth J. Evans, and Mohamed Sahnoun. 2001. *The Responsibility to Protect: Report of the International Commission on Intervention and State Sovereignty*. Ottawa: International Development Research Centre.

International Criminal Court. 2010. "Statement by Mrs. Fatou Bensouda, Deputy Prosecutor of the International Criminal Court." February 19. www.icc-cpi.int/NR/rdonlyres/

C200208B-5375-41B2-8967-FFFC05528E34/281566/FatousstatementGuinesENG1.pdf (May 27, 2020).

International Crisis Group. 2011. "Côte d'Ivoire: Is War the Only Option?" March 3. www.crisisgroup.org/africa/west-africa/c%C3%B4te-divoire/cote-d-ivoire-war-only-option (February 17, 2020).

Ipinyomi, Foluke. 2012. "Is Côte d'Ivoire a Test Case for R2P? Democratization as Fulfillment of the International Community's Responsibility to Prevent." *Journal of African Law* 56 (October): 151–174. DOI:10.1017/S0021855312000071.

Karlsrud, John. 2016. "Mali." In *The Oxford Handbook of the Responsibility to Protect*, eds. Alex J. Bellamy and Tim Dunne. Oxford: Oxford University Press, 786–800. DOI:10.1093/oxfordhb/9780198753841.013.42.

Kikoler, Naomi. 2015. "Guinea. An Overlooked Case of the Responsibility to Prevent in Practice." In *The Responsibility to Prevent: Overcoming the Challenges of Atrocity Prevention*, eds. Serena K. Sharma and Jennifer M. Welsh. Oxford: Oxford University Press, 304–323. DOI:10.1093/acprof:oso/9780198717782.003.0012.

Koga, Kei. 2016. *Reinventing Regional Security Institutions in Asia and Africa. Power Shifts, Ideas, and Institutional Change*. London: Routledge.

Lacher, Wolfram and Dennis Tull. 2013. *Mali: Beyond Counterterrorism. SWP Comments* 7. Berlin: Germany Institute for International and Security Affairs.

Lederer, Edith. 2018. "France Proposes Sanctions against Mali Peace Deal Spoilers." *AP*. August 31. https://apnews.com/a6852182c3c94aaa89820d1f9e5ad660/France-proposes-sanctions-against-Mali-peace-deal-spoilers (May 30, 2020).

Look, Anne. 2012. "ECOWAS Imposes Sanctions on Mali." *Voice of America*. April 1. www.voanews.com/a/west-african-leaders-impose-sanctions-on-mali-145801255/180314.html (March 10, 2022).

Lopez, Elisa. 2014. "Discourses and Practices of the Regionalisation of Foreign and Security Policies: The Cases of West Africa and South America." Ph.D. diss. University of Warwick and LUISS Guido Carli.

Nigeria. 2009. "Statement of Nigeria at the UNGA Debate on the Secretary-General's Report Entitled "Implementing the Responsibility to Protect." www.globalr2p.org/media/files/nigeria-2009-r2p-debate.pdf (February 17, 2020).

Nigeria. 2018. "Statement of Nigeria at the UNGA Plenary Meeting on the Responsibility to Protect (R2P) and the Prevention of Genocide, War Crimes, Ethnic Cleansing and Crimes against Humanity." June 25. https://papersmart.unmeetings.org/media2/19407297/statement-by-nigeria.pdf (February 16, 2020).

Nussbaum, Ania. 2020. "West Africa Backs French Military Presence Amid Protests." *Bloomberg*. January 13. www.bloomberg.com/news/articles/2020-01-13/west-africa-backs-french-military-presence-amid-protests (April 15, 2020).

PBS Frontline. 2004. "Interview Kofi Annan." *PBS Frontline*. April 1. www.pbs.org/wgbh/pages/frontline/shows/ghosts/interviews/annan.html (April 15, 2020).

Reuters. 2011. "ECOWAS Calls for Strict UN Sanctions on Ivory Coast." *Reuters*. March 24. www.reuters.com/article/ivorycoast-ecowas/ecowas-calls-for-strict-un-sanctions-on-ivory-coast-idUSLDE72N1TV20110324 (February 14, 2020).

Reuters. 2012. "Neighbours Launch Sanctions against Mali: Ouattara." *Reuters*. April 2. www.reuters.com/article/ozatp-mali-sanctions-20120402-idAFJOE83108Y20120402 (May 12, 2022).

Sierra Leone. 2009. "Statement of Sierra Leone. Follow-Up on the Outcome of the Millennium Summit Report of the Secretary-General." www.responsibilitytoprotect.org/Sierra%20Leone-ENG.pdf (February 16, 2020).

Streitfeld-Hall, Jaclyn. 2015. "Preventing Mass Atrocities in West Africa." *Global Centre for the Responsibility to Protect*. Occasional Paper Series No. 6, 1–26.

Thakur, Ramesh and Thomas Weiss. 2009. "R2P: From Idea to Norm – and Action?" *Global Responsibility to Protect* 1 (1): 22–53. DOI:10.1163/187598409X405460.

Togo. 2013. "Statement of Togo. Unofficial Translation from Published Statement." www.globalr2p.org/media/files/togo_en.pdf.

Traore, Oury. 2016. "Annex. Economic Community of West African States (ECOWAS)." In *African Regional Communities and the Prevention of Mass Atrocities*, ed. African Task Force on the Prevention of Mass Atrocities. Budapest: Foundation for the International Prevention of Genocide and Mass Atrocities, 1–28.

UN General Assembly. 2005. "Resolution adopted by the General Assembly on 16 September 2005." 60/1.2005 World Summit Outcome. ttps://www.un.org/en/development/desa/population/migration/generalassembly/docs/globalcompact/A_RES_60_1.pdf (October 11, 2019).

UN General Assembly. 2018. "Responsibility to Protect." www.un.org/pga/72/2018/06/25/formal-debate-of-the-general-assembly-under-agenda-item-the-responsibility-to-protect-and-the-prevention-of-genocide-war-crimes-ethnic-cleansing-and-crimes-against-humanity/ (February 17, 2020).

UN News. 2011. "Death Toll in Ivorian Post-election Violence Surpassed 1,000 – UN." May 26. https://news.un.org/en/story/2011/05/376492-death-toll-ivorian-post-election-violence-surpassed-1000-un (February 17, 2020).

UN Security Council. 2011. "Resolution 1975. S/RES/1975." http://unscr.com/en/resolutions/doc/1975 (February 18, 2020)

UN Security Council. 2012a. "Letter Dated 18 April 2012 from the Secretary-General addressed to the President of the Security Council." S/2012/237. https://undocs.org/S/2012/237 (February 17, 2020).

UN Security Council. 2012b. "Resolution 2085. S/RES/2085." www.securitycouncilreport.org/atf/cf/%7B65BFCF9B-6D27-4E9C-8CD3-CF6E4FF96FF9%7D/s_res_2085.pdf (February 17, 2020).

United Nations. 2011. "The Role of Regional and Subregional Arrangements in Implementing the Responsibility to Protect." A/65/877 – S/2011/393. https://undocs.org/A/65/877 (February 18, 2020).

Vanheukelom, Jan. 2017. "Understanding the Economic Community of West African States Political Traction with Africa's Oldest Regional Organisation." *ECDPM Policy Brief.*

Voice of America. 2013. "International Donors Pledge Aid for Mali Force." *VOA News*. January 29. www.voanews.com/a/international-donor-pledge-aid-for-mali-force/1592760.html (July 31, 2022).

WANEP policy officers. 2019. Interviewed by Jochem Rietveld, Skype, June 2019.

Welsh, Jennifer M. 2013. "Norm Contestation and the Responsibility to Protect." *Global Responsibility to Protect* 5 (4): 365–396.

Williams, Abiodun. 2017. "The Responsibility to Protect and Institutional Change." *Global Governance* 23 (4): 537–544.

Witt, Antonia. 2013. "Convergence on Whose Terms? Reacting to Coups d'État in Guinea and Madagascar." *African Security* 6 (3/4): 257–275. DOI:10.1080/19392206.2013.854113.

World Bank. 2020. "The World Bank in Nigeria." *The World Bank*. www.worldbank.org/en/country/nigeria/overview (April 15, 2020).

6 Conclusion

Introduction

The aim of this book is to elucidate how and to what extent regional organisations have internalised the norm of R2P. The EU and ECOWAS served as case studies to better understand these regional normative processes. The theory chapter noted that, in the light of this research, there was a need to better connect the regional security governance literature with the norms literature. The review of the norms literature demonstrated the great progress made in the field since its emergence in the 1990s. Finnemore and Sikkink (1998) laid the foundations with their norms life cycle model. Multiple scholars built on Finnemore and Sikkink's work by expanding and criticising it. First, Acharya (2004, 2011, 2013) exposed the norms life cycle model's implicit and underlying cosmopolitanism (or Western-centrism) and gave agency to local actors from the Global South through the concepts of norm localisation, norm circulation, and subsidiarity norms. It is against this context that this book proposed the concept of local norm construction, which builds on Acharya's work but gives local actors a more direct role in constructing the local building blocks of subsequent 'global norms'. Second, a range of scholars criticised the assumptions of norm stability and linearity inherent in the early norms literature and, instead, argued to see norms as "inherently contested" and emphasised the importance of the cultural validity of norms (Welsh 2013; Wiener 2008). Third, Bloomfield (2016) and others demonstrated that the existing norms research had focused too much on norm entrepreneurs and examples of successful normative change. To get a more rounded picture, Bloomfield (2016) urged to study opponents of normative change as well, so-called 'norm antipreneurs'.

In the review of the literature on regional organisations in the field of security, it was shown that some accounts mainly focus on the benefits that regional organisations provide to the UN and other global actors. In doing so, they generally do not give pride of place to the agency of these regional organisations. Other literature, such as the regional security governance literature, does account for the agency of regional organisations. Other aspects of the literature that were reviewed were the role of power in regions, regional leadership, and regional hegemony.

DOI: 10.4324/9781003230731-6

The analytical framework of this book reviewed the relevant literature and proposed an analytical model on the basis of that. First, it introduced the concept of local norm construction that fits in with Acharya's earlier work on norm localisation and circulation (Acharya 2004, 2013), but that gives local actors an even more distinct role in norm construction. Whereas localisation has local actors alter global norms to have them fit with their local priors and norm circulation has them feed back some of their own norms (Acharya 2004, 2013), there is always an (implicit) assumption that there already are global norms 'out there' to which these local actors contribute. The norm of R2P has demonstrated that the role of local actors can go beyond that: West African norm entrepreneurs and European norm entrepreneurs directly built the building blocks of R2P, before the norm emerged and crystallised at the global level in the shape and form which is now recognised as 'the R2P norm'. These aspects are also further discussed in the discussion of different regional normative contexts and their implications for norm entrepreneurs and antipreneurs, which builds on Bloomfield's (2016) model. Second, the analytical framework formulated a number of factors linking the regional security governance literature to likely regional dispositions to the norm of R2P. The remaining factors focused on the different aspects of internalisation of R2P, ranging from the expression of formal support to the responsibility to rebuild. These factors were key to answering the 'how'-part of the research question of this book, while the concepts of the Europeanisation literature enabled to answer the 'to what extent'-part.

The EU and ECOWAS were selected as regional case studies for the study of the regional internalisation of R2P based on a most different systems design. The organisations differ in many aspects that are deemed relevant for the regional diffusion and internalisation of R2P: whereas the EU is a Western regional organisation, is deemed to have a low risk of mass atrocity crimes, is generally seen as a security community, and has two permanent Security Council members, ECOWAS is a African (sub-)regional organisation, is deemed to have a medium to high risk of mass atrocity crimes, is generally seen as a hegemonic power system, and has no permanent Security Council members. The fact that the organisations differ in many aspects is important in terms of case selection: to better understand the drivers of regional norm diffusion and internalisation of R2P, one has to look at regional systems that are very different from one another to understand which factors matter and which do not or only to a lesser extent.

The crisis case studies within these two regional cases were selected according to the occurrence or threat of atrocity crimes, which makes them of R2P concern and according to a variety in regional responses, ranging from diplomatic measures and sanctions to a military response. For both the EU and ECOWAS, a case has been included with a robust application of R2P – the case of Libya for the EU and the case of Mali for ECOWAS – and several cases where measures were taken short of the use of force – the cases of Syria and

Myanmar for the EU and the cases of Guinea and Ivory Coast for ECOWAS. This variety in response was an important selection criterion as it shed light on how the norm of R2P has been internalised and on which measures were taken under varying circumstances.

Contextual comparisons

The contextual chapter's aim was to analyse how the regional organisations under analysis dealt with questions of security, sovereignty, and human rights since their founding until the norm of R2P emerged. The three themes were chosen as they clearly relate to different elements of the R2P norm, so they could provide an understanding of what kind of experience the regional organisations built in these areas throughout their history and how this might impact on their disposition towards R2P when the norm emerged in the early 2000s.

In the case of the EU, it was shown that security was a driving factor behind the creation of the ECSC, as it pooled the war resources of coal and steel. In the first few decades, various attempts were made towards European defence and foreign policy integration, although these were generally not too successful (Urwin 1995). During this time, the security situation in Western Europe was characterised by the Cold War and security was usually conceived in a traditional way, i.e. as national security, with threats predominantly coming from other states, in this case the Soviet Union. After the end of the Cold War, the security agenda widened and deepened, and the concept of human security emerged. EU-elites such as Solana and Ferrero-Waldner and various member states proved to be strong advocates of human security and they aimed to popularise the principle within the EU and implement it in regional policies (Christou 2014; Harnisch 2017). The advocacy for human security is important as it directly relates to R2P: both concepts embrace non-traditional notions of security, although R2P is a narrower concept than human security (Christou 2014)

The EU and its member states built considerable experience with sovereignty-pooling since the organisation's founding, even though preferences on integration have differed at the institutional level and between member states and they have evolved over time. This experience with sovereignty-pooling is relevant to R2P as the norm has a qualified notion of sovereignty, as opposed to an absolute notion. Finally, the section on human rights showed that the EU has an elaborate human rights architecture in place. When human rights violations took place during the Yugoslav conflicts, the EU was, however, ill-equipped to deal with this, as the CFSP was only in the making at the time (Gross 2007). The EU's ineffectiveness and dependence on others during the Yugoslav conflicts provided an impetus for further security cooperation, of which the 1998 St. Malo Summit was the first real expression (Gross 2007). For R2P, the Srebrenica massacre was a powerful event that laid bare the inadequacy of the international community to deal decisively with mass atrocities and thus to find new ways to respond to these situations. Together with the

Rwandan genocide, the Srebrenica massacre therefore prompted the international community to tackle this issue, which was crucial in creating the right structural conditions for norm entrepreneurship of R2P.

The discussion of ECOWAS showed that security has been a challenge since the independence of West African states following decolonisation. Some of the states had to fight an independence war to secure their independence. Once the states in the region had (re)gained their independence, this did not mean that peace returned to the West African region. Soon, civil wars started to erupt as rival elites fought for the newly won power (Marc et al. 2015). ECOWAS, which had been founded in the 1970s for economic purposes, lacked the mandate to respond to these intrastate conflicts, which destabilised the region and endangered its mandate for economic development of the region. Nigeria did not wait for a regional institutional response and decided to take matters in its own hands with its interventions in the late 1980s and 1990s in Liberia and Sierra Leone through ECOMOG, a multilateral ad hoc intervention force led by Nigeria (Olonisakin 2011). Against this backdrop of regional instability and insecurity and unmandated interventions, ECOWAS realised it needed to reform itself to stay relevant. To this end, it revised its founding treaty in 1993, which introduced the organisation's regional security mandate, and it adopted the 1999 Mechanism, with its regional security provisions, and the 2001 Protocol on Democracy and Good Governance, introducing standards on democracy and good governance (ECOWAS 1993, 1999, 2001).

On sovereignty, ECOWAS member states initially had a 'traditional' perspective: having recently won their independence, they were not willing to give up their sovereignty when ECOWAS was founded in the 1970s. This meant that ECOWAS operated on an intergovernmental basis and that it had a narrow, economic mandate. Söderbaum (2004) argued that ECOWAS is, in fact, a sovereignty-boosting regional organisation, through which ruling elites gain legitimacy while giving up only limited sovereignty. Although this may be the case to some extent, the practice of ECOWAS' interventions in member states shows that in some areas, the organisation is able to take regional measures that can be very intrusive vis-à-vis the sovereignty of its member states. One could make the argument that, at least in the area of security, the ECOWAS member states have gone much further than their EU-counterparts in pooling sovereignty as well, with ECOMOG (now: ECOWAS Standby Force) coming close to a West African standing force, something which the EU is still only aspiring to (Piccolino 2016).

Concerning human rights, it was noted that West African states lacked the sovereignty to sign important human rights treaties in the aftermath of the Second World War, such as the Universal Declaration of Human Rights in 1948. When ECOWAS was founded in 1975, there was no human rights language in its founding document. It was only in 1991 that the organisation first alluded to human rights as part of its declaration on political principles (ECOWAS 1991). The 1993 Revised Treaty made a further step by making specific references to human rights in its preamble and by recognising the promotion and protection of human rights as one of the fundamental principles to which ECOWAS member states will adhere in the pursuit of ECOWAS objectives (ECOWAS 1993). Human rights subsequently got a central place in the 1999 Mechanism and particularly the 2001 Protocol (ECOWAS 1999, 2001). The conflicts in ECOWAS member states witnessed massive human rights violations, which ECOWAS sought to address through its interventions. This intervention practice emerged from Nigeria's increased security role in the region through ECOMOG and later also through regional security institutionalisation in the 1999 Mechanism and the 2001 Protocol.

When comparing the historical experiences of the two regional organisations, a few things stand out. First, given their vastly different historical experiences, their initial approaches to regional integration and sovereignty-sharing were markedly different. Whereas the ECSC-founders felt a strong impetus to pool sovereignty against the backdrop of yet another destructive war on the European continent, West African states initially engaged in more modest forms of regional integration, cognisant of their newly regained sovereignty after years of colonial rule. Over time, this dynamic changed to some extent. Especially in the area of security, ECOWAS member states made great strides in regional integration and in building a regional intervention mechanism, as well as shared expectations around democracy and good governance (ECOWAS 1993, 1999, 2001). These developments have been so significant that in the area of regional security, ECOWAS has arguably gone further in sovereignty-pooling than the EU. These more recent regional integration developments in both regions also reflect different regional security environments. Whereas the EU generally enjoys a stable security environment, especially internally, West Africa has long been plagued by state instability, civil unrest, and civil wars. These opposite security environments offered different incentives for security cooperation and integration to the two regional organisations: whereas ECOWAS was to some extent forced to develop a regional security role in order to stay relevant, the EU was not confronted with similar pressures. Against this, however, one could argue that the EU has faced significant threats to its security from external sources in more recent years, particularly from Russia, and that its response to this so far has not been as transformative as ECOWAS' response to its internal sources of insecurity.

Both regional organisations put an emphasis on human rights and atrocity prevention. For the EU, this was strongly inspired by the lessons from the Holocaust resulting in the 'Never Again'-credo, and in more recent years by the failings of the international community in Rwanda and Srebrenica (EEAS 2018; Schmidt 2019). It led to the creation of and participation in an elaborate human rights architecture, codified in *inter alia* the Lisbon Treaty (EU 2007). In the case of ECOWAS, its attention for human rights started in the early 1990s and was later built into the 1999 Mechanism and 2001 Protocol (ECOWAS 1999, 2001). This reflected the high occurrence of mass atrocities in the region and therefore the need to put more robust mechanisms in place to respond to gross human rights violations. In both cases, historical experiences with mass atrocities, whether recent or more distant in the past, played a key role in creating the right structural conditions for a strong human rights culture and a commitment to prevent and put a halt to mass atrocities.

A comparative assessment of the EU's and ECOWAS' internalisation of R2P

It is now time to turn to comparative reflections of the two regional case studies that were analysed in this research. The regional factors that were outlined in the analytical framework will help in making this comparison (see Table 6.1 for a comparison of the EU and ECOWAS on the various regional factors). It was noted that in both regions, there was fear of the (threat of the) use of hard power, which was expected to decrease the likelihood of internalisation of R2P. With regard to the use of hard power by external powers, some EU member states fear a potential Russian intervention since the Crimean annexation of 2014 and even more so after the invasion of Ukraine of 2022, while some ECOWAS member states are wary of France's interventionism in the region. In both cases, however, this did not seem to impact the likelihood of internalisation of R2P. In the case of the EU, the geopolitical situation vis-à-vis Russia and the norm of R2P are, apart from an unsuccessful Russian attempt to invoke R2P during the 2008 Georgia intervention (GCR2P 2008), seen as two completely different issue areas and a connection will unlikely be made, whereas in ECOWAS a significant number of member states actually welcome France's involvement in the region in the fight against terror, even though population support is often more contested (Nussbaum 2020; France24 2022). Regarding the use of hard power by regional powers, there was an important difference between the two regions: while in the EU, it is unconceivable that the states with significant hard power would use this power *within* the region, in ECOWAS this happens on a regular basis, usually with Nigeria in the lead. While some states in the region have voiced their concern about this from time to time, no evidence was found that these 'hegemonic interventions' have created significant resistance against R2P, or West African mechanisms predating the global norm, in the region. In the case of the EU, as hard power projection *within* the region is a remote possibility, this factor also had little impact on the likelihood of internalisation of R2P. To conclude, in both cases, the fear of the use of hard power, whether threatened by external or regional powers, does not seem to have made a significant impact on the likelihood of internalisation of R2P in the regional organisations under analysis. While this is a tentative finding based on an exploration of two regional case studies, it will be important to assess whether this lack of relationship between these two factors is visible in other regions as well, especially given the lengths the ICISS and other R2P norm entrepreneurs have gone to disassociate R2P from (humanitarian) intervention (International Commission on Intervention and State Sovereignty et al. 2001).

Concerning the regional actor type and regional self-perception, the EU was characterised as a regional security community (Adler and Greve 2009). References to the EU in official circles and the academic community, such as the 'EU as a peace project'-discourse and the 'civilian/normative/cosmopolitan-Europe-debate', suggest that EU elites and observers also perceive the EU as such (Von der Leyen 2019; Tusk 2019; Duchene 1972; Habermas 2003; Manners 2002). As was argued in the analytical framework of this book, a security community subscribes to shared norms and values and facilitates peace among its members (Deutsch 1957; Adler and Barnett 1998; Adler and Greve 2009). This allows member states to focus on matters beyond state security, such as the defence of human rights through for instance R2P. The norm-based nature of security communities further amplifies the attention for human rights issues. The EU, as a security community, could therefore be expected to have a positive disposition to R2P. This expectation has been supported by the empirical evidence: the EU issued strong rhetorical support for R2P in international fora in the early years of R2P and continues to do so, and has more recently, starting in 2016 with the appointment of the EU R2P Focal Point and the creation of a new division in the EEAS, followed up on this at the policy level.

ECOWAS, as a regional actor, has the characteristics of a regional hegemonic system, in which Nigeria is clearly the hegemon, evidenced by its large share in West Africa's GDP and population (African Development Bank Group 2018; World Bank 2020). Both Nigeria itself and other ECOWAS member states recognise the leadership role Nigeria plays in the region (Lopez 2014). Implications for R2P internalisation are less clear in regional hegemonic systems than in regional security communities and they depend on the role of the hegemon in the region, which is assessed in the second regional factor. In this context, it was discussed how Nigeria has positively contributed to the regionalisation of ECOWAS and how this role is being recognised by other ECOWAS member states (Lopez 2014, 215). Relevant to R2P, Nigeria led a first regional intervention in Liberia in the late 1980s and it continued its leadership in these kinds of interventions in the region's civil wars in the 1990s. It therefore contributed to the emergence of a regional intervention practice, which also spurred ECOWAS to catch up institutionally through the development of several institutional protocols and mechanisms in the area or regional security (ECOWAS 1999, 2001). Nigeria thus acted in line with the expectations based on the hegemonic stability thesis and it contributed to the institutionalisation of ECOWAS' broadly conceived regional security role that preceded the emergence of the global R2P norm. The lack of a clear hegemon in the EU might have hampered leadership on the norm in that regional organisation. In the case of Libya, for instance, one witnessed disagreement between the bigger member states, with France and the UK pushing for a robust application of R2P, and Germany resisting this (Brockmeier et al. 2014). The conflicting agendas of the EU's leading member states prevented the emergence of collective leadership on R2P that could somehow mirror hegemonic leadership at the EU level. An ALDE MEP at the time alluded in an interview that the need for consensus in CFSP decision-making has proved an important obstacle to achieving EU wide consensus on R2P (ALDE MEP 2018). Arguably, collective leadership from the EU's leading states on R2P would have gone a long way in forging this consensus. The absence of a hegemon, or in the EU's case, collective leadership, could thus be seen as a factor that hampered the internalisation of R2P at the European level. Additional case studies will need to be conducted to see whether the presence of a regional hegemon and/or collective leadership is a facilitating factor for the regional internalisation of R2P across regions. The exploration of this factor in the EU and ECOWAS seems to suggest it has a role to play.

The third regional factor focused on the available and preferred foreign policy resources and capacities in the region. For the EU, this would mean that one should see internalisation of R2P most pronounced in areas where the regional organisation has an edge, such as in diplomacy, conflict prevention and development. Concerning R2P internalisation, one would thus expect a strong internalisation of formal support (as it relates to diplomacy), prevention (as it relates to conflict prevention and diplomacy, and, when assessing long-term prevention, also on development cooperation). As significant hard power is for many member states less readily available and the use of it often contested, one would expect a less ready internalisation of the military component of the responsibility to react. For ECOWAS, this would mean that one should see internalisation of R2P most pronounced in areas where the organisation is well-equipped, such as in diplomacy, conflict prevention, and conflict management. Concerning R2P internalisation, one would thus expect a strong internalisation of formal support (as it relates to diplomacy), prevention (as it relates to conflict prevention and diplomacy), and reaction (as it relates to conflict management). In the cases, we saw these expectations confirmed. EU institutions, especially the EP, frequently refer to R2P in R2P cases, while the EU engages in preventive diplomacy, applies sanctions, and engages in long-term prevention, including through rebuilding. ECOWAS, for its part, engages in preventive diplomacy, often in the form of shuttle diplomacy, it applies sanctions, and it does not shy away from the use of force when needed in R2P cases.

The degree of regional institutionalisation was the last regional factor assessed in the analytical framework. It was noted that both regional organisations have a high degree of regional institutionalisation (for ECOWAS, this is the case in the area of regional security, less so outside), which would make one expect an institutionalised response to the R2P norm. In the EU, this turned out to be the case, with the appointment of a regional focal point, a creation of a division within the EEAS that focused on R2P among other things and the development of the Atrocity Prevention Toolkit. In ECOWAS, this was less the case, mostly because it had already developed elaborate provisions related to R2P in its existing protocols. This means that a high degree of regional institutionalisation does not automatically translate into institutional responses to new global norms, especially when there are already strongly developed regional norms in

Table 6.1 EU-ECOWAS comparisons on the regional factors

No.	*Factor*	*EU*	*ECOWAS*
1	Expressed fear of the use of hard power	Significant (of Russia)	Limited (of French and Nigerian-led interventions, although mostly these are welcomed by member states)
2	(Self-perception of) regional actor type	Regional security community	Regional hegemonic stability system
3	Capacities Availability Preference	Diplomacy, conflict prevention, development	Diplomacy, conflict prevention, and conflict management
4	Degree of regional institutionalisation	High (in general)	High (in security)

place in the same policy area. Adding regional case studies with a low degree of regional institutionalisation, such as a regional organisation in the Middle East, would be helpful in elucidating regional responses to R2P in those contexts.

Table 6.1 sums up the above findings and comparisons.

The second part of the analytical framework focused on different normative contexts and their implications for norm entrepreneurs and antipreneurs. In the contextual and empirical chapters, it was discussed that in both regional cases traditional notions of sovereignty were not or no longer entrenched when R2P as a norm emerged. In the EU, member states had built decades of experience of sovereignty-pooling and the 'people-centred' human security enjoyed significant support. Concerning ECOWAS, the protocols it had adopted in the 1990s and the early 2000s and the intervention practice that had first emerged in the late 1980s allowed for sovereignty to be overridden in cases of the unconstitutional seizure or maintenance of power or in cases of massive human rights violations. Given the fact that traditional notions of sovereignty were no longer entrenched in the regions, 'sovereignty-antipreneurs' were not expected to be advantaged over entrepreneurs, nor were they expected to be successful in exploiting blocking opportunities. In both cases, this seems to have been the case, as no significant norm antipreneurship against R2P in either region has been documented in the lead up to and during the 2005 World Summit negotiations.

When assessing the regional roots of the R2P norm and local norm construction, norm entrepreneurs could be found in both regions. In West Africa and ECOWAS, former UN Secretary General Kofi Annan and former Nigerian President Obasanjo were key norm advocates for R2P (Annan) or West African precursors to the norm (Obasanjo), while in the EU, former UK Prime Minister Blair, former French Foreign Minister Kouchner and former German Foreign Minister Fischer advocated for (precursors of) R2P and interventions on humanitarian grounds more broadly. The origins of their norm leadership were different, though. Annan advocated for R2P being shaped by events in his home region West Africa and the UN's failures over Rwanda and Srebrenica, while Obasanjo as newly democratically elected Nigerian President pushed the adoption of the 1999 Mechanism to protect fragile democracies in West Africa. Blair, Kouchner, and Fischer were all inspired by different shades of similar principles, such as 'liberal interventionism' (Blair) and *'droit d'ingérence'* (Kouchner). Fischer attempted to redefine the German lessons of the Holocaust and the Second World War, arguing that the default lesson should not be the non-use of German force abroad, but instead instilling a special responsibility on Germany to accept the use of force where this serves the aim of halting (imminent) mass atrocities (Brockmeier et al. 2014, 434). These norm entrepreneurs all delivered important contributions to the eventual global R2P norm. The ICISS recognised the important work of ECOWAS in its 2001 report, while some of Blair's principles and the criteria for the use of force originating from Just War Theory found their way into the ICISS report, albeit not into the 2005 World State Outcome Document (International Commission on Intervention and State Sovereignty et al. 2001; UNGA 2005).

With regard to the facilitating factors related to processes of local norm construction as outlined in the analytical framework, it seems that these were more met in the case of ECOWAS than in the case of the EU. While both the EU and ECOWAS responded to policy challenges that resonated beyond their localities, ECOWAS' response seems to have been generally more successful or at least less controversial (while ECOMOG's interventions were hotly debated in West Africa, they did not stir global controversy at the scale that, for instance, the 1999 Kosovo operation did). It was also a West African norm entrepreneur, former Secretary General Annan, who left the biggest mark on the global R2P norm. The most influential European norm entrepreneur, former UK Prime Minister Blair, played a more ambiguous role, on the one hand making an important contribution through his support for sovereignty as responsibility and liberal interventionism, while on the other hand doing damage to the nascent R2P norm through association with the unmandated Iraq war.

Regarding internalisation of the R2P norm (see Table 6.2), it was shown that both EU- and ECOWAS-member states have expressed formal support

Table 6.2 EU-ECOWAS comparison on the different aspects of R2P internalisation

No.	*Aspect*	*EU*	*ECOWAS*
1	Formal support	Yes, to a significant extent	Limited (present in UNGA debates and direct reference in 2008 ECPF, but no reference in R2P cases)
2	Responsibility to prevent	Partial	Partial
3	Responsibility to react		
3a	Sanctions	Yes	Yes
3b	Military intervention	Limited; highly contested	To a significant extent, sometimes contested
4	Responsibility to rebuild	Partial, improving	Limited

for R2P during the annual UNGA debates on R2P. At the regional-institutional level, however, there is an important difference: while EU institutions, such as the EP and the Council, frequently refer to R2P in their communications, this is not the case for ECOWAS institutions. The explanation for this is that these institutions generally refer to ECOWAS' own protocols, which include provisions relevant to R2P. Both regional organisations have adopted institutional provisions to internalise the responsibility to prevent (the EU: Atrocity Prevention Toolkit; ECOWAS: the 2008 ECPF), they have expressed authoritative support for atrocity prevention measures during regional crises, and they have taken measures under the responsibility to prevent, such as the use of preventive diplomacy (think of ECOWAS' 'shuttle-diplomacy' in the region). The cases of Myanmar and Ivory Coast showed that the regional organisations have difficulty to adequately prevent atrocities and respond to these when they have competing considerations, such as democracy promotion (the EU in Myanmar) or upholding the principle of constitutional maintenance and assumption of power (ECOWAS in Ivory Coast). Overall, considering both institutional provisions and case responses (authoritative support and policy action), one can speak of a partial internalisation of the responsibility to prevent in both regional organisations. On the responsibility to react, both organisations have adopted sanctions in R2P cases, but the decision to intervene has been much more hotly contested in the EU, in the case of Libya, than in ECOWAS, in the case of Mali. On the responsibility to rebuild, both organisations have taken rebuilding measures in the aftermath of conflicts, although generally without a specific mass atrocity prevention lens (the EU in Libya and ECOWAS in Mali). An exception to this are the measures taken by the EU in the aftermath of the August 2017 Rohingya crisis, which generally had a clear protection aim. This shows that the EU seems to have learnt from rebuilding deficiencies in Libya and, at least based on the Rohingya case, is increasingly internalising the responsibility to rebuild after atrocity cases.

Overall, it was concluded that the EU's internalisation of R2P amounts to norm accommodation, signified by changes in policy and discourse in response to the R2P norm that are too significant to qualify as norm absorption but arguably lacking the complete overhaul of policies and policy actions characteristic of norm transformation. ECOWAS' engagement with its regional crises *has* been transformative since the 1980s: the regional organisation developed itself from an organisation with a rather limited economic mandate to a fully fledged regional organisation that, particularly in the area of regional security broadly conceived, goes much further than the EU is willing or able to. The caveat here is that given its strong pre-existing records in this area, ECOWAS tends to refer to its own protocols and mechanisms when responding to regional R2P crises, so the norm is less visible in the regional discourse than in the EU. Its actions are nevertheless testament to the norm and indeed show that ECOWAS as a whole, member states such as Ghana and Nigeria (*inter alia* through ECOMOG), as well as influential leaders such as Kofi Annan and Obasanjo, have been critical regional norm entrepreneurs. They all have, through processes of local norm construction in the ECOWAS region and through advocacy at the global level, co-constituted one of the main building blocks of the global R2P norm as we know now it.

Figure 6.1 sums up the above empirical findings of this book in the theoretical model that was designed in the theory chapter of this book:

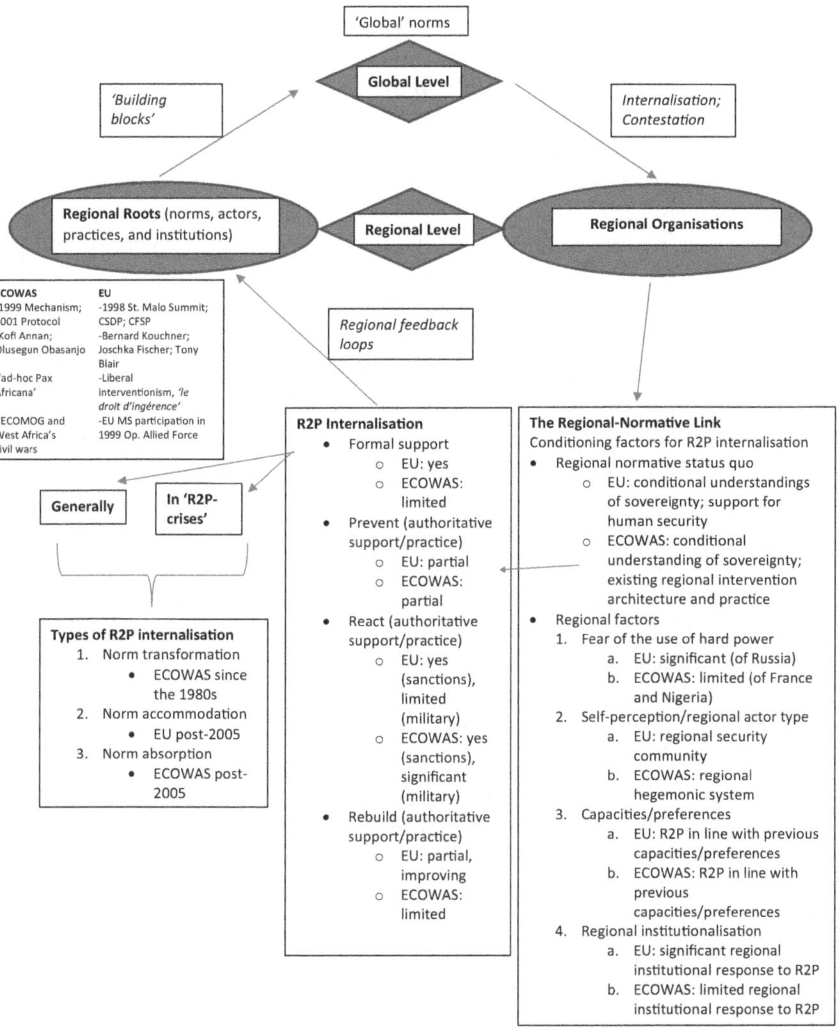

Figure 6.1 Empirical findings related to the analytical model of norms, R2P, and regional organisations

Source: Author's creation

Contributions to the literature, limitations, and implications for future research

This book has made a few core contributions to the literature. Theoretically, it has expanded on Acharya's work by introducing and demonstrating the importance of the concept of local norm construction, in which local actors build the building blocks of subsequent global norms. This book has also engaged analytically with the concept of 'norm internalisation': it has differentiated this concept from neighbouring concepts such as norm consolidation, it has delimited to which instances it applies and it has operationalised this concept vis-à-vis the R2P norm. Based on this conceptualisation and operationalisation of norm internalisation, this book has subsequently systematically assessed the internalisation of different components of R2P in the different case studies in the empirical chapters and it has assessed the depths of change based on the Europeanisation literature. Third, this book has introduced a regional application of Bloomfield's norm role spectrum and it has more generally made connections between the regional security governance literature and the norms literature.

Empirically, this study has shown that rhetorical support for R2P and presence of the norm in the regional discourse does not automatically translate in internalisation in regional policies. This was especially the case in the early years after the adoption of R2P in the EU, when strong rhetorical support, for instance at the UN, was not matched with specific regional R2P policies. In more recent years, improvements have been made, among others through the development of the Atrocity Prevention Toolkit and efforts to integrate mass atrocity prevention in existing policies and programs. It is striking, however, that in the regional organisation where R2P appears much less visible in the regional discourse, we have witnessed a stronger internalisation of the norm in regional policies. ECOWAS has responded to R2P cases using all tools in the R2P toolbox, ranging from diplomatic measures to military intervention. When it decided to use military means, these decisions were much less hotly contested among member states than in case of the EU, where the Libyan intervention led to major divisions. While ECOWAS has responded to R2P cases in a very comprehensive way, it has generally not framed its response in terms of R2P, but with reference to its own protocols that it adopted before R2P as a global norm emerged. The inclusion of the case study of ECOWAS has been important to address the current imbalance in the R2P literature, which heavily focuses on the EU's approach to the norm. Moreover, while many authors have recognised Africa's and the African Union's contributions to the R2P norm, few have recognised the key groundwork ECOWAS had laid prior to this in this area in the pre-World Summit era. Scholars that have recognised this contribution are generally from the West African region (see, for instance, Aning and Atuobi (2012)), with a few exceptions (Hartmann and Striebinger 2015; Arthur 2019).

There are a few theoretical and empirical limitations to the research at hand. Theoretically, it was challenging to connect the norms literature on the one hand and the regional security governance and R2P literature on the other. This was primarily because these bodies of literature do not often overlap or directly speak to each other, with some notable exceptions, such as Acharya's work (Acharya 2004, 2011, 2013). The identification and formulation of the regional factors should therefore be seen as a first attempt to start theorisation in the intersection of these literatures. At the moment, the regional factors identified serve as exploratory, tentative, factors rather than more robust hypotheses. Some of these factors have received initial support when they were explored in the regional case studies of the EU and ECOWAS, while others, sometimes surprisingly, have not received this support. The factor of expressed fear of the use of hard power was one that was expected to receive significant support, especially as this was an important concern for R2P norm entrepreneurs who have gone to great lengths to disassociate R2P from humanitarian intervention (International Commission on Intervention and State Sovereignty et al. 2001). The factor has, however, so far not been corroborated by the empirical evidence presented in the EU and ECOWAS chapters. The eventual aim is that the regional factors identified and explored in this book will be subjected to more regional case studies, which will be further discussed in avenues for future research below.

Empirically, there were some limitations to this research as well. First, by necessity, choices had to be made with regard to the number of regional crises analysed in the empirical chapters. The analysed crises should offer a rich assessment of R2P challenges the EU and ECOWAS have dealt with in recent years, both internally and externally, and varying in both the severity of atrocities committed and the level of regional response. There are nevertheless other cases that would have been interesting to study in the context of this book, such as the EU's response to Islamic State, which was briefly touched upon in the analysis of the Syrian crisis. For ECOWAS, the intervention in The Gambia in 2016/2017 would have been instructive as another electoral crisis that could have realistically relapsed into the commission of atrocities, as did in fact occur during the Ivory Coast crisis. Second, there were data availability challenges. While the EU's approach to R2P has been widely discussed in the R2P literature and the regional crises analysed in the EU chapter have received much attention (see, for instance De Franco et al. 2016; Newman 2018; Newman and Stefan 2020; Staunton and Ralph 2019 to name just a few), this was not always the case for ECOWAS and the crises there. Added to that was the fact that it was easier to get in touch and set up interviews with EU officials and experts than with their ECOWAS counterparts, partly due to geographical reasons, but also because there is less public information available on who works for ECOWAS and in which departments officials and civil servants work. Contact information of ECOWAS officials and civil servants is also generally publicly unavailable. This challenge was partly overcome through a snowballing method once I had been able to make some initial contacts within ECOWAS through colleagues and conference attendance, but the fact remains that more interviews were conducted with EU officials and experts than with their ECOWAS counterparts. These data availability challenges have sometimes limited the robustness and the specification of certain empirical findings. An example would be the difficulty in establishing instances of norm antipreneurship of ECOWAS member states in the period following the 2001 ICISS report up to and including the 2005 World Summit negotiations. Although no direct norm antipreneurship was observed, this may have been due to a lack of empirical information rather than a certainty that norm antipreneurship or more subtle forms of resistance and contestation did, in fact, not take place in this time period.

A promising way to carry this research forward would be to develop a typology of regional organisations and their approaches to R2P. To do this convincingly, one would need to analyse more regional cases to account for the diversity of regional organisations and regional approaches to R2P. The cases of the EU and the ECOWAS have already provided a sense of the diversity of approaches to R2P. In some ways, they were also similar though, as both regional organisations have a high degree of regional institutionalisation and are willing to pool sovereignty to significant degrees. For this reason, it would be interesting to analyse regional cases where member states have been less willing to pool sovereignty. ASEAN would be a case in point (Ginsburg 2005).

There has been scepticism among ASEAN member states about the R2P norm, given their emphasis on non-interference emblematic of the 'ASEAN way', although Bellamy (2009, 549) warns against dismissing the region's governments all too readily as "R2P-sceptics and spoilers." The fact is though, that the regional organisation has struggled to respond to atrocity crises in its region: in the face of the genocide committed against the Rohingya in ASEAN member state Myanmar, a crisis analysed in the EU chapter of this book, the ASEAN member states stayed muted in their response and failed to even condemn the atrocities (UN Human Rights Council 2022; Al Jazeera 2020; Human Rights Watch 2019). The lack of an appropriate regional response to the crisis that may have reasonably been expected given the severity of the crimes inflicted upon the Rohingya was even noted by a critical report of ASEAN regional parliamentarians (Al Jazeera 2020). ASEAN's focus on repatriating the Rohingya minority to Myanmar runs the real risk of putting them at mercy again of the government that inflicted atrocities upon them (Al Jazeera 2020). Given these observations pertaining to the regional response to the Rohingya crisis, which is exemplary of a strong tradition of regional non-interference up to the point where at least the impression has been made that a blind eye has been turned on genocide, ASEAN is probably the least likely candidate for regional internalisation of R2P. That would make the organisation, precisely for this reason, a crucial case study for regional internalisation of the R2P norm. It is expected that in the case of ASEAN one will witness levels of norm contestation and resistance against the R2P norm that could not be observed in equal measure in either the EU or ECOWAS.

When looking from the angle of regional institutionalisation, ASEAN still represents quite a developed regional project, though. It would therefore also be important to include a regional case that is loosely institutionalised across the board. One of the regional organisations in the Middle East would be an obvious candidate (Pinfari 2016). Such a case could investigate the claim presented in this section that loosely based regional organisations are likely to have challenges creating and implementing prevention and rebuilding policies based on R2P.

The Middle East has long been characterised by political protests, civil wars, terrorism, religious strife, and foreign intervention, many of which coincide with high levels of mass atrocities, as witnessed in Iraq, Libya Syria, and Yemen (GCR2P 2022). This makes this region another critical candidate for the assessment of the regional internalisation of R2P. Other than in many other parts of the world, the Middle East has not witnessed high levels of regional institutionalisation. Regional organisations such as the League of Arab States are quite loosely institutionalised when compared to their regional peers (Barqueiro et al. 2016). These two observations – a high incidence of mass atrocities coupled with a low degree of regional institutionalisation – make for another important regional case study of the internalisation of the R2P norm. Whereas the first observation should speak for the internalisation of R2P, as there should be a high demand for protection against mass atrocities in the Middle East, the other – the low degree of regional institutionalisation – is expected to operate against effective regional approaches against these mass atrocities. It will be important to assess how the balance between these counteracting factors has played out with regard to the regional internalisation of R2P in the Middle East. The Libyan crisis that was analysed in this book has already given away that there is no rejection in principle of the R2P norm, as the League of Arab States, for instance, called for the imposition of a no-fly zone over Libya following Gaddafi's attacks on Libyan civilians (Adler-Nissen and Pouliot 2014). This position shows the organisation is at least in principle open to the norm. Whether it would be willing to take measures itself to implement the R2P norm in different contexts within its region is a question that can only be answered through an in-depth case study.

The analysis of other regional approaches to R2P should, apart from resulting into important empirical findings, deliver new theoretical insights as well. The study of the additional regional cases would allow for further investigation of the regional factors identified in the analytical framework in other regional contexts. Some of the factors may be dropped against more empirical evidence that their analytical utility is limited, which would make the theoretical model proposed in this book more parsimonious. Other factors may receive further support and/or could be further refined. Equally important would be to establish if some of the local and regional roots of the R2P norm can be found in the Middle East and South East Asia as well. With regard to the latter, Acharya (2004) has conducted an important study into the history of engagement with intervention norms in the Asia Pacific, while Bellamy (2009) has done so more directly with regard to the R2P norm in the post-World Summit era. It is expected that preliminary evidence for some of the potential regional roots for the R2P norm (or lack thereof) can be found in these articles, although more research is needed in this area. Finally, conducting additional regional case studies would in time allow for the creation of a typology of different types of regional organisations and their approaches to R2P. This would be an important theoretical contribution to both the regional security governance literature and the specific literature on R2P.

Bibliography

Acharya, Amitav. 2004. "How Ideas Spread: Whose Norms Matter? Norm Localisation and Institutional Change in Asian Regionalism." *International Organisation* 58 (Spring): 239–275.

Acharya, Amitav. 2011. "Norm Subsidiarity and Regional Orders: Sovereignty, Regionalism, and Rule-Making in the Third World." *International Studies Quarterly* 55 (1): 95–123.

Acharya, Amitav. 2013. "The R2P and Norm Diffusion: Towards a Framework of Norm Circulation." *Global Responsibility to Protect* 5 (4): 466–479.

Adler, Emanuel and Michael Barnett, eds. 1998. *Security Communities*. Cambridge: Cambridge University Press.

Adler, Emanuel and Patricia Greve. 2009. "When Security Community Meets Balance of Power: Overlapping Regional Mechanisms of Security Governance." *Review of International Studies* 35 (1): 59–84.

Adler-Nissen, Rebecca and Vincent Pouliot. 2014. "Power in Practice: Negotiating the International Intervention in Libya." *European Journal of International Relations* 20 (4): 889–911.

African Development Bank Group. 2018. "West Africa Economic Outlook 2018." *African Development Bank*. www.afdb.org/fileadmin/uploads/afdb/Documents/Publications/2018AEO/African_Economic_Outlook_2018_West-Africa.pdf (April 15, 2020).

Al Jazeera. 2020. "Myanmar's Rohingya Crisis Exposes ASEAN Weaknesses: Report." *AL JAZEERA*. October 20. www.aljazeera.com/news/2020/10/20/myanmars-rohingya-crisis-exposes-asean-weaknesses-report (July 4, 2022).

ALDE MEP. 2018. Interviewed by Jochem Rietveld, Email Correspondence, July 2018.

Aning, Kwesi and Samuel Atuobi. 2012. "The Economic Community of West African States and the Responsibility to Protect." In *The Routledge Handbook of the Responsibility to Protect*, eds. Andy W. Knight and Frazer Egerton. London: Routledge, 216–231.

Arthur, Peter. 2019. "Economic Community of West African States, Regional security and the Implementation of Humanitarian Intervention and the Responsibility to Protect: Rhetoric or Reality?" *Insight on Africa* 11 (2): 162–183. DOI:10.1177/0975087819845195.

Barqueiro, Carla, Kate Seaman and Katherine Teresa Towey. 2016. "Regional Organizations and Responsibility to Protect: Normative Reframing or Normative Change?" *Politics and Governance* 4 (3): 37–49.

Bellamy, Alex. 2009. "The Responsibility To Protect in the Asia-Pacific Region." *Security Dialogue* 40 (6): 547–574.

Bloomfield, Alan. 2016. "Norm Antipreneurs and Theorising Resistance to Normative Change." *Review of International Studies* 42 (2): 310–333.

Brockmeier, Sarah, Gerrit Kurtz and Julian Junk. 2014. "Emerging Norm and Rhetorical Tool: Europe and a Responsibility to Protect. *Conflict, Security & Development* 14 (4): 429–460.

Christou, George. 2014. "The European Union's Human Security Discourse: Where Are We Now?" *European Security* 23 (3): 364–381.

De Franco, Chairo, Christoph Meyer and Karen Smith. 2016. "Europe and the European Union." In *The Oxford Handbook of the Responsibility to Protect*, eds. Alex Bellamy and Tim Dunne. Oxford: Oxford University Press, 391–408.

Deutsch, Karl. 1957. *Political Community and the North Atlantic Area: International Organization in the Light of Historical Experience*. Princeton: Princeton University Press.

Duchene, Francois. 1972. "Europe's Role in World Peace." In *Europe Tomorrow: Sixteen Europeans Look Ahead*, ed. Richard Mayne. London: Fontana/Collins, 32–47.

ECOWAS. 1991. *Declaration of Political Principles of the Economic Community of West African States*. Abuja: ECOWAS.

ECOWAS. 1993. *Revised Treaty of ECOWAS*. Abuja: ECOWAS.

ECOWAS. 1999. *Mechanism for Conflict Prevention, Management, Resolution, Peace-Keeping and Security*. Abuja: ECOWAS.

ECOWAS. 2001. *Protocol on Democracy and Good Governance*. Abuja: ECOWAS.

European External Action Service. 2018. "Statement by High Representative/Vice-President Federica Mogherini on the International Holocaust Remembrance Day." *EEAS*. January 26. www.eeas.europa.eu/node/38794_en (July 28, 2022).

European Union. 2007. "Treaty of Lisbon. Amending the Treaty on European Union and the Treaty Establishing the European Community." 2007/C 306/01. *Official Journal of the European Union*. https://eur-lex.europa.eu/legal-content/EN/TXT/?uri=celex%3A12007L%2FTXT (May 5, 2019).

Finnemore, Martha and Kathryn Sikkink. 1998. "International Norm Dynamics and Political Change." *International Organisation* 52 (4): 887–917.

France24. 2022. "In Mali, 'France is Paying the Price for its Own Ambiguity,' Expert Says." *France24*. www.france24.com/en/africa/20220114-in-mali-france-is-paying-the-price-for-its-own-ambiguity-expert-says (July 7, 2022).

GCR2P. 2008. "The Georgia-Russia Crisis and the Responsibility to Protect: Background Note." *GCR2P*. www.globalr2p.org/wp-content/uploads/2021/07/the-georgia-russia-crisis-and-the-r2p-background-note.pdf. (July 7, 2022).

GCR2P. 2022. "Populations at Risk." *GCR2P*. www.globalr2p.org/populations-at-risk/2022. (July 8, 2022).

Ginsburg, Tom. 2005. "The State of Sovereignty in Southeast Asia." *American Society of International Law Proceedings* 99: 419–422.

Gross, Eva. 2007. "European Union Foreign Policy towards the Balkans." In *European Foreign Policy in an Evolving International System*, eds. Nicola Casarini and Costanza Musu. Basingstoke: Palgrave Macmillan, 97–111.

Habermas, Jurgen. 2003 "Making Sense of the EU: Towards a Cosmopolitan Europe." *Journal of Democracy* 14 (4): 86–100.

Harnisch, Sebastian. 2017. "Theory and Practice of Human Security concerns in EU-Japan relations: The EU Perspective." *EU-Japan Security Cooperation: Challenges and Opportunities* (Spring/Summer): 1–11.

Hartmann, Christoff and Kai Striebinger. 2015. "Writing the Script? ECOWAS's Military Intervention Mechanism." In *Governance Transfer by Regional Organizations. Patching Together a Global Script*, eds. Tanja Börzel and Vera van Hüllen. Basingstoke: Palgrave Macmillan, 68–82.

Human Rights Watch. 2019. "ASEAN: Don't Whitewash Atrocities Against Rohingya." *Human Rights Watch*. June 19. www.hrw.org/news/2019/06/19/asean-dont-whitewash-atrocities-against-rohingya (July 4, 2022).

International Commission on Intervention and State Sovereignty, Gareth J. Evans, and Mohamed Sahnoun. 2001. *The Responsibility to Protect: Report of the International Commission on Intervention and State Sovereignty*. Ottawa: International Development Research Centre.

Lopez, Elisa. 2014. "Discourses and Practices of the Regionalisation of Foreign and Security Policies: The Cases of West Africa and South America." Ph.D. diss. University of Warwick and LUISS Guido Carli.

Manners, Ian. 2002. "Normative Power Europe: A Contradiction in Terms?" *Journal of Common Market Studies* 40 (2): 235–258.

Marc, Alexandre, Neelam Verjee and Stephen Mogaka. 2015. *The Challenge of Stability and Security in West Africa*. Washington, DC: The World Bank.

Newman, Edward. 2018. "The Limits of Liberal Humanitarianism in Europe: The 'Responsibility to Protect' and Forced Migration." *European Review of International Studies* 4 (2 + 3): 59–77.

Newman, Edward and Christina Stefan. 2020. "Normative Power Europe? The EU's Embrace of the 'Responsibility to Protect' in a Transitional International Order." *Journal of Common Market Studies* 58 (2): 472–490.

Nussbaum, Ania. 2020. "West Africa Backs French Military Presence Amid Protests." *Bloomberg*. January 13. www.bloomberg.com/news/articles/2020-01-13/west-africa-backs-french-military-presence-amid-protests (April 15, 2020).

Olonisakin, Oluwafunmilayo. 2011. "ECOWAS from Economic Integration to Peacebuilding." In *ECOWAS and the Dynamic of Conflict and Peace-building in West Africa*, eds. T. Jaye, D. Garuba and S. Amadi. Dakar: Council for the Development of Social Science Research in Africa, 11–26.

Piccolino, Giulia. 2016. "International Diffusion and the Puzzle of African Regionalism: Insights from West Africa. *UNU-CRIS Working Papers 2016/1* 1–32.

Pinfari, Marco. 2016. "Regional Organizations in the Middle East." In *The Oxford Handbook Online in Political Science*. Oxford: Oxford University Press.

Schmidt, Julia. 2019. "The European Union and the Responsibility to Protect." *European Foreign Affairs Review* 24 (3): 309–326.

Söderbaum, Fredrik. 2004. "Modes of Regional Governance in Africa: Neoliberalism, Sovereignty Boosting, and Shadow Networks." *Global Governance* 10 (4): 419–436.

Staunton, Eglantine and Jason Ralph. 2019. "The Responsibility to Protect Norm Cluster and the Challenge of Atrocity Prevention: An Analysis of the European Union's Strategy in Myanmar." *European Journal of International Relations* 26 (3): 1–27.

Stefan, Christina and Edward Newman. 2020. "Europe's Progress and the Road ahead at R2P's 15th Anniversary." *Global Responsibility to Protect* 12 (4): 369–371. DOI:10.1163/1875-984X-01204004.

Tusk, Donald. 2019. "Remarks by President Donald Tusk after his meeting with Taoiseach Leo Varadkar." February 6. www.consilium.europa.eu/en/press/press-releases/2019/02/06/remarks-by-president-donald-tusk-after-his-meeting-with-taoiseach-leo-varadkar/ (October 2, 2020).

United Nations General Assembly. 2005. *2005 World Summit Outcome. Resolution 60/1* (GA/RES/60/1). New York: United Nations General Assembly.

United Nations Human Rights Council. 2022. "Independent International Fact-Finding Mission on Myanmar." *United Nations Human Rights Office of the High Commissioner*. www.ohchr.org/en/hr-bodies/hrc/myanmar-ffm/index (July 8, 2022).

Urwin, Derek. 1995. *The Community of Europe: A History of European Integration since 1945*. 2nd ed. London: Routledge.

Von der Leyen, Ursula. 2019. "A Union that Strives for More. My Agenda for Europe." https://ec.europa.eu/commission/sites/beta-political/files/political-guidelines-next-commission_en.pdf (October 2, 2020).

Vorster, Nico. 2015. "Just War and Virtue: Revisiting Augustine and Thomas Aquinas." *South African Journal of Philosophy* 34 (1): 55–68.

Welsh, Jennifer M. 2013. "Norm Contestation and the Responsibility to Protect." *Global Responsibility to Protect* 5 (4): 365–396.

Wiener, Antje. 2008. *The Invisible Constitution of World Politics*. Cambridge: Cambridge University Press.

World Bank. 2020. "The World Bank in Nigeria." *The World Bank*. www.worldbank.org/en/country/nigeria/overview (April 15, 2020).

Index

Note: Page numbers in *italics* indicate a figure and page numbers in **bold** indicate a table on the correspoindin page.

For Product Safety Concerns and Information please contact our EU representative GPSR@taylorandfrancis.com Taylor & Francis Verlag GmbH, Kaufingerstraße 24, 80331 München, Germany